Sound Studio Production Techniques

Sound Studio Production Techniques

Dennis N. Nardantonio

TAB BOOKS

Blue Ridge Summit, PA

FIRST EDITION
SECOND PRINTING

Library of Congress Cataloging-in-Publication Data

Nardantonio, Dennis N.
    Sound studio production techniques / by Dennis N. Nardantonio.
       p.   cm.
    ISBN 0-8306-9250-9   ISBN 0-8306-3250-6 (pbk.)
    1. Sound—Recording and reproducing.   2. Sound studios.
    I. Title.
    TK7881.4.N37   1990
    621.389′3—dc20   89-29163
                                                                    CIP

TAB Books offers software for sale. For information and a catalog, please contact TAB
Software Department, Blue Ridge Summit, PA 17294-0850.

Acquisitions Editor: Roland S. Phelps
Production: Katherine G. Brown
Cover Illustration: Kajem/Victory West Studios, Gladwyne, PA

Contents

Preface

This book is a tutorial on the craft of professional recording. The objective is to acquaint the user with studio equipment and its application in a production cycle. It focuses on the technical aspects of microphones, tape decks, signal processing gear, mixing consoles, and software-based addressable devices. There is intense coverage on "how it works" and the device's proper application in a production environment.

   This book can serve as a training manual. Furthermore, prospective studio owners, recording engineers, home studio users, and musicians should find it valuable as a starter for personal and career goals in recording and producing. Though much of the material is technical, many visual aids are provided to demonstrate a point. A background in electronics and some math skills are helpful in order to grasp many of the technical concepts presented (the Appendix provides a math review), although without such background, you can still benefit from the information.

Introduction

This book is dedicated to the craft of professional recording. Although recording is fun, learning it does require some academic effort. Knowing how to record properly means grasping an understanding of acoustics and recording equipment operation. Only then can engineers develop their creative recording potentials. To some extent, recording can be considered a marriage of science and art. This profession has gone a long way toward the capture of sound and reproducing it with such detail, elegance, and accuracy so as to please the most sensitive listeners. This means there is a call for high-performance integrity of microphones, mixing consoles, signal processors, tape decks, amplifiers, and loudspeaker systems to faithfully record and reproduce sonic information.

Humans are sentient creatures that perceive through sense of touch, taste, smell, hearing, and sight. The gifts of sight and hearing are important because most of what is learned is through these two senses. In recording, hearing is the final gauge that judges the quality of sound. Sonic information is acoustically coupled to our ears using air as a medium to transmit vibrations. The ear is a delicate microphone that translates these vibrations into a form that the brain registers as sound. In a way, the mind is like a tape recorder. It can recognize a sound that was heard before by virtue of memory. The brain compares an entry with those in memory and identifies it when there is a match. Somehow the mind can process the dynamics and harmonic content information into storage. Perhaps a bigger mystery is why some sounds are significantly more pleasing than others. Is this music?

Imagine how an alien or extraterrestrial observation report would read concerning human behavior patterns with regard to sound. The report might say "This specie makes equipment to polarize rust (record on magnetic tape) and then processes it to vibrate air. In certain cases, it appears to induce euphoria, which sometimes motivates their body parts to move in sync to the rhythm of these vibrations (dance). Not any of the other sentient creatures (cats, dogs, etc.) react this way.''

As was stated, sight is also a very powerful sense in the learning process; and, it might seem strange to announce that you require vision to make use of this book in order to learn about sound. But humans are image-intensive learners, so that is why there is a proliferation of illustrations and photos in this book. In order to make sense of controls and indicators on recording equipment, some kind of visual impression must take place in your mind of what sound is.

This book is written to reach an audience with a broad range of aptitudes. There are no prerequisites to use this book although your personal background and related experiences can be an asset. For that reason, the Appendix is a tutorial covering all the math skills necessary to comprehend the technical portions in the chapters. Hence, anyone who has an intense interest on this subject and makes an attempt to absorb all the technical information has a sporting chance. Others who just want the fundamental know-how can skip the equations and derivations. The point is that this training will be valuable for a broad range of people being prospective recording engineers, studio owners, home studio operators, producers, and musicians.

The first chapter is a lesson on electronics. Chapters 2 and 3 are dedicated to acoustics. Chapters 4 through 11 cover recording equipment and system integration. The last two chapters, 12 and 13, are dedicated to session procedures and practices and the Appendix (math review) is followed by a complete glossary. This book not only exposes the reader to recording equipment but also its application in a production cycle. There is a major emphasis on signal routing and system integration in which you can learn how to make all the equipment work together effectively as a system as opposed to just treating each piece as an isolated case. Explaining the philosophy of application can help the new engineer from feeling disoriented and intimidated in a control room environment. If a control room is set up for professional recording, an engineer should be able to adapt if he or she understands equipment applications from a systems perspective.

Finally, there are those individuals worthy of mention who were supportive on this project. Special thanks to Roland S. Phelps, Electronics Acquisitions Editor at TAB Books for discovering this manuscript, to Lillian Ruoff, administrative assistant at General Instrument Corporation for her clerical support, to Nick Starr, a longtime friend who gave me my first production lessons, to all the product manufacturers that submitted photos for publication, and to the recording studios in the Philadelphia, PA area who cooperated in obtaining many of the photos in this book.

1

Audio Electronics Fundamentals

THIS CHAPTER REVIEWS BASIC ELECTRONIC THEORIES AND COMPONENTS. Very often readers are confronted with graphs, electronic symbols, schematics, and block diagrams used in manuals to describe equipment operation. To best grasp production concepts, it is important to understand the common, fundamental devices used in the recording industry.

ELECTRICITY BASICS

Theory supports that electrons (negatively charged particles) flow through a conductive medium if a potential difference is applied to the medium. The electron flow is *current* and the potential difference is *voltage*. Voltage sources are two types: dc *(direct current)* and ac *(alternating current)*. A battery is an example of a common dc voltage source. Ac sources are numerous, ranging anywhere from high-voltage household electricity down to microvolt sources such as microphones or musical instrument transducers. Typical dc voltage sources are either chemical (like a battery), or a dc power supply can be derived from an ac source (a process known as *ac-to-dc conversion*). All audio equipment requires a dc power supply to operate. Every audio device that is plugged into a wall socket converts this electricity into usable dc sources.

All ac audio sources are generated from physical motion (a moving part) in which mechanical energy is converted into an electrical signal. Some power plants that provide residential electricity use water flow as a mechanism to operate generators. The flowing water rotates the generator's armature (a part with wire windings), which cuts through a magnetic field, inducing a voltage. On a much smaller scale, a microphone generates a signal as sound vibrations (voice) cause displacement of the microphone's *diaphragm*. Then, this diaphragm has windings that cut through a magnetic field when in motion, inducing a voltage. The illustration in FIG. 1-1 shows the electrical symbols for a dc and an ac source.

FIG. **1-1.** *Depiction of dc voltage source and ac voltage source.*

DC Source   AC Source

FIGURE 1-2 shows a schematic circuit that is powered by a battery. The battery is an active dc voltage source applied to the resistor R. The resistor is a conductive medium that regulates the current flow, which is expressed in *amperes* (often abbreviated as *amps*). The degree of current flow (amps, also abbreviated as A) depends on the value of the resistor, which is expressed in *ohms* (Ω). Larger resistor values impede the current flow more. The mathematical relationship between the variables of voltage (V), current (I), and resistance (R) is known as *Ohms Law*, which states that voltage is equal to the resistance times the current:

$$V = R \times I$$

Consequently, by algebraic manipulation, current is calculated as:

$$I = V/R$$

Electrons flow from negative (−) to positive (+) poles. Another accepted convention is to think of "positron" flow for current (positively charged particles) in which these particles flow in the opposite direction—from (+) to (−). In either case, the numbers come out the same in the Ohm's Law equation.

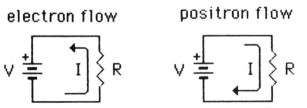

FIG. **1-2.** *Two conventions for expressing current direction.*

As an example, if the applied voltage is 12 Vdc and the resistor is 6 ohms, then current is:

$$I = V/R$$
$$= 12/6$$
$$= 2 \text{ amps}$$

In electronics, it is not uncommon for current to have very small values. Expressions for small values are *milliamps* (mA) and *microamps* (μA). The prefix *milli* means one-thousandth (1/1000) and *micro* means one-millionth (1/1,000,000). As an example, let's increase the resistor value to 6000 ohms. Current would be:

$$I = 12/6000$$
$$= 0.002 \text{ A}$$

To convert this to milliamps, multiply by 1000:

$$I = 0.002 \text{ A} \times 1000$$
$$= 2 \text{ mA}$$

To convert 0.002 amps to microamps, multiply by 1,000,000:

$$I = 0.002 \text{ A} \times 1,000,000$$
$$= 2000 \ \mu\text{A}$$

Therefore, 0.002 A = 2 mA = 2000 μA.

Large resistor values are often expressed as kilohms (the prefix *kilo* means *thousand*). Therefore, the resistor value 6000 ohms can also be expressed as 6 kilohms (6 kΩ or simply 6 k). For even larger values, resistors are expressed in megohms (the prefix *mega* means *million*). The value 5,600,000 ohms is more easily written as 5.6 MΩ or simply as 5.6 M. In summary, the letter k means multiply by 1000, and the letter M means multiply by 1,000,000.

Sinusoidal Signals

Audio electronics deals primarily with ac signals (sounds). In the circuit shown in FIG. 1-3, an ac source is applied to the resistor and the circuit is grounded. The ground symbol indicates that the circuit has a *zero potential reference*. The current reverses direction or alternates as a result of the constantly reversing voltage polarity of the ac source.

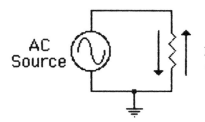

FIG. **1-3.** *Alternating current source powering circuit contains a ground.*

A component of sound can be thought of as a *sinusoidal signal*. A *cycle* of this signal constitutes a positive portion and a negative portion that occurs over a specific time period. This is graphically shown in FIG. 1-4. During the positive half of the cycle, current travels in one direction around the circuit and then reverses direction for the negative portion.

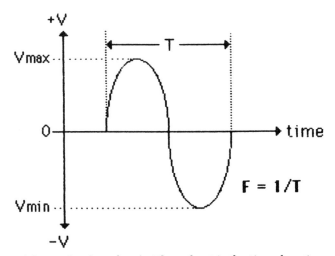

FIG. **1-4.** *Sinusoidal signal, where* f = 1/t. *The value* t *is the time duration, or period, of one cycle.*

An example of such an ac source would be a microphone picking up a tuning fork vibration. The microphone converts the mechanical vibration into an electrical sinusoidal signal. The time period of the cycle defines the *frequency* of the signal given by:

$$f = 1/t$$

where f is the frequency, 1 is for one cycle, and t is the *period* or time expressed in seconds. Thus, frequency is expressed in *cycles per second*, or cps; however, the current convention for expressing cycles per second is *hertz*, abbreviated as Hz. For example, 1000 cps is the same as 1000 Hz. Remembering that k means one thousand, 1000 Hz = 1 kHz.

Capacitors and Inductors

If voltage is sinusoidal, the resulting current is sinusoidal too. The value of resistors is not affected in any way by the frequency of the signal; however, other components are sensitive to frequency: *capacitors* and *inductors*. With an ac source, resistors act *resistive* and capacitors and inductors act *reactive*. *Reactance* (symbolized with X) is the opposition of alternating current flow by a capacitance, inductance, or combination of both. In fact, the reactance of these types of components is determined by the frequency. The reactance expression for a capacitor is:

$$X_C = 1/(2\pi f C)$$

where f is frequency, C is the value of the capacitor expressed in *farads* (abbreviated F), and $\pi = 3.14159$. The reactance expression for an inductor is:

$$X_L = 2\pi f L$$

where L is the inductance expressed in henries (abbreviated H). Ohm's Law applies to these components the same way a resistance does:

$$V = I \times X_C \text{ and } V = I \times X_L$$

Current can be solved for in each case by dividing reactance into the voltage.

Given the *peak-to-peak* voltage, which is the total amount of voltage from the highest positive peak (V_{max}) to the lowest negative peak V_{min}, we can determine the peak-to-peak current. Let's plug in a couple of values and compare results. Using a 800 mV (peak-peak), 5 kHz voltage source, calculate the peak-to-peak current for a 4.7 kΩ resistor, a 0.02 μF capacitor, and a 12 mH inductor. First calculate the reactances X_C and X_L:

$$
\begin{aligned}
X_C &= 1/(2\pi f C) \\
&= 1/(2 \times 3.14159 \times 5000 \times 0.00000002) \\
&= 1592 \ \Omega
\end{aligned}
$$

$$X_L = 2\pi fL$$
$$= 2 \times 3.14159 \times 5000 \times 0.012$$
$$= 377 \ \Omega$$

Note that as frequency increases, X_C decreases and X_L increases. Now solve for the current for each component:

Resistor: $\quad I \quad = \text{V/R}$

$= 0.8/4700$

$= .00017$ A

$= 170 \ \mu\text{A}$

Capacitor: $\quad I \quad = \text{V/}X_C$

$= 0.8/1592$

$= .0005025$ A

$= 502.5 \ \mu\text{A}$

Inductor: $\quad I \quad = \text{V/}X_L$

$= 0.8/377$

$= .0021$ A

$= 2.1$ mA

FIGURE 1-5 pictures typical versions of these three common components.

Phase Relationships

Reactive components like capacitors and inductors in a circuit cause *phase shift*, which is the time relationship between voltage and current. A resistor causes no phase change, but when using a capacitor, current *leads* voltage, or another way of saying it is that voltage *lags* current. As shown in FIG. 1-6, the capacitor current peak of I_{min} occurs before that of the source voltage and the resistance current. With inductors, current lags voltage or voltage leads current. Therefore, in the figure the I_{min} peak occurs on the "time line" after the voltage source (it's delayed). Also note in the figure the schematic symbols for each component.

The expression for voltage of a sinusoidal waveform is:

$$v(t) = V\sin(2\pi ft)$$

where V is the peak amplitude and sin is the trigonometric function of the quantity $2\pi ft$ which is the angle. The quantity $2\pi f$ is a radian expression for frequency and is usually referred to as *omega* (ω) where:

$$\omega = 2\pi f$$
$$v(t) = V\sin(\omega t)$$

The ωt represents an angle called theta (θ). Therefore:

$$v(t) = V\sin(\theta)$$

The expression for current in a resistor is:

$$i(t) = (V/R)\,[\,\sin(\omega t)\,]$$

A current that leads voltage, as for a capacitor, is expressed as:

$$i(t) = I\sin(\omega t + \beta)$$

where β (beta) is the number of degrees the current leads the voltage. In the previous diagram (FIG. 1-5), the capacitor current is shown to lead voltage by one quarter of a cycle, or 90 degrees (because a full cycle equals 360 degrees, as in a circle). In radians, 90 degrees is $\pi/2$, which means that $\beta = \pi/2$. The amplitude *I* is voltage divided by resistance.

The lagging inductor current is similar:

$$i(t) = I\sin(\omega t - \beta)$$

The current lags the voltage by one quarter of a cycle, or 90 degrees.

TRANSIENT AND STEADY-STATE RESPONSES

Now consider what would happen if a dc source is applied to a capacitor or even an inductor. The answer is easy when you realize that the frequency for a dc source is zero. Plugging a zero into the reactance expressions, $X_C = 1/0 = \infty$ (infinity) and $X_L = 0$. This means that capacitors do not permit any dc current flow, but inductors act like a *short* (no resistance). A short circuit allows the voltage source to deliver its maximum current (why shorts blow fuses).

These dc behaviors for capacitors and inductors are how these devices act after settling into a steady state. A *transient* response also occurs when the dc voltage is initially applied. Initially, these components act quite opposite of how they normally do. There is a current surge that charges the capacitor before

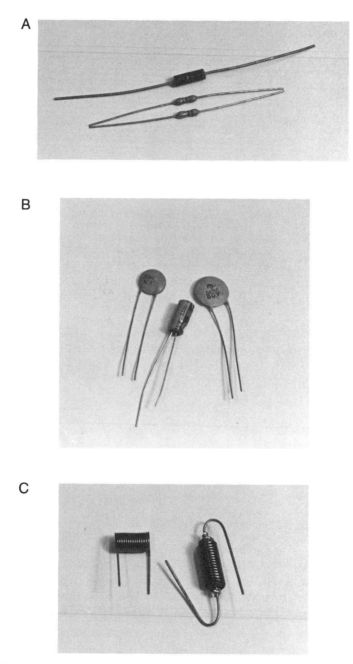

FIG. 1-5. *Circuit elements: (A) resistors, (B) capacitors, and (C) inductors.*

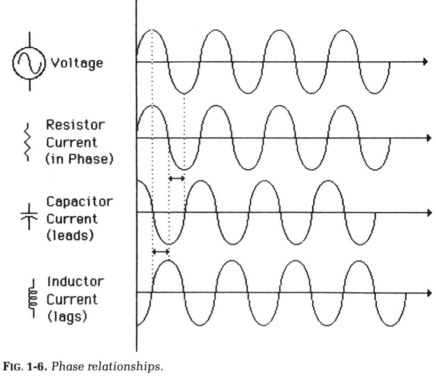

FIG. **1-6.** *Phase relationships.*

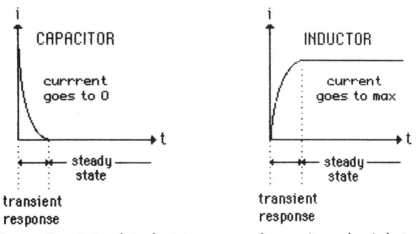

FIG. **1-7.** *Transient and steady-state responses of a capacitor and an inductor.*

the current reduces to zero and initially the inductor *chokes* or blocks current when dc voltage is applied. The graphs in FIG. 1-7 show the transient responses followed by the steady-state responses.

9

VOLTAGE DIVIDER

A *voltage divider* circuit is shown in FIG. 1-8. The current flow through the circuit is determined by the sum of the two resistors, which are configured in *series*. What is of interest here is the voltage at their junction. *Kirchhoff's Voltage Law* states that the sum of the voltage *drops* across each component in a series circuit must equal the applied source voltage. This means that:

$$V_S = V_1 + V_2$$

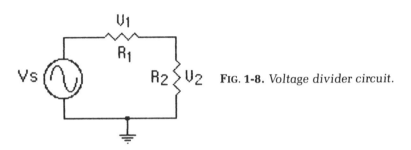

FIG. 1-8. *Voltage divider circuit.*

where V_1 is the voltage drop across R1 and V_2 is the drop across R2. Since the current is the same for both resistors, then it follows that from Ohm's law:

$$V_1 = I \times R_1 \text{ and } V_2 = I \times R_2$$

Therefore,

$$V_S = IR_1 + IR_2$$

$$= I(R_1 + R_2)$$

The voltage at the junction of the two resistors is V_2. If $V_2 = IR_2$ and $I = V_S/(R_1 + R_2)$, then $V_2 = V_S R_2/(R_1 + R_2)$. The junction voltage ($V_2$) is a portion of the voltage source (V_S) given by the ratio $R_2/(R_1 + R_2)$. This is the principle of the voltage divider. V_2 is a percentage of V_S by devising a resistor ratio.

A special component that is used to create a variable voltage divider is a *potentiometer*. This variable resistor simulates two series resistors but with the flexibility to adjust any R_1/R_2 combination desired. This is a very common application to control volume or signal level. A potentiometer or "pot" in a circuit is shown schematically in FIG. 1-9. The *wiper* or pointer can be positioned to create a junction to establish the desired ratio between R_1 and R_2. The variable V_0 is the portion of the V_S value that can vary from V_S to zero volts.

10

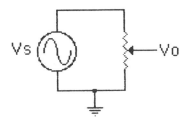

FIG. 1-9. *Potentiometer in circuit with ac source.*

FIGURE 1-10 shows a common rotary potentiometer. Some audio applications requiring linear movement use a sliding type of potentiometer referred to as a *fader.*

FIG. 1-10. *Potentiometer (rotary type).*

FILTERING

Another form of "divider" that is frequency dependent is a *filter.* FIGURE 1-11 shows a filter circuit using a series resistor and a capacitor. The capacitor's reactance X_C relative to R determines the junction voltage (V_2). Realize that X_C depends on the V_S frequency in such a way that the higher the frequency, the smaller the X_C. This also means that a smaller X_C results in a smaller V_2, which then implies that the division ratio can be altered by changing the V_S frequency. The V_2 output is larger for lower frequencies and diminishes as frequency increases. This configuration that favors lower frequencies and blocks, or *attenuates,* higher ones is known as a *low-pass filter.*

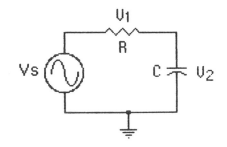

FIG. 1-11. *Low-pass filter.*

Bear in mind that there is a phase shift induced by this capacitor. The relationship between X_C and R_1 is not as simple as the voltage divider calculation for the two-resistor network of FIG. 1-8. A vector math technique called *phasor math* is used to calculate the magnitude and phase angle of the junction voltage (V_2). Phasor math is a vector analysis in which the capacitor and inductor reactances are treated as imaginary numbers. These numbers are dimensionally at right angles (90 degrees) with respect to the zero-phase, or real axis. FIGURE 1-12 shows the dimensional relationship between resistance, capacitance, and inductance. The resistance lies on the positive real axis, the inductance lies on the positive imaginary axis, and the capacitance is on the negative imaginary axis. Mathematically, the imaginary reactances are written as jX_L for the inductor, and $-jX_C$ for the capacitor. Recall the voltage division expression:

$$V_2 = V_S \left(\frac{R_2}{R_1 + R_2} \right)$$

Substituting $-jX_C$ in the voltage divider expression in the same position where R_2 is gives:

$$V_2 = V_S \left(\frac{-jX_C}{R - jX_C} \right)$$

The denominator $R - jX_C$ can be added vectorally. Adding a resistor value with a capacitive reactance creates a new vector *magnitude* (M). From the geometric

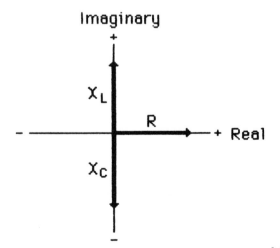

FIG. **1-12.** *Impedance vectors for resistance, capacitance, and inductance.*

formula, the magnitude is the square root of the sum of the squared imaginary and real components:

$$M = \sqrt{R^2 + X_C^2}$$

The phase angle θ would be somewhere between 0 and -90 degrees and can be calculated by taking the arctangent of X_C over R:

$$\theta = \tan^{-1}(X_C/R)$$

The expression $R - jX_C$, expressed as a phasor quantity (M) with the phase angle θ, is shown as a vector in FIG. 1-13 and is written as $M\{\theta\}$. Substituting $M\{\theta\}$ for $R - jX_C$, the ratio $-jX_C/(R - jX_C)$ is now $-jX_C/M\{\theta\}$. The capacitor impedance $-jX_C$ can be expressed in phasor form as $X_C\{-90\}$. Now the ratio is $X_C\{-90\}/M\{\theta\}$. The rule for phasor division is to divide the magnitudes and subtract the angles. Therefore, the complete expression is:

$$V_2 = V_S\left(\frac{X_C}{M}\right)\{-90 - \theta\}$$

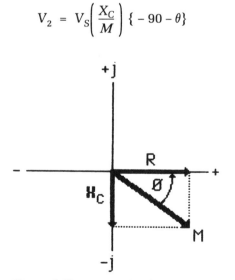

FIG. 1-13. *Vectoral illustration for the expression* $R - jX_C$.

FIGURE 1-14 shows the vector relationship of the source V_2 to V_S. (If necessary, refer to the Appendix for a review of some algebra, trigonometry, phasor math, and logarithms that are used throughout the book.)

13

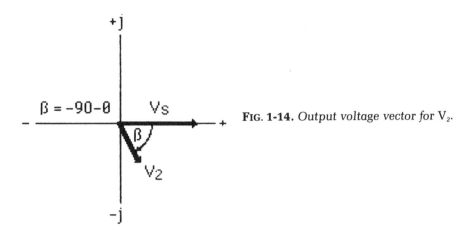

FIG. **1-14.** *Output voltage vector for* V$_2$.

Though not demonstrated here, the rule for multiplying two vectors is to multiply the magnitudes and add the angles. When adding or subtracting vectors, the magnitudes must be converted into their real and imaginary components in which real = Mcos (β) and imag = Msin (β). Then add all the real parts and all the imaginary parts to form total real and total imaginary components.

There is a formula used to determine at what frequency the roll-off becomes significant. This is called the *cut off frequency* (f_C) and is the frequency at which V$_2$ is about 70 percent of V$_S$. This is also referred to as the -3 dB or ''3 dB down'' point. This is a logarithmic expression that represents power lost:

$$dB = 20 \log (V_2/V_S)$$

If the positions of R and C are reversed in FIG. 1-11, this creates a high-pass filter network. The higher frequencies are passed because R is in the output position and looks large in comparison to X$_C$ for high frequencies. Similarly, we can use inductor/resistor combinations to consider high-pass and low-pass networks. The science of making filter networks is broad, but this gives a feel for how components can be used for special functions in audio.

TRANSISTORS

Once a signal is generated, there is a need to amplify it. Such amplification can be achieved via an *active* device. Where the resistor, capacitor, and inductor are all *passive* devices (incapable of amplification), the *transistor* is an active one. The two common types of transistors are shown in FIG. 1-15. The signal to be amplified is ac-coupled by a capacitor into the *base* input of the transistor. The circuit shown in FIG. 1-16 is a basic amplifier configuration using an npn type of transistor.

14

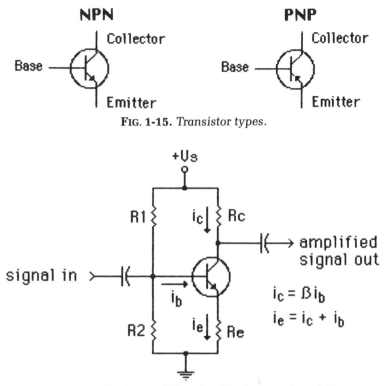

FIG. **1-15.** *Transistor types.*

FIG. **1-16.** *Basic amplifier circuit using npn transistor.*

A transistor requires a dc voltage supply (V_S) to operate. It must be applied to the collector path as well as to the base. Resistors R1 and R2 form the divider network that feeds dc voltage to the base. Thus, the base sees a portion of the supply (V_S) determined by the values of R1 and R2. This base voltage *biases* or "turns on" the transistor, meaning that dc base current (i_b) flows from the base, through the base-emitter junction, and through resistor R_e. Collector current (i_c) can then flow through resistor R_c through the collector-emitter junction and it then joins the base current at resistor R_e. The base and collector currents combine to form the emitter current (i_e). There is a relationship between the base current and the collector current. The collector current is the amplified base current in which $i_c = \beta i_b$, where β is the gain factor. The collector current follows changes in the base current.

The signal that is coupled in via the capacitor combines with the dc base current, adding to it with the positive half of the cycle and subtracting from it with the negative half. Because the collector current tracks (follows) the base current, a magnified version of the signal reproduces in the collector and emitter branches. This amplified signal is then coupled out through the collector

15

capacitor and passed on to another stage. Bear in mind that the coupling capacitors prevent any dc bias current from bleeding into the signal source or passing on to the output. (Recall that the dc current cannot exit through the capacitors because dc frequency is zero, making the capacitor impedance look infinitely large.)

The ratio of the amplified signal to the input signal is the *gain*, and it is usually a voltage ratio. The voltage of the output is determined by load of the next stage. Where R_L is the load, the output voltage is that portion of the amplified current (i_c') that leaves the stage multiplied times R_L:

$$V_o = i_c' \times R_L$$

OPERATIONAL AMPLIFIERS

Large-scale integrated (LSI) circuits have been developed for compactness and versatile application. A common building block for audio use is the *operational amplifier* or *op-amp*. Also an active device, the op-amp is a network of transistors packaged in a compact component to save space. FIGURE 1-17 shows a basic op-amp configuration and the equation relating output V_o to inputs V_1 and V_2. If V_2 is grounded ($V_2 = 0$), the equation is simplified. The gain, in this case, can easily be controlled by selecting two resistors—an input resistor R_1 and a feedback resistor R_f.

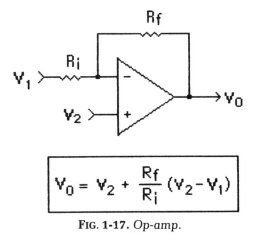

$$V_0 = V_2 + \frac{R_f}{R_i}(V_2 - V_1)$$

FIG. **1-17.** *Op-amp.*

Refer to FIG. 1-18, a common configuration for an inverting op-amp and its corresponding equation. The negative sign in the equation implies 180-degree phase shift, or the signal is said to be *inverted*. Hence, the negative input of the op-amp is called the inverting input and the positive one is the non-inverting input.

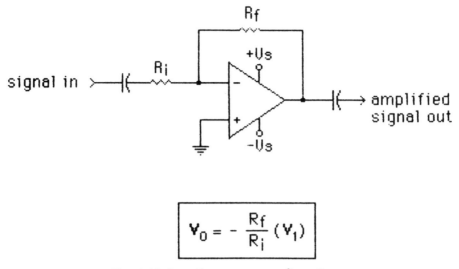

$$V_0 = - \frac{R_f}{R_i} (V_1)$$

FIG. **1-18.** *Inverting op-amp configuration.*

The ratio of the feedback resistor R_f over the input resistor R_i determines the voltage gain. Op-amps used for audio applications usually have both a positive and a negative power supply.

Note that in any block diagram, a triangular symbol similar to that of an op-amp represents amplification.

Another possible configuration for the op-amp is the *summing amp*, which accommodates a multiple of inputs and combines them as one output (FIG. 1-19). Mixers that utilize summing amps usually represent them in their diagrams with input lines shown connected to a common output line or *bus* rather than showing a symbol (FIG. 1-20).

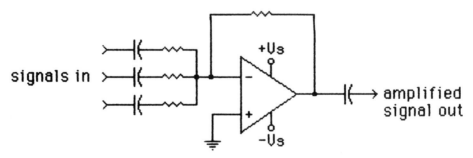

FIG. **1-19.** *Summing amp.*

17

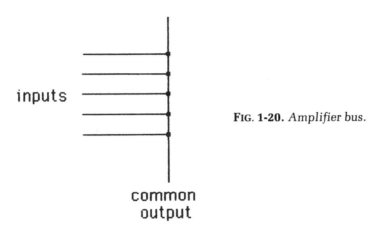

inputs

FIG. 1-20. *Amplifier bus.*

common
output

There are many types of op-amp configurations, particularly with active filters that use R-C combinations to make high-pass, low-pass, bandpass, and other circuits (covered in future chapters). But for now, these basics should be helpful for tackling the mixing console block diagrams and system diagrams to come. FIGURE 1-21 shows what some of these active devices look like.

A

FIG. 1-21. *Active circuit elements: (A) transistors and (B) op-amps.*

B

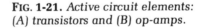

POWER SUPPLIES

Basic dc power supplies consist of transformers, diodes, electrolytic capacitors, and voltage regulators. Residential and commercial service entrance is 220/110 Vac, however these are not practical voltages to work with. A transformer is used to step down 110 Vac to something lower. A transformer is made up of wire windings or *turns* around a core. There are two sets of windings called the *primary* and the *secondary* windings, as shown in FIG. 1-22. The primary accepts the high voltage (110 Vac) and the secondary produces the stepdown output voltage. The stepdown voltage is proportional the turns ratio of the secondary over the primary. For example, a 5:1 turns ratio steps down 110 Vac to 22 Vac (110 ÷ 5 = 22). With a lower ac voltage to work with, it now can be converted to a dc source using four diodes and a capacitor.

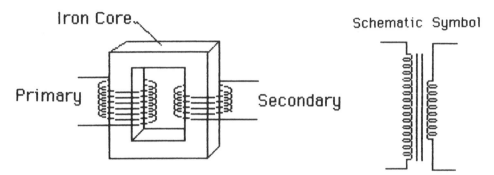

FIG. 1-22. *Transformer illustration and symbol.*

A *diode* is a component that controls current direction. All the components discussed so far permit current to flow in either direction. A diode permits current to flow in one direction only (FIG. 1-23). The diode has an *anode* (positive) end and cathode (negative) end. The schematic representation is an arrow-like symbol indicating current direction. Diodes block current in the reverse direction.

FIG. 1-23. *Diode illustration and symbol.*

FIGURE 1-24 shows a schematic of an ac source applied to resistor with a diode in the path. Only the positive portion of the cycle can get through because the positive voltage on the anode forward biases the diode. On the negative half cycle, the negative voltage does not affect the diode, so it is blocked.

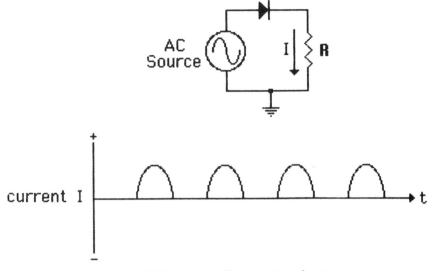

FIG. **1-24.** *Half-wave rectifier circuit and output.*

For this reason, diodes can operate as *half-wave rectifiers* (or just *rectifiers*). Configuring four diodes in a ring makes a *full-wave rectifier* or *diode bridge* as in FIG. 1-25. In this arrangement, the negative peak is not lost but is recovered into a positive peak.FIGURE 1-25A shows current flow during the positive peak and FIG. 1-25B shows the path during the negative peak. Thus, the capacitor is charged in one direction. The capacitor *integrates* or smooths out the peaks.

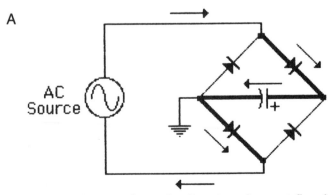

FIG. **1-25.** *Full-wave rectifier: (A) shows the direction of current flow for the positive part of the cycle*

B

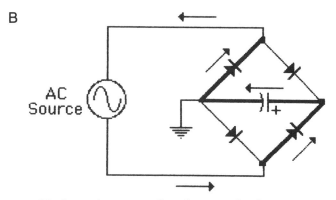

FIG. 1-25. *(B) shows the current flow direction for the negative portion.*

The capacitor charges only to 70 percent of its peak value. The result is illustrated in FIG. 1-26. This is the rectified, or dc, voltage that can now be used for other stages.

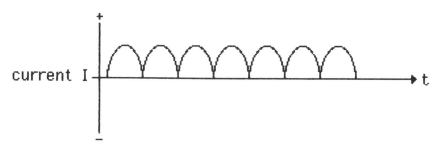

FIG. 1-26. *The output of the full-wave rectifier is a continuous, positive dc voltage.*

When a dc voltage is then produced, a *voltage regulator* is utilized to get a specific dc voltage. Voltage regulators can only step down a dc voltage, meaning that the applied dc voltage must be higher than the desired (rated) output voltage. FIGURE 1-27 shows a schematic of a power supply that produces both positive and negative dc voltages.

LOGIC ELEMENTS

Logic elements are *binary* devices, which means that only two voltages are used for inputs and outputs. The two logic states are typically 0 volts and +5 volts where 0 volts represents a binary 0, and +5 volts is a binary 1. This is the whole basis of computer technology. In audio equipment, logic elements play a large role in motor control circuitry in tape transports, synthesizers, and mixing console automation. Combinations of ones and zeros become electronic passwords to perform various operations.

21

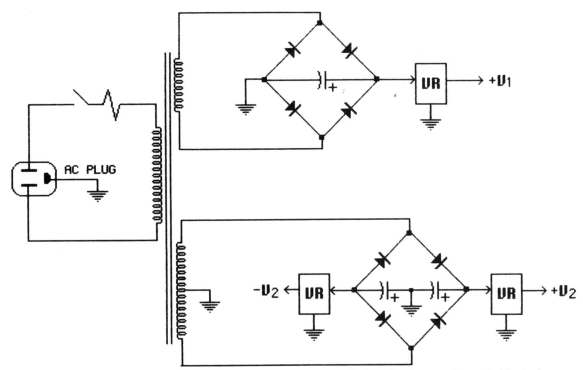

FIG. 1-27. *Power supply that converts ac to dc. The voltage regulating circuits are shown in block diagram form for simplicity. The supply provides both positive (V₁ and V₂) and negative (−V₂) dc voltage sources.*

FIGURE 1-28 shows three basic logic devices: the AND gate, the OR gate, and the inverter. Their operation is described by a *truth table*. This table shows the output response of the device in terms of applied inputs. FIGURE 1-29 shows the truth tables for AND and OR gates. Note that the only time the AND gate output is "high" (logic level #1) is when both inputs are high. The OR gate is high when either input is high. The inverter simply converts a 1 to a 0 or vice versa. If an AND gate has an inverter on the output, the AND gate is drawn with a bubble at the output and called a NAND gate. Similarly, an OR becomes a NOR, as shown in FIG. 1-30.

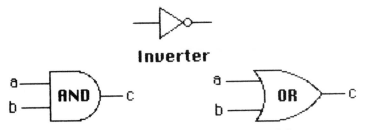

FIG. 1-28. *Symbols for logic gates: AND, OR, and the inverter.*

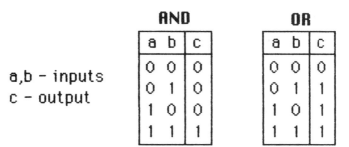

FIG. **1-29.** *Truth tables for the AND and OR gates.*

a,b – inputs
c – output

AND		
a	b	c
0	0	0
0	1	0
1	0	0
1	1	1

OR		
a	b	c
0	0	0
0	1	1
1	0	1
1	1	1

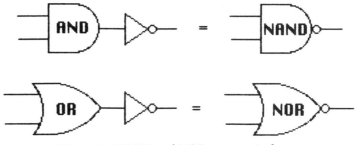

FIG. **1-30.** *NAND and NOR gate equivalents.*

As a small example of operation, refer to the logic schematic and timing diagram in FIG. 1-31. Signals are applied to inputs A, B, and C, as described in the timing diagram in FIG. 1-32. The final output F can be determined using the truth tables. Output D is in accordance with the OR truth table in which D is high when either of the inputs B or C is high. Output E is simply an inversion of input A. Output F is then in accordance with the AND truth table in which F is high only when both inputs D and E are high.

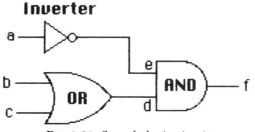

FIG. **1-31.** *Sample logic circuit.*

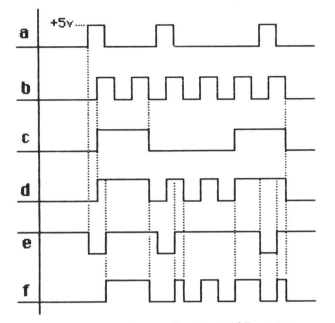

FIG. **1-32.** Timing diagram for circuit of FIG. 1-31.

2

Monitoring

MONITORING, THE FINAL LINK IN THE RECORDING CHAIN, IS AUDIOPHILE lingo for the word "listening." The expression *monitor* is also another word for "loudspeaker." Most people already have a familiarity with loudspeakers as being cabinets that house speaker cones. The cabinet is more than just a place to conceal the speaker. Its construction is carefully designed to suit the speaker used, and therefore the cabinet is a functional part of the loudspeaker system. Attempting to use speakers without any housing is impractical because the efficiency of the speaker to reproduce sound is greatly reduced when not mounted on a *baffle*. When mounted on a speaker board (the baffle), the board partitions the forward sound pressure from dispersing back to the rear of the speaker which is important for efficient sound reproduction. Professional studio monitors are enclosure-mounted speakers that are designed for high-fidelity performance to faithfully reproduce the audio spectrum for critical listening applications.

Technically, speakers are electromechanical converters. An electrical signal is converted into a mechanical vibration we call sound. To understand how this works, consider a permanent magnet and an iron core with wire windings as shown in the FIG. 2-1. The permanent magnet has a north and south pole. When current is applied to the windings, the iron core becomes magnetic and also develops north and south poles. The polarity depends on current direction: if ac current is applied, the north and south poles alternate as current direction alternates. When two magnetic sources are merged, opposite poles attract and like poles repel. The alternating current keeps switching poles, so the iron core is alternately attracted and repelled by the permanent magnet. Thus, there is mechanical motion as a result of these magnetic forces.

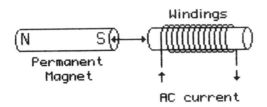

FIG. 2-1. *Magnetic attraction and repulsion of a coil and a permanent magnet.*

Principally, this is how a speaker works. The speaker cone has windings coiled at its base (the *voice coil*), backed by a permanent magnet. An amplifier delivers the electrical signal to the voice coil and the speaker cone moves back and forth through a series of magnetic attractions and repulsions to the permanent magnet. The illustration in FIG. 2-2 shows a basic speaker and its components.

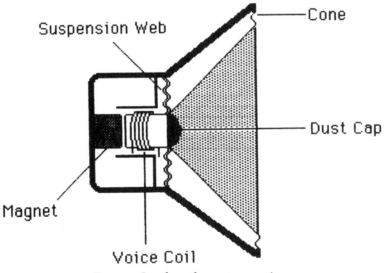

FIG. 2-2. *Loudspeaker cutaway view.*

ENCLOSURES, BAFFLING, AND CROSSOVER NETWORKS

Sound is produced by cone displacement. But as aforementioned, a speaker must be enclosed or baffled to operate effectively. The cabinet or speaker enclosure acts as a barrier to prevent sound pressure in front of the cone from cancelling the pressure developed at the rear of the cone. The lower frequencies suffer from these phase cancellations the most. That is why an unmounted speaker sounds "thin."

Speakers have various dimensions: they can be designed as a full range speaker or only dedicated to handle a portion of the audio frequency spectrum.

In most cases, monitor systems use two or more different individual *drivers* in an enclosure to cover the audio range. This way, there is more power-handling capability because the sonic energy is distributed among several drivers. Drivers with diameters ranging from 8 to 15 inches are generally called *woofers*. They cover the low end of the audio spectrum (bass response). For higher frequencies, speakers with smaller diameters are more efficient. Drivers with diameters less than 8 inches are regarded as *midrange* to cover the frequency spectrum between the low and high end. Finally, *tweeters* reproduce the high end. The diagram in FIG. 2-3 shows an example of the woofer, midrange, and tweeter frequency ranges for a given system.

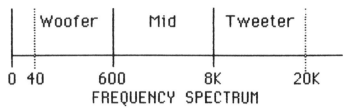

FIG. **2-3.** *Frequency distribution for monitor components.*

As illustrated in FIG. 2-4, an enclosure with a woofer, midrange, and tweeter is called a three-way system. The individual and overall frequency boundaries vary from system to system. Crossover boundaries from woofer to midrange can fall anywhere from 500 to 1200 Hz, and the midrange to tweeter transition point could start at 5 kHz. This all depends on the design concepts and the speaker components used.

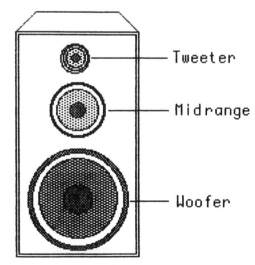

FIG. **2-4.** *Three-way monitor.*

In a multidriver system, the frequency allocation for each speaker component is accomplished by means of a *crossover network* inside the enclosure. A crossover is a passive electrical circuit made up of capacitors and inductors that filters or sorts out that part of the frequency spectrum for each speaker component. A three-way system requires three filters—a low-pass filter for the woofer, a bandpass filter for the midrange speaker, and a high-pass filter for the tweeter. FIGURE 2-5 shows a diagram of a three-way system and a sample schematic of a filtering network is in FIG. 2-6.

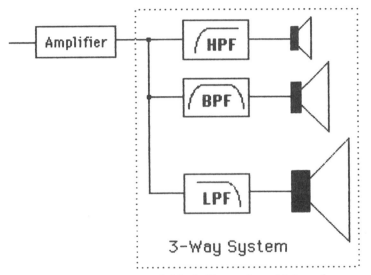

FIG. 2-5. *Three-way monitor with block illustration of internal crossover.*

The crossover network distributes the frequencies so that each speaker receives only that part of the spectrum it is supposed to reproduce efficiently. Speakers are considered to be 8-ohm devices. The voice coil is actually a complex *impedance* composed of a combined resistance and inductance (reactance). This means that this impedance varies with the frequency of the signal. For example, a midrange speaker might be 8 Ω only at 1 kHz. The crossover network is also designed to be 8 Ω to match the impedance of the speakers. The electrical theory used when interfacing networks is that *maximum power transfer is achieved when impedances are equal, or matched.*

The diagram in FIG. 2-7 shows a *Bode plot* of the crossover network. A Bode plot (pronounced ''bohdee'') is a graphical display in which the horizontal, frequency axis is exponential (the frequency doubles for each equal spacing). Each spacing division is an *octave*. The frequency span from *f* to *2f* defines an octave.

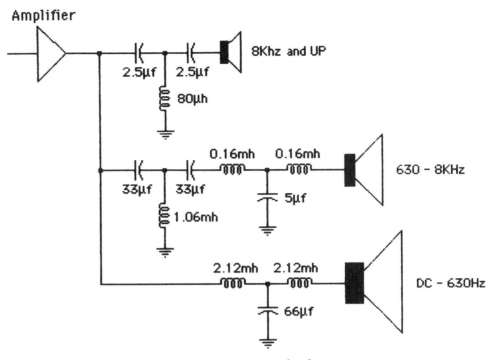

FIG. 2-6. *Crossover network schematic.*

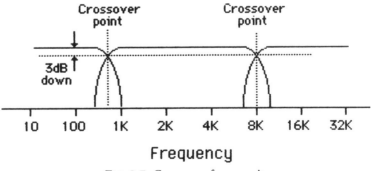

FIG. 2-7. *Crossover frequencies.*

The vertical axis represents power level expressed in decibels in which ''3 dB down'' (– 3 dB) means a 50 percent reduction in power. The crossover point is the frequency at which one filter intersects another at the 3 dB down point. If the top or flat part of the filter response is at the 0 dB level, then the crossover points should be 3 dB down.

The expression for power in decibels is $dB = 10 \log (P_{out}/P_{in})$. If at a certain frequency a filter reduces the power of P_{in} by $1/2$ on its output such that $P_{out} = P_{in}/2$, then $dB = 10 \log (1/2) = -3$. This might be a bit confusing, but logarithmic expressions are a way to escape working with large numbers on small scales. It so happens that if two speakers at the crossover point both produce the same frequency at 50 percent, then the total is 100 percent or 0 dB. Then there is theoretically no *dropout* at the crossover points.

Two-way monitors are very common in studios, too. Typically, this is an enclosure with a woofer and a *horn*. A horn is a special type of speaker construction that does the job of midrange and tweeter in a two-way application. The horn has a compression driver and a flared extrusion, giving its name, as illustrated in FIG. 2-8. This physical construction improves efficiency of a tweeter or midrange device. The driver compresses the air at the narrow neck opening, raising the pressure. An acoustical thrust is developed when the compressed air is coupled with the lower air pressure at the flared end of the horn. Usually the higher powered systems resort to a horn application. FIGURE 2-9 shows a two-way studio monitor, the UREI 809, with a horn centered in the woofer. This kind of speaker construction can be described as being *axial, coaxial,* or *dual concentric.*

Compression Driver

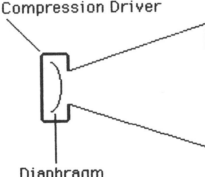

FIG. **2-8.** *Horn components.*

Diaphragm

There are two types of monitor enclosures—*acoustic suspension* and *bass reflex.* Acoustic suspension cabinets are completely sealed for an airtight enclosure. Bass reflex cabinets have a hole on the enclosure face that allows air passage from the interior to the exterior. The *port* hole is tuned or placed in such a way as to reinforce the bass response. The Tannoy PBM-6.5 (two-way) pictured in FIG.2-10 is an example of an acoustic suspension enclosure and the Tannoy Little Gold Monitor is a bass reflex type (FIG. 2-11). Note the port hole in the upper right corner. The Tannoy is a dual concentric two-way system (the horn is barely visible behind the dust screen).

FIG. 2-9. *UREI 809 Time Align monitor. (Time Align is a registered trademark of E.M. Long & Associates)*

FIG. 2-10. *Tannoy PBM-6.5 two-way monitor.*

FIG. **2-11.** *Tannoy Little Gold two-way concentric monitor.*

In both two-way and three-way systems, the woofer is positioned near the bottom of the enclosure and the higher frequency components are more elevated. FIGURE 2-12 features JBL two-way and three-way enclosures (models 4406, 4408, 4410, and 4412).

FIG. **2-12.** *JBL 4406, 4408, 4410, and 4412 monitors.*

A professional monitor is designed to give a flat response across the audio spectrum, meaning that all frequencies reproduce equally in energy level (in accordance with the applied signal). Some units have a control on the monitor face to alter a response, like to boost or cut the high end, depending on the listening environment.

Monitors are tested for frequency response in an *anechoic chamber*. This special chamber has its interior surfaces acoustically treated such that there will virtually be no reflections to influence test readings. The chamber surfaces are covered with large pyramid-type structures to absorb the sound. A microphone is placed in front of the monitor at a prescribed distance to register the acoustic power levels as the monitor is driven with uniform audio signals across the band.

DISPERSION

A speaker system has a sound dispersion characteristic called its *radiation pattern*. This has to do with the way sound intensity varies with regard to radial direction. A location directly in front of the monitor is the "on-axis" position and is the direction where the sound is most intense as shown in FIG. 2-13. As the listener moves "off-axis" to another angle, the high-frequency content becomes less perceptible. More off-axis movement begins to further diminish the highs and the midrange. A position behind the enclosure sounds very "bassy." The lowest frequency content has a very radial dispersion pattern as opposed to high-frequency content, so low-frequency intensity is consistent at off-axis locations. The mids and especially the highs are more directional and focus into narrower beams of sound. This spectral radiation pattern is depicted in FIG. 2-14.

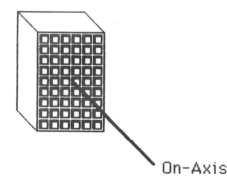

On-Axis

FIG. 2-13. *The on-axis location has the highest sound intensity.*

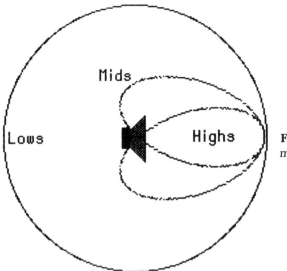

FIG. 2-14. *Radiation patterns of low, midrange, and high frequencies.*

The fact that the lows ''wrap around'' the monitor forces a concern for proper monitor placement and mounting. Consider a monitor placed near a wall or mounted flush to a wall as shown in FIG. 2-15. The low-frequency content reflects off the wall surface and is time delayed with respect to the direct sound wave in front of the monitor. The overall bass sound is intensified, but the time lag in the reflected sound discolors the purity of the direct sound when they both blend together. However, this is not an uncommon situation because this is how many listen to music at home.

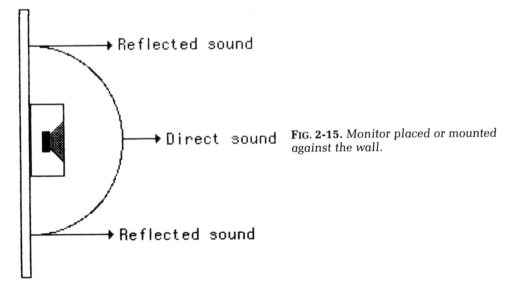

FIG. 2-15. *Monitor placed or mounted against the wall.*

A remedy for wall reflections is to apply sound absorption materials on the wall surface to reduce the reflected intensity. Another choice is to flush mount the cabinet into the wall as shown in FIG. 2-16. Any reflected sound remains radial (the bass response is still more intense) but it is noninterfering. In the following chapter on studio acoustics, creating a proper listening environment is covered in detail.

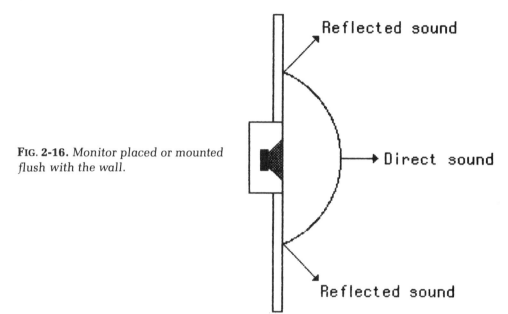

FIG. 2-16. *Monitor placed or mounted flush with the wall.*

STEREO PHASING

There is a polarity requirement for a stereo monitoring application. Monitors are two-terminal devices with a positive and a negative input. Both monitors must be in phase for a proper stereo hookup. The diagram in FIG. 2-17 shows this arrangement. Note that the (+) and (−) monitor terminals must match the amplifier terminals to keep the speakers in phase. To explain what is meant by *in phase*, consider an amplified sinusoidal signal that drives both monitors. The speaker cones move back and forth corresponding to the negative and positive sinusoidal peaks. When the speakers are in phase, the cones in both monitors move in the same direction. If a pair of terminals is reversed, then as one monitor cone moves forward, the other will move backward. In this condition, the speakers are out of phase. *Phase cancelling* results when a system is not in phase. As one speaker is compressing air, the other is reducing air pressure. This state of low pressure or suction is termed *rarefaction*. The acoustical air pressures oppose each other and tend to neutralize or drop out some of the sound, which disturbs the sonic tonal purity.

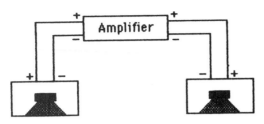

FIG. 2-17. *Monitors hooked up correctly for stereo listening.*

AMPLIFICATION AND ACTIVE CROSSOVERS

For more powerful systems, post-crossover amplification techniques are used known as *biamping* and *triamping*. In these cases, each speaker component is driven by its own amplifier. The crossover network is external and feeds the amplifiers as shown in FIG. 2-18. The external crossover network serves the same purpose as an internal one by separating the various frequency bands and routing them to each amplifier. However, these crossover networks are designed for low-power preamplification levels (they handle only small signals).

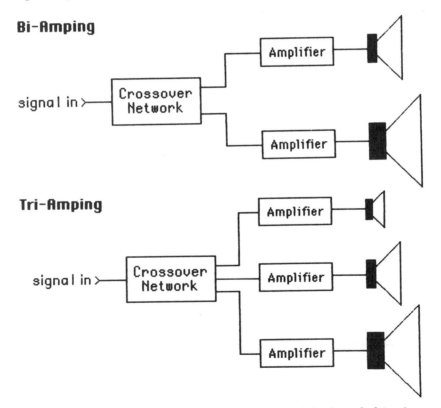

FIG. 2-18. *In biamping and triamping, the crossover network feeds each driver's separate amplifier.*

FIGURE 2-19 shows a Loft Model 603S frequency-dividing network. This is a stereo unit for triamping. Each channel has adjustments to set the two crossover points. The low/mid point has a selectable range. The point can be set from 40 to 800 Hz or from 400 Hz to 8 kHz. The mid/high point has only one range. The point can be set from 600 Hz to 12 kHz. Each band (low, mid, and high) has a gain control that can boost up to 9 dB. The model 603M, pictured in FIG. 2-20, is a single-channel unit with the same range controls as the 603S but has a limiter for each band to suppress peak power levels to protect the speaker components.

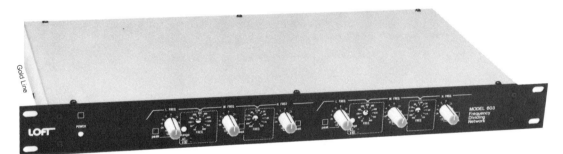

FIG. 2-19. *Loft 603S stereo frequency-dividing network.*

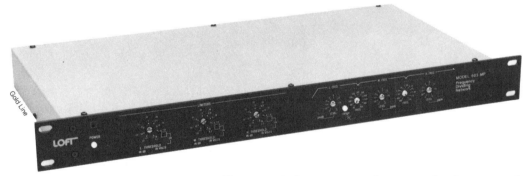

FIG. 2-20. *Loft 603M mono frequency-dividing network.*

There are some interesting advantages to biamping and triamping. The most obvious advantage is the power availability per component as opposed to one amplifier driving everything. A single amplifier handling the whole spectrum can easily be overloaded, causing its output to *clip*. When this happens, the signal becomes highly distorted and all components are affected. An *overload* is the condition when an incoming signal exceeds the maximum rated input level for the amp. In other words, overloading overdrives the amplifier

37

input with too much level. When an input signal is too high or "too hot," it forces the amplifier to saturate and clip the signal. To understand what clipping is, consider a 100-watt power amplifier with a gain of 26 dB driving an 8-ohm monitor. Knowing that the amplifier can deliver 100 watts into 8 ohms, what does this mean in terms of peak-to-peak voltage? Power is defined as the root mean square (rms) voltage squared over resistance:

$$P_{watts} = \frac{V_{rms}{}^2}{R}$$

Solving algebraically for V_{rms}:

$$V_{rms} = \sqrt{PR}$$
$$= \sqrt{(100)\,(8)}$$
$$= \sqrt{800}$$
$$= 28.28$$

To convert V_{rms} to peak-to-peak voltage V_{p-p}:

$$V_{p-p} = \sqrt{2}(2)\,V_{rms}$$
$$V_{p-p} = 80$$

FIGURE 2-21 shows the 80-volt peak-to-peak signal. Knowing that the amplifier gain is 26 dB, the maximum peak-to-peak input signal can be calculated from the decibel expression:

$$dB = 20 \log (V_{out}/V_{in})$$

Algebraically solving for V_{in}:

$$dB/20 = \log (V_{out}/V_{in})$$

Taking the antilog for base 10 by using the form where

$$a = \log (x),\ then\ x = 10^a$$

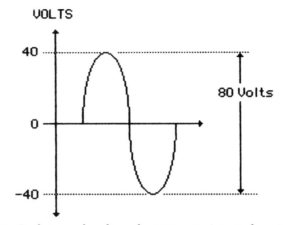

FIG. 2-21. *Peak-to-peak voltage for 100 watts into 8 ohms is 80 volts.*

$$\frac{V_{out}}{V_{in}} = 10^{db/20}$$

$$V_{in} = \frac{V_{out}}{10^{dB/20}}$$

Since the gain is 26 dB and V_{out} = 80, substitute these numbers for the above expression:

$$V_{in} = \frac{80}{10^{\,26\,/\,20}} = \frac{80}{10^{1.3}} = \frac{80}{20}$$

$$V_{in} = 4(\text{Max p} - \text{p volts})$$

Thus a 26 dB power gain will amplify a 4-volt signal into an 80-volt signal. That is a voltage gain of (80/4) = 20. This 4-volt input can be expressed in rms voltage:

$$V_{rms} = \frac{V_{p-p}}{\sqrt{2}\,(2)}$$

$$V_{rms} = \frac{4}{\sqrt{2}\,(2)}$$

$$V_{rms} = 1.414$$

Examine what would happen if the incoming signal exceeded 4 volts peak-to-peak (1.414 V_{rms}). Because the 100-watt amplifier cannot do better than 80 V_{p-p}, then the hot input would force it to clip as shown in FIG. 2-22. As an example, if a 5 V_{p-p} input were applied, an amplifier voltage gain of 20 would make an attempt to generate an output voltage of 100 V_{p-p} rather than 80. But as soon as +40 or −40 volts is reached, the output stays at these saturation levels for that portion of the input signal exceeding +2 and −2 volts.

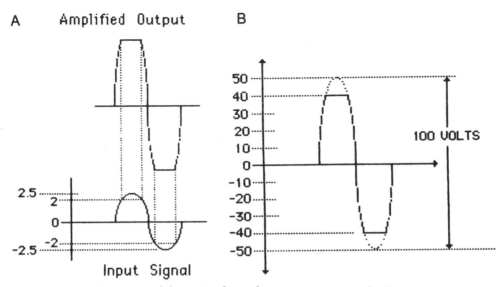

FIG. 2-22. *Overdriven amplifier: (A) shows how an input signal of $5V_{p-p}$ clips when it exceeds the $4V_{p-p}$ limit. (B) shows the clipped output of an overdriven amplifier.*

When a signal clips, it resembles a square wave. This kind of distortion translates into a lot of high-frequency energy that threatens to blow out tweeters. An amplifier should have plenty of "headroom," meaning that the amplifier power rating should be well above the nominal use. Most preamp devices that drive a power amplifier can deliver signal levels as high as 6 V_{p-p}. For a 26 dB-gain power amp, that would mean about 245 watts into an 8-ohm monitor load.

$$V_{rms} = \frac{V_{p-p}}{2.83} = \frac{6}{2.83} = 2.12$$

$$V_{out} = V_{in}10^{dB/20}$$
$$= (2.12)\ 10^{26/20}$$
$$= (2.12)\ (20)$$
$$= 42.4$$

$$P = \frac{V^2}{R} = \frac{(42.4)^2}{8}$$
$$= 244.7 \text{ watts}$$

If another 8-ohm monitor is hooked up in *parallel* (as opposed to *series*), the power output from the amplifier increases, provided the amplifier is capable. If two monitor loads share the same source, the loads are said to be in parallel. The schematic representation is shown in FIG. 2-23. R1 and R2 represent monitor loads and both experience the same voltage V applied by the amplifier. The current passing through each load is:

$$I_1 = \frac{V}{R_1} \text{ and } I_2 = \frac{V}{R_2}$$

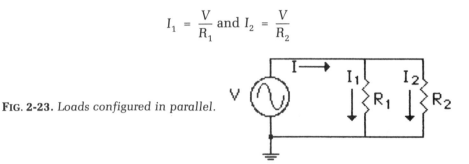

FIG. 2-23. *Loads configured in parallel.*

The total current $I = I_1 + I_2 = V/R_1 + V/R_2$. The equivalent resistance of the parallel loads is $R = V/I$.

$$R = \frac{V}{I} = \frac{V}{I_1 + I_2}$$

$$= \frac{V}{\dfrac{V}{R_1} + \dfrac{V}{R_2}}$$

$$= \frac{1}{\dfrac{1}{R_1} + \dfrac{1}{R_2}}$$

Therefore,

$$R = \frac{R_1 R_2}{R_1 + R_2}$$

In the case where two parallel monitor load impedances are the same, the equivalent impedance is equal to one-half of one of the loads. Where R_m is the monitor load, and $R_1 = R_2 = R_m$, then:

$$R = \frac{R_m R_m}{R_m + R_m}$$

$$= \frac{R_m R_m}{2R_m}$$

$$= \frac{R_m}{2}$$

41

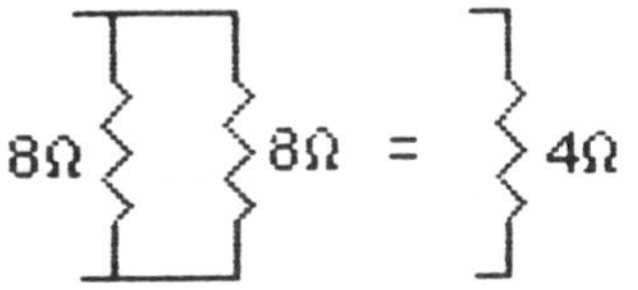

FIG. 2-24. *Reducing parallel resistances.*

FIGURE 2-24 shows the equivalent load of two parallel 8-ohm speakers.

Speakers have a power rating that represents the maximum continuous power. A transient power burst will be forgiven, but a sustained level above its rating will damage the components. Excessive power can overheat the voice coil.

SENSITIVITY AND EFFICIENCY

By now, you might have the impression that electrical power and acoustical volume must have a proportional relationship. In general, this is true, but not all monitors sound equally as loud for the same power input. How much input power that is converted into acoustical power depends on the *efficiency* of the monitor. Actually, only a small percent of the applied power is converted into sonic energy. The part that does not convert dissipates as heat. Therefore, power input equals heat plus acoustical energy.

The specification of *sensitivity* indicates efficiency. The *sound pressure level* (SPL) is a measurement observed 1 meter from the speaker along its on-axis using a 1-watt input. This information can be used to determine the acoustic power density in terms of watts per square meter. The expression that relates SPL to electrical power is:

$$SPL(dB) = 10 \log\left(\frac{\delta}{10^{-12}}\right)$$

where δ is watts/square meter and SPL is decibels. Solving for δ,

$$\delta = 10^{(dB/10)-12}$$

Sometimes this sensitivity measurement is made in an anechoic chamber or in a room environment where this measurement is boosted, say by a wall reflection. As an example, an anechoic sensitivity measurement yields 90 dB at 1 meter with a 1-watt input. From the power density expression:

$$\delta = 10^{(90/10)-12}$$
$$\delta = 10^{(9-12)}$$
$$\delta = 10^{-3} = 0.001 \text{ W/m}^2$$

Assuming that the monitor is a point source and that the sound is omnidirectional (radiates in all directions), the surface area for a sphere at a given radial distance is:

$$A = 4\pi r^2$$

where r = 1 meter,

$$\begin{aligned} A &= 4\pi \\ &= 4(3.142) \\ &= 12.57 \text{ m}^2 \end{aligned}$$

If a monitor has 100 percent efficiency where it would convert 1 electrical watt into 1 watt of acoustical power, then the acoustical power density is 1 watt divided by the surface area of the sphere (A).

$$\delta = \frac{P}{A} = \frac{1 \text{ W}}{12.57 \text{ m}^2} = 0.08 \text{W/m}^2$$

The efficiency of the monitor is the ratio of the sensitivity power density (δ_s) to the applied power density (δ_a).

$$\begin{aligned} \text{Efficiency} &= (\delta_s/\delta_a) \times 100 \\ &= (0.001/0.08) \times 100 \\ &= 1.25 \text{ \%} \end{aligned}$$

This means that very little of the applied electrical power is converted into acoustical energy. The other 98.75 percent dissipates as heat.

It is interesting to note that in free space, the SPL drops 6 dB every time the distance away from the speaker doubles (FIG. 2-25). If there is an SPL of 90 dB at 1 meter, then it will be 84 dB at 2 meters, 78 dB at 4 meters, 72 dB at 8 meters, etc.

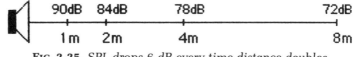

FIG. 2-25. *SPL drops 6 dB every time distance doubles.*

This SPL change can be calculated from the equation:

$$\Delta \text{SPL} = 10 \log(\delta_2/\delta_1)$$

FIG. 2-26. *Power density (δ) at distance (r).*

in which δ_1 is the power density at r_1 and δ_2 is the power density at r_2 (FIG. 2-26).

$$\delta_1 = P/4\pi r_1{}^2$$

$$\delta_2 = P/4\pi r_2{}^2$$

$$\frac{\delta_2}{\delta_1} = \left(\frac{r_1}{r_2}\right)^2$$

$$\Delta\text{SPL} = 10 \log \left(\frac{r_1}{r_2}\right)^2$$

If $r_1 = D$ *and* $r_2 = 2D$:

$$\left(\frac{r_1}{r_2}\right)^2 = \left(\frac{D}{2D}\right)^2 = 0.25$$

then:

$$\Delta\text{SPL} = 10 \log (0.25)$$

$$= -6.02 \text{ dB (drop)}$$

The negative sign implies a drop or loss of power. The logarithm of any number less than one is negative.

AMPLIFIER SPECIFICATIONS

Amplifier specification is performance information. This is standard information that serves as a basis for comparison between one product and another. The main specifications are discussed here, and most of them apply to all the other audio gear in the recording link.

power output—The continuous power output capacity of the amplifier stated for both 8 ohm and 4 ohm loads. In general, expect almost 50 percent more power when going into 4 ohms. For example, an amplifier rated at 170 watts into 8 ohms might deliver 250 watts into 4 ohms.

gain—The amount of amplification expressed in dB. Typically, gain is about 26 dB for amplifiers. A 3 dB gain means the power is doubled. A 26 dB gain means that the power is doubled almost nine times and voltage is increased 20 times. Conversely, a 3 dB decrease is half power. The following equations apply: $dB = 10 \log(P_{out}/P_{in})$ or $dB = 20 \log(V_{out}/V_{in})$ and $P_{out}/P_{in} = 10^{(dB/10)}$ or $V_{out}/V_{in} = 10^{(dB/20)}$. For a 26 dB gain, $P_{out}/P_{in} = 10^{(26/10)} = 400$.

sensitivity—The maximum input voltage required to drive the amplifier to its rated power output into a 4 ohm load.

input impedance—The load seen by a preamplifier or mixer when plugged into the power amplifier, which is generally 15 kilohms.

frequency response—Should represent the bandwidth for which the response is flat or uniform. Most modern amplifiers cover a range that greatly exceeds the human hearing range (down as low as 5 Hz and beyond 50 kHz).

THD—Total Harmonic Distortion. Anytime a signal is processed by an amplifier, the penalty is some distortion. All distortion disturbs the spectral purity of a signal and results in generating harmonics or overtones that are multiples of the input frequency. Fortunately, these unwanted overtones are not very audible. Expect spec values to be less than 0.5 percent.

intermod distortion—Intermod is short for *intermodulation* and is a phenomenon that occurs when at least two signals are mixed together. They tend to spin off unwanted frequencies called *spurs*, which are the sum and difference of all the harmonic combinations. Expect to see spec values less than 0.1 percent.

signal-to-noise ratio—A ratio of signal power over noise power (S/N), expressed in decibels. The drawback of using any active device is its contribution of noise or "hiss." Most amplifiers have a S/N of about 110 dB or better. Look for signal-to-noise ratios that exceed 80 dB. See FIG. 2-27.

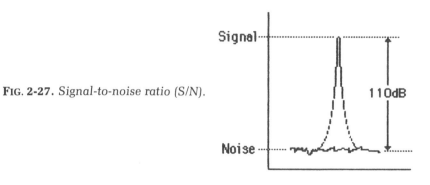

FIG. **2-27.** *Signal-to-noise ratio (S/N).*

slew rate—Describes the amplifier's transient performance, or how fast it can react to an input signal. Certain audio signals, particularly percussion sounds, have a fast attack or rise time, meaning that the signal goes from 0 volts to its peak level in a very short period of time, which is measured in millionths of a second (microseconds or μs). An amplifier must be able to respond in order to faithfully reproduce the signal. Most amplifiers have a slew rate of about 25 V/μs. See FIG. 2-28.

Pictured in FIG. 2-29, FIG. 2-30, and FIG. 2-31 are several power amplifiers—the Ramsa (Panasonic) WP-9220, the QSC MX 2000, and the Carver PM-2.0t. FIGURE 2-32 pictures a headset amplifier made by Tascam, the MH-4. It has four stereo outputs to drive four headphones.

45

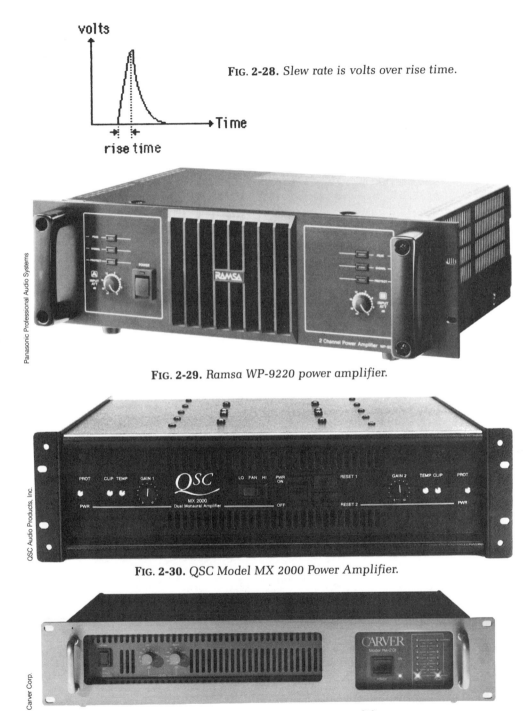

FIG. **2-28.** *Slew rate is volts over rise time.*

FIG. **2-29.** *Ramsa WP-9220 power amplifier.*

FIG. **2-30.** *QSC Model MX 2000 Power Amplifier.*

FIG. **2-31.** *Carver PM-2.0t power amplifier.*

FIG. 2-32. *Tascam MH-40 Multiheadphone amplifier.*

3

Studio Acoustics

IN SPITE OF EQUIPMENT PERFORMANCE SPECIFICATIONS AND ENGINEERING application skills, the recording and listening environment has a critical bearing on the final results. Undesirable room acoustics can interfere with proper miking applications in the recording cycle as well as deceive the listener in the control room. The first thing is to identify the types of acoustical phenomena that occur in an enclosure and then deal with it in order to make the studio a suitable recording and listening environment.

SOUNDPROOFING

One of the first considerations is how to isolate a studio from its external environment. Noises such as auto traffic, airplanes, trains, storms, and other activities threaten to contaminate recordings. There are some methods to resist the penetration of outside disturbances as well as prevent studio sounds from escaping to the outside world. The degree of effectiveness of soundproofing depends on the material construction of the floor, ceiling and walls. In general, the denser the materials, the better the isolation. Most buildings do not have adequate construction for acoustic isolation where a recording environment is concerned. Therefore, additional reinforcement might be required, depending on your location. There are cost-effective solutions as opposed to expensive ones such as six-foot-thick concrete walls and ceilings.

Walls can be acoustically reinforced by constructing a parallel wall using standard materials such as studs, sheet rock, and fiberglass insulation as shown in FIG. 3-1. For best results, leave an air gap about 4 inches wide between the existing wall and the new wall. The purpose of the air gap is to decouple the walls from vibrations that can easily transfer from the existing wall to the new wall via the studs. The objective is to avoid making contact using rigid materials because such materials transfer vibrations more efficiently than flexible ones.

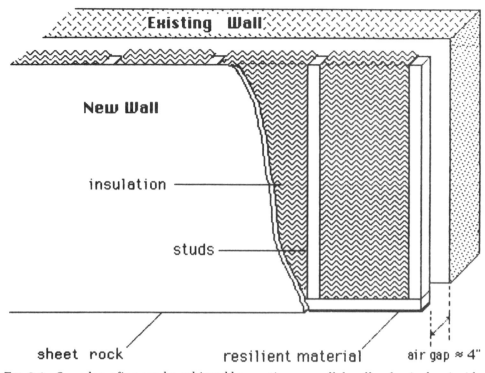

FIG. 3-1. *Soundproofing can be achieved by erecting a parallel wall a few inches inside the existing wall.*

But the new wall has to be attached somewhere, so make points of contact with other surfaces using resilient materials such as rubber, sponge, or springs. The base of the new wall should sit on a rubbery material avoiding a rigid contact with the floor.

Materials are described in terms of *transmission loss*, which is a value expressed in dB. It represents a material's ability to reflect or absorb (attenuate) sound. This attenuation characteristic is frequency dependent. High-frequency content is transmitted (attenuated) less than low-frequency content. That means a siren would be less audible than the rumble of a truck at the same sound intensity. The diagram in FIG. 3-2 shows a material being subjected to an incident sound wave. A portion of the incident wave is absorbed and the rest is reflected. A consequence of absorption is transmission on the other side. Transmission loss (TL) is defined mathematically as:

$$TL = 10 \log \left(\frac{S_i}{S_t} \right)$$

49

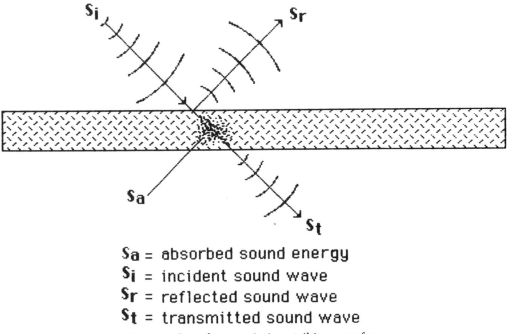

S_a = absorbed sound energy
S_i = incident sound wave
S_r = reflected sound wave
S_t = transmitted sound wave

FIG. 3-2. *Sound transmission striking a surface.*

For example, if 20 percent of the incident sound is transmitted through a barrier, then,

$$TL = 10 \log \left(\frac{100}{20} \right)$$

$$= 10 \log(5) \approx 7 \text{ dB}$$

This implies that the incident sound energy is attenuated 7 dB. If the environmental noise is 50 dBa (adjusted decibels) then the interior noise will be 43 dBa. It is interesting to note that if the S_i/S_t ratio is inverted in the TL expression to read $TL = 10 \log (S_t/S_i)$, the number will be negative, but numerically the same. This inverted ratio (S_t/S_i) is called the *transmission coefficient*. Coefficient charts for various materials are given for several frequencies because transmission loss is frequency dependent. The larger the coefficient value, the poorer the attenuation property is for isolation. A brick wall might have a profile like the one pictured in FIG. 3-3. The worst case is at about 4000 cps where the transmission coefficient is about 0.025. This means a brick wall can at best offer 16 dB of isolation. Most information sources provide coefficient values up to 4 kHz. The curve in FIG. 3-3 is only realistic up to that frequency.

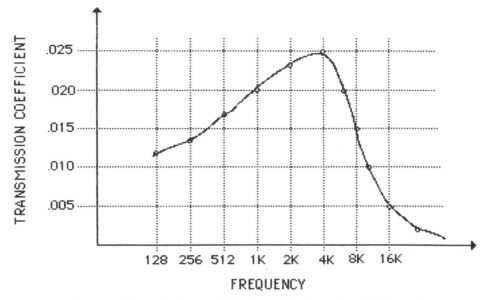

FIG. 3-3. *Transmission coefficient profile of a painted brick wall.*

A studio should pursue an interior noise level goal of about 10 dBa. Small openings such as door jambs and windows can seriously degrade isolation attempts. All air leaks must be plugged. An alternative to this is to have an isolation booth and use it for sensitive acoustical recording as well as isolation from other instruments in the studio. The approach as to how extensive isolation construction should go depends on the location. Noise measurements can be made with metering devices. But to get a good idea of what dBa sound pressure level values really mean, the chart in FIG. 3-4 should be helpful. The "a" in dBa stands for the a-weighted scale from the Fletcher-Munson curves. These curves show the human ear response to sound pressure level over the audio spectrum. Our ears are most sensitive in the area of 3 to 4 kHz, so we require more sound intensity for lows and highs to experience equal volume.

If a budget is permitting, some studios go to the extent of making the walls, floor, and ceiling suspended from the exterior construction and foundation using resilient hardware. Rooms constructed in this manner are called "floating" rooms. After a studio is made soundproof in which exterior sounds are blocked as well as studio sounds are contained, the next step is to condition the studio for tonal balance. There are several adverse acoustical phenomena that occur and affect a recording environment.

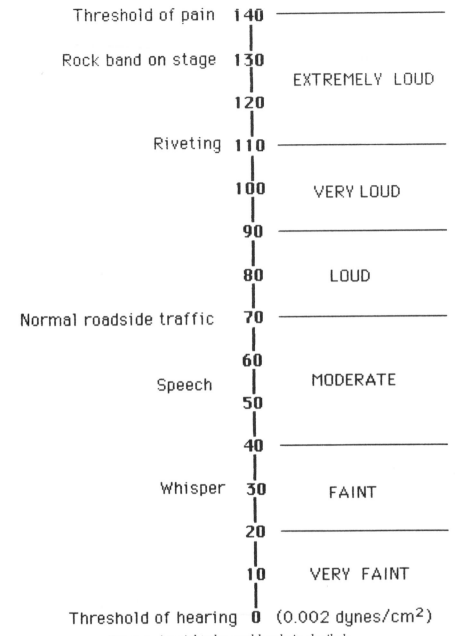

Threshold of pain	140	
	130	
Rock band on stage	130	EXTREMELY LOUD
	120	
Riveting	110	
	100	VERY LOUD
	90	
	80	LOUD
Normal roadside traffic	70	
	60	
Speech		MODERATE
	50	
	40	
Whisper	30	FAINT
	20	
	10	VERY FAINT
Threshold of hearing	0	(0.002 dynes/cm^2)

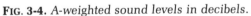

FIG. 3-4. *A-weighted sound levels in decibels.*

STANDING WAVES

Standing wave is a term that describes a sound that resonates between parallel surfaces. Because most room constructions have parallel surfaces, this can be a problem. Depending on the distance between the two surfaces, certain frequencies are reinforced by the reflections as the sound bounces back and forth between the surfaces. To the ear or to a microphone, there is a tonal imbalance, creating unwanted *coloration* in the natural sound. Fortunately, the frequencies that become standing waves are predictable. The fundamental resonant frequency has a wavelength that is twice the distance between the parallel surfaces (FIG. 3-5). The formula is:

$$F = \frac{V}{2D} = \frac{565}{D}$$

where F = fundamental frequency
V = velocity of sound (1130 ft/sec)
D = distance between surfaces

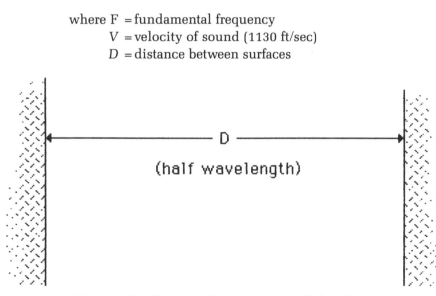

FIG. **3-5.** *Standing wave between two parallel surfaces.*

Once the fundamental is determined, the rest of the resonant standing waves are the frequency's *harmonics*, or multiples. For example, if the distance between two parallel walls is 20 feet, then the fundamental is 565/20 ≈ 28 Hz. The other standing waves are the harmonics, 56 Hz, 84 Hz, 112 Hz, 140 Hz, and so on. Fortunately, the harmonics are not as severe as the fundamental. In fact, the higher the harmonic frequency, the less severe it is (the smaller its amplitude).

Because a room has three sets of parallel surfaces, standing waves occur in three axial directions. It is desirable to have room dimensions that do not have the potential of reinforcing the same frequencies. The worst case obviously is a room where all three dimensions (*modes*) are the same (a cube). The graph in FIG. 3-6 represents the relative length and width ratios recommended for a reasonable modal distribution, where the height has a relative value of 1. As an example, if the height z is 1, a set of coordinates that would work is $y = 2$ (length) and $x = 1.5$ (width). So if there is a 10-foot ceiling, then the length of the room should be 20 feet and the width 15 feet. If the ceiling is 8 feet, then the length should be 16 feet and the width 12 feet.

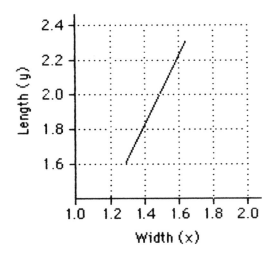

FIG. **3-6.** *Room dimension ratios where height is 1 (x:y:1).*

One way to avoid standing waves is to have nonparallel surfaces. This might not be convenient unless a studio is being built from scratch. A method that is effective is the construction of a *bass trap*. Due to the fact that fundamental frequencies are low, a bass trap is designed to absorb lows, thus damping a reflection that would echo back to reinforce the fundamental.

Bass Trap

Recall that an incident wave results in reflection, absorption, and transmission. The law of the conservation of energy supports that the incident energy equals the reflected energy plus the absorbed and transmitted energy.

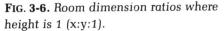

$$S_i = S_r + S_a + S_t$$

The principle of a bass trap is to have a large $(S_a + S_t)$ total, keeping S_r small as opposed to a soundproofing application in which S_t is kept small and S_r large. Dense, rigid materials have a high degree of reflectivity in which most of the incident sound energy bounces back. But if flexible materials are used, then sound energy can be converted into another form of mechanical energy. Sound energy is dissipated when flexible materials give way. This is the principle of a bass trap.

Plywood is a common material used in making bass traps. From the standing wave formula, resonant fundamental frequencies are calculated based on room dimensions. A bass trap is designed or "tuned" to absorb a particular resonant frequency. In the construction of a bass trap, an air gap dimension must be calculated as a function of plywood density and the fundamental frequency. The diagram in FIG. 3-7 shows the physical construction of a bass trap. The air space (x) between the front plywood face and the wall dampens the plywood motion, thus dissipating the energy of the resonant wave. The formula to calculate this air space (x) is:

$$x = \frac{28,900}{\delta f^2}$$

where x = air space dimension (inches)
δ = density of plywood (lbs/ft^2)
f = fundamental frequency (Hz)

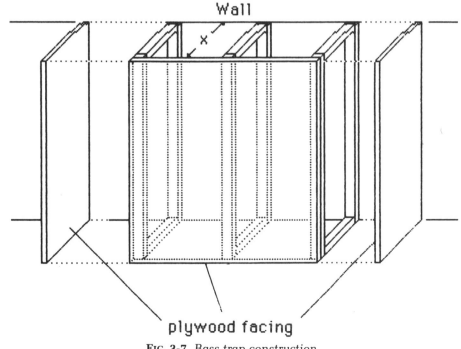

FIG. 3-7. Bass trap construction.

For $1/2$-inch plywood, $\delta = 1.375$ lbs/ft^2. Because density is proportional to thickness, this means that δ for $1/4$-inch plywood is half as much. As an example, a wall-to-wall room dimension of 20 feet has a resonant standing wave frequency of 28 Hz. Using $1/2$-inch plywood, the required air space (x) is approximately 27 inches.

$$x = \frac{28,900}{(1.375)(28)^2} \approx 27 \text{ inches}$$

Note from the formula that the denser the material (larger δ), the smaller the required air space. Using $3/4$-inch plywood ($\delta = 2.063$), only 18 inches is needed. The supporting studs should be spaced by a minimum of 24 inches. The attachment of the studs will reinforce the plywood and alter the density (δ) value. For convenience, substitute for the variable F in the equation and calculate x in terms of room dimension D where $F = 565/D$.

$$x = \frac{28,900}{\delta \left(\dfrac{565}{D} \right)^2}$$

Therefore,

$$x = \frac{(.091)D^2}{\delta}$$

Needless to say, trapping an entire wall can eat up floor space, so only a portion of a surface can be considered, but probably no less than 25 percent. Another method that resembles the bass trap technique is the *Helmholtz resonator* where cubical or cylindrical compartments are employed to resist standing waves. These cavities work on the principle of phase cancellation.

REVERBERATION

Reverberation is the result of multiple reflections on all the room surfaces. The intensity and duration of the reverberation depends on room dimensions as well as the absorption characteristics of the surfaces. Although reverb can be a desirable effect applied in production, control should be exercised in the studio. Materials such as carpet, curtains, acoustical tiles, and convoluted foam have a damping property called the *absorption coefficient*. It is the ratio of the absorbed sound energy over the incident sound energy. For purposes of discussion, consider that any transmitted sound lost is part of the absorption. From a reflection perspective, the absorbed sound (S_a) is that which is not reflected. Then the coefficient of absorption $(\beta) = S_a/S_i$.

Fiber and porous materials have good absorption coefficients except at low frequencies. Just as transmission coefficients are frequency dependent, so are absorption coefficients. Heavy carpet on a concrete floor has an absorption coefficient of 0.65 at 4000 Hz. This means that the reflected sound is expected to be 35 percent of the initial incident sound. Thus, reverberation can be reduced using fiber and porous materials. Reverberation time can be approximated using this expression:

$$T_{60} = \frac{.049V}{-S\ln(1-\beta)}$$

where $T_{60} = 60$ dB reverberation reduction (sec)

V = room volume (cubic feet)

$\ln$ = natural log

β = average absorption coefficient of room

S = total surface area

The subscript 60 implies the time it takes for a vibration to diminish 60 dB down from its initial SPL. As an example, consider a room with dimensions of $10 \times 15 \times 20$ feet (FIG. 3-8) with an average absorption coefficient of 0.5. Plugging in the numbers, the estimated reverberation time using the 60 dB down point as a reference is:

$$V = 10 \times 15 \times 20 = 3000$$

$$S = 2(10 \times 15) + 2(15 \times 20) + 2(10 \times 20) = 1300$$

$$1 - \beta = 1 - 0.5 = 0.5$$

$$T_{60} = \frac{0.049(3000)}{-1300\ln(0.5)} = \frac{147}{-1300\,(-0.693)} = 0.163 \text{ sec}$$

This room would be considered a "dead" room, meaning that there is negligible sound reflection. Modern recording usually prefers a room to be somewhat dead (0.4 sec) as opposed to a "live" room that has a long reverberation time. Natural reverberation can be a nuisance when trying to achieve isolation within the studio. Engineers and producers prefer to apply reverberation electronically

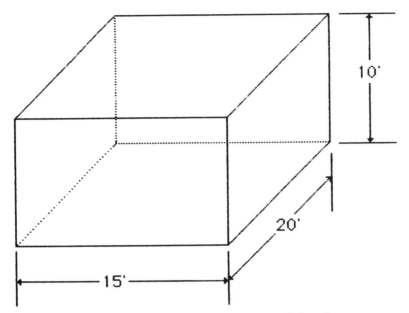

FIG. 3-8. *Room dimensions that have parallel surfaces.*

in the mixdown because of all the programmable features offered in digital reverb devices.

ECHOES

An echo is a discrete reflection or repeat of a sound that has a substantial time delay, long enough for human perception (FIG. 3-9.) Reverberation is the random scattering of sound, a multiplicity of echoes so closely spaced so as to make the repeats unintelligible. If incident sound is perpendicular to a surface, the reflection is directed back towards the source along the same axis. A time travel exceeding 35 milliseconds can be detected and perceived as an echo. If sound travels at 1130 ft/sec, then only 40 feet are needed for a 35-millisecond delay (1130 ft/sec × 0.035 sec ≈ 40 ft). On a per foot basis, sound travels 1 foot in 0.885 ms (1/1130). The impact of this is that a singer 20 feet away from a wall will hear an echo, because the forward and return path totals to 40 feet. What is even worse is the condition set up by parallel walls that creates a series of echoes called *flutter echo*.

Diffusers

Although walls might be treated for absorption, it might not be sufficient to eliminate echoes. Geometric structures called *diffusers* can break up echoes.

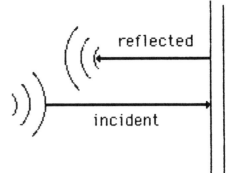

FIG. 3-9. *Echo is a discrete audible reflection.*

Diffusion is a technique that is used to create an irregular surface area that will deflect sound in random directions. A diffuser can run vertically from floor to ceiling or horizontally from wall to wall, dissolving echoes and aiding in breaking up standing waves. FIGURE 3-10 shows an illustration of a vertical diffuser and a control room photograph of a horizontally constructed diffuser.

Convoluted foam, such as Sonex (pictured in FIG. 3-11), has peak and valley contours that have diffusive characteristics because of the irregular surface area, but it is only effective for high-frequency content. Its porous character makes it effective for high-frequency absorption. FIGURE 3-12 shows egg-carton-type convoluted foam mounted on a wall surface. FIGURE 3-13 shows hinged louvers mounted on the studio wall surface. One side is a hard wood surface and the other is soft for sound absorption. These panels can be swiveled to expose either side. Hard surfaces such as control room and isolation booth glass should be angled to avoid parallelism with an opposing wall.

ISOLATION BOOTHS AND GOBOS

A studio should have one or more isolation booths to separate activities going on at the same time. This is to prevent *crosstalk* (also called *spillover* or *bleed*) from one mike into another. It is certainly desirable, for example, to keep the guitar amplifier mike isolated from the drums and vice versa. An isolation booth is usually a small room within the studio. Once again, walls should be nonparallel and surfaces treated with absorption materials. The viewing window should be angled to avoid standing waves. An isolation booth is pictured in FIG. 3-14. The diagram in FIG. 3-15 shows an example of a wall construction for a booth. The air space absorbs sound transmission for both internal and exterior concerns.

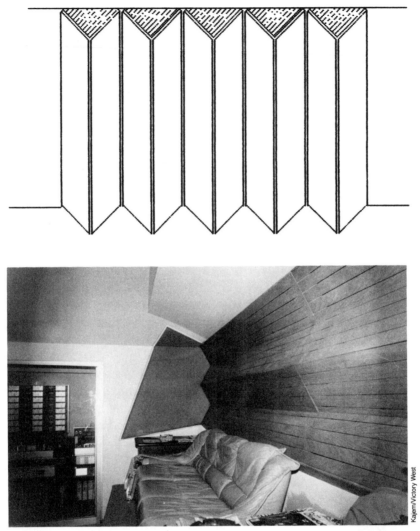

Kajem/Victory West

FIG. 3-10. *Diffusers: (A) illustrates one construction technique of a panel diffuser, and (B) shows the Kajem control room rear diffuser.*

Another method used for partial isolation is placement of portable partitions called *gobos*. These gobos help reduce crosstalk. Gobos are isolating the amplifiers shown in FIG. 3-16. The diagram in FIG. 3-17 shows a construction of a gobo. This gobo has both hard and soft surfaces. Hard obviously for reflection and soft for absorption. Used in sets, they can be manipulated to control the dispersion of sound by using the soft, absorptive sides for a ''dry'' sound or the hard sides for a ''live'' sound. FIGURE 3-18 pictures a three-sided set for vocal isolation.

Alpha Audio Acoustics

FIG. 3-11. *Sonex convoluted foam for diffusing high frequencies.*

Strata Recording Studio

FIG. 3-12. *Convoluted foam panels.*

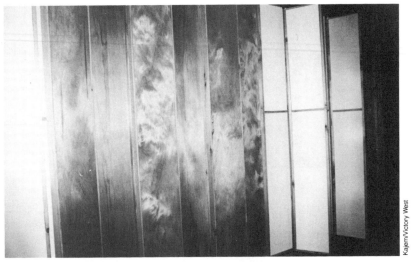

Kajem/Victory West

FIG. 3-13. Hinged panels.

Strata Recording Studio

FIG. 3-14. Isolation booth

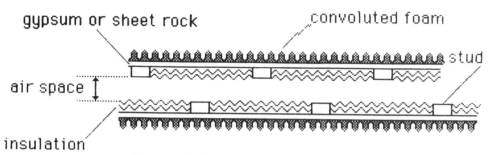

FIG. 3-15. *Isolation wall cross section.*

Sigma Sound Studios

FIG. 3-16. *Gobos isolating two amplifiers.*

CONTROL ROOM

The control room should have the same tonal balance integrity as the studio section by employing bass traps, diffusers, absorbers, and nonparallel walls. The common wall that separates the engineer in the control room and the musicians in the studio should be a solid acoustical barrier to prevent sound transmission from the studio from interfering with the engineer's perception of the sound delivered by the monitoring speakers. Because this common wall needs a viewing window, it should have double-glass construction (to form an air space) and be angled for proper sound deflection. Additionally, the glass panes should be angled with respect to each other, in a nonparallel fashion, to avoid standing waves in the air space. The diagram in FIG. 3-19 depicts this construction. As an added measure, some control rooms conceal tape machines behind sliding glass doors in spaces called *mosfits*.

63

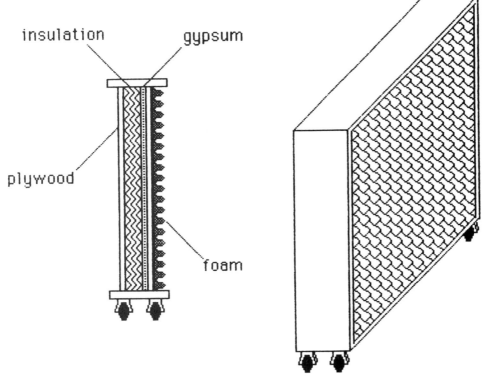

FIG. 3-17. Gobo construction.

FIG. 3-18. Multifaceted gobo isolating a vocal setup.

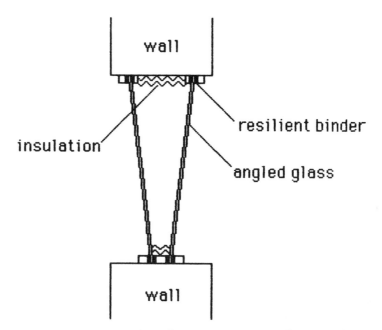

FIG. 3-19. *Cross section of window separating control room and studio.*

Stereo monitoring speakers should be placed 8 to 12 feet apart and aimed towards the listener, who should be located the same distance from each speaker as the speakers are apart. The diagram in FIG. 3-20 shows this spatial relationship. The listener, with respect to the speakers, should form an equilateral triangle in which all the triangle sides are equal in dimension. If the speakers are elevated in any way, they should be aimed towards the listener. The recommended listening level, especially for mixing, is 85 decibels.

A control room is considered to have good tonal balance if it can produce a flat frequency response. This means there is unity gain across the audio spectrum. To test for this, inject a source that delivers energy across the spectrum such as a white- or pink-noise generator. A *white-noise* source fills the entire spectrum with equal energy, where a *pink-noise* source is filtered white noise that is rolled off at 3 dB per octave as shown in FIG. 3-21. An octave is the span between two frequencies in which the higher frequency is twice the lower one. These bands correspond to standard frequency points found on graphic equalizers. The conventional frequencies for equalizers are 16.5 Hz, 31.5 Hz, 63 Hz, 125 Hz, 250 Hz, 500 Hz, 1000 Hz, 2000 Hz, 4000 Hz, 8000 Hz, and 16000 Hz.

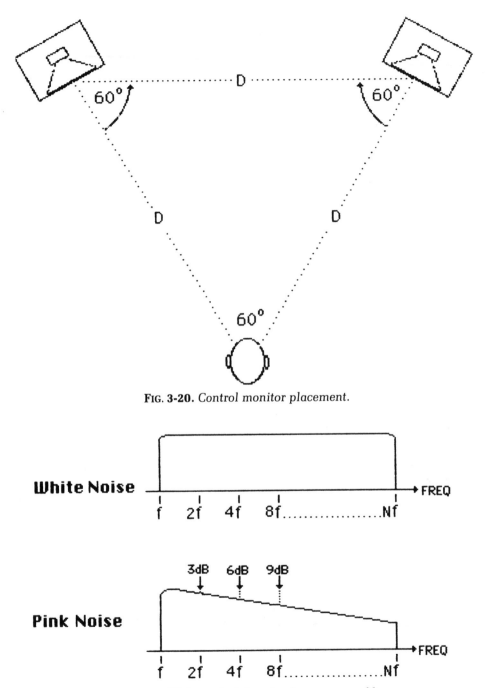

FIG. **3-20**. *Control monitor placement.*

FIG. **3-21**. *White and pink noise frequency profiles.*

The purpose of a graphic equalizer, in this application, is to compensate for coloration by boosting deficiencies or attenuating resonances. An audio analyzer is used in conjunction with a pink-noise generator to tune a room. An audio analyzer graphically displays the acoustic power levels at each of the frequency bands. These power levels are registered by a mike placed in the listening position. The graphic equalizer slide controls are used to boost or cut frequency power levels until the audio analyzer displays a flat response. Most audio analyzers have vertical LED bar displays. The diagram in FIG. 3-22 shows the setup for this procedure. A graphic equalizer should not be used as a substitute for poor room characteristics by making radical compensations. It is good practice to first achieve tonal balance by the methods described before resorting to an equalizer.

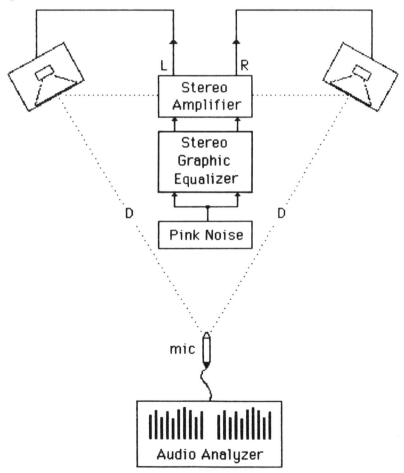

FIG. 3-22. *Setup for tuning the control room.*

FIGURE 3-23 pictures two graphic equalizers made by Rane, the GE27 and GE14. The GE27 is a ⅓-octave, single-channel unit with 27 fixed frequency settings that can be boosted or cut. The GE14 is a 14-band dual-channel unit. FIGURE 3-24 features a Gold Line hand-held audio analyzer, ASA 10B, and the PN2

FIG. **3-23.** *Rane GE27 and GE14 graphic equalizers.*

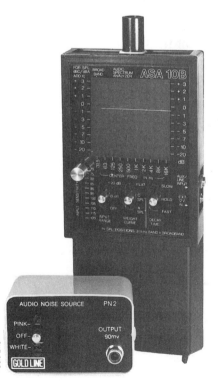

FIG. **3-24.** *Gold Line ASA 10B analyzer and PN2 noise generator.*

audio noise source having selectable pink or white noise. This is a 10-band analyzer. FIGURE 3-25 shows a Gold Line model ASA 30B ⅓-octave real-time audio analyzer. Both of these units have a built-in microphone. FIGURE 3-26 shows a rack-mounted Gold Line Model 30 ⅓-octave analyzer with a pink-noise generator.

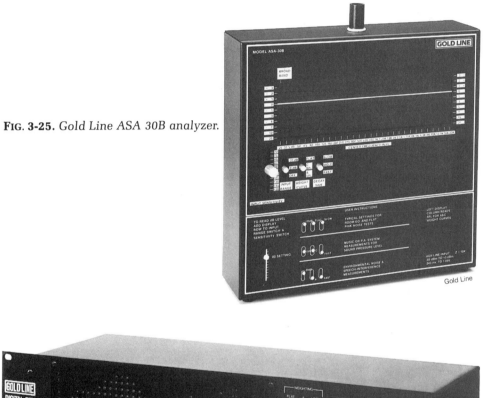

FIG. **3-25.** *Gold Line ASA 30B analyzer.*

FIG. **3-26.** *Gold Line Model 30 analyzer.*

4

Mixing-Console Architecture

THE HEART OF A RECORDING STUDIO IS THE MIXING CONSOLE. IT IS LOCATED centrally in the control room. FIGURE 4-1 is an example of a studio layout. The console is the interface between the microphones and the tape deck and signal-processing devices. It is very important to get a grasp on the architecture by concentrating on signal routing and application philosophy, beginning with simple concepts and developing into complex ones.

See the Tascam M-520 console, pictured in FIG. 4-2, as an example. What you learned about this unit can be transferable to other manufacturer's units as well because in many ways all mixers are principally the same. Do not confuse recording consoles with sound reinforcement boards used for live performance applications. The most significant difference is that a recording mixer has monitoring facilities for *tape deck returns,* a more elaborate *submixing group,* and in many cases, an *integral patch bay.* As shown in FIG. 4-3, a console can be perceived as a composite of three sections:

- ✇ Input module section
- ✇ Monitoring group
- ✇ Subgroup

When inquiring about consoles, typical questions that engineers ask are:

	Tascam M-520
How many inputs?	20
How many auxiliary sends?	4
What is the equalizer configuration?	3-band quasi-parametric
How many sub buses?	8
How much track monitoring?	16

70

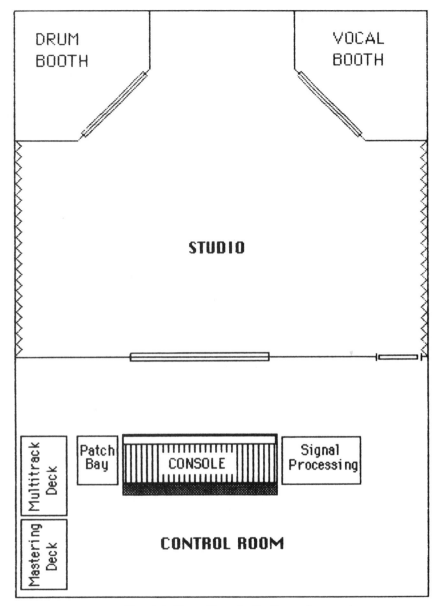

FIG. 4-1. *Recording studio floor plan.*

INPUT MODULES

To start the discussion on the input section, the *channel input modules* are basically identical (except for a couple of minor points that are explained later in this chapter). FIGURE 4-4 shows an input module in considerable detail.

Tascam Teac Corp. of America

FIG. 4-2. *Tascam M-520 recording console.*

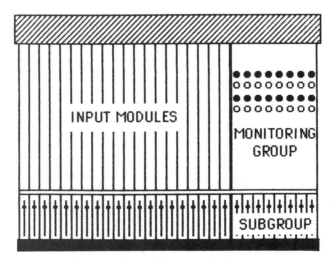

FIG. 4-3. *Recording console layout.*

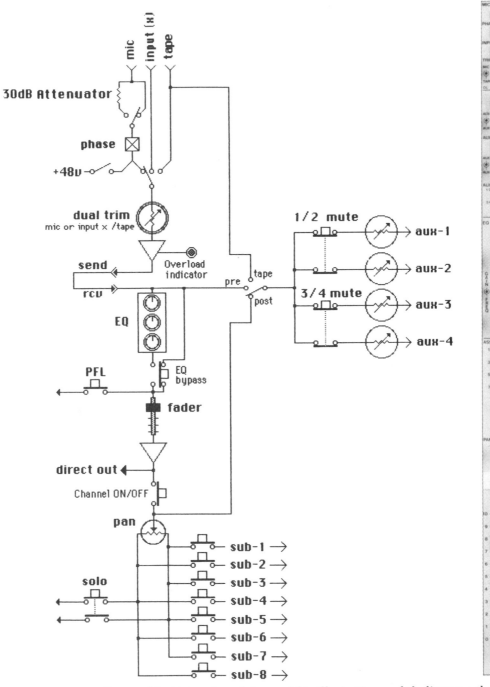

FIG. 4-4. *Tascam M-520 input module on right; illustration on left diagrams the module's interconnections.*

73

Assume you want to record a vocal track. In the studio, there is a balanced input jack for all 20 channels that accepts low-impedance microphones. It does not matter which channel you select because all channels are functionally identical in this application. But, suppose you choose channel #3. Plug the mike in at the junction box input #3. There is a physical connection from the studio junction box to the console in the control room. In the control room, focus attention on input module #3 and set the selector switch to MIKE. The vocal signal travels through the module and exits it at the place on the schematic marked DIRECT OUT. Now take a patch cord and make a connection from the DIRECT OUT to the tape deck. When using a 16-track transport, this vocal signal can be applied to any one of these tracks. Now suppose you choose track input #5. All you have done so far is to route the vocal signal into the console and from the console to the deck, as shown in FIG. 4-5.

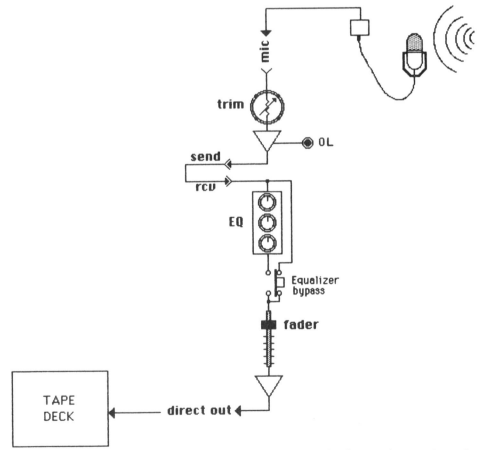

FIG. 4-5. *Part of the console input module showing the path of a vocal input from the microphone to the tape deck.*

The signal coming from the microphone alone is not strong enough to drive the tape deck, so the console amplifies it. The first stage of amplification is controlled by the trim dial. If the incoming signal is *too* strong for the preamp, the overload indicator flickers. The proper thing to do is to attenuate the signal using the trim until the flickering stops. The signal then moves on to the equalizer (EQ), which can alter its sound character. A pushbutton switch is provided to bypass this function if desired. Finally, the signal passes through the fader (sliding volume control) to regulate the signal level applied to the tape deck. Note that there is a send/receive jumper above the equalizer in FIG. 4-5. This is a facility to interrupt the signal path for the purpose of inserting a device such as a compressor. Removing the jumper from the console and connecting the external device is called a *channel patch*. FIGURE 4-6 shows a compressor "patched into" the signal path.

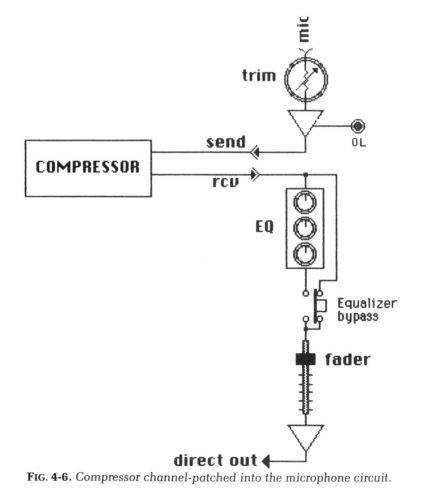

FIG. 4-6. *Compressor channel-patched into the microphone circuit.*

PATCH BAY

Most devices have connectors in the rear. Since it is inconvenient trying to make connections where they are hard to reach or view, the solution is a *patch bay* system. A patch bay is a piece of hardware that centralizes all the connection points of the console, tape deck, and signal-processing devices. This provides a means of viewing all the "rear" connectors from the front. FIGURE 4-7 is a picture of a Switchcraft patch bay with its mirror image to show the connectors in the rear. Patch bays are normally located to either the left or right of the console and in many cases are integrated as part of the console. These patch bay connector sockets are stacked in rows with labeling for identification of each socket as shown in FIG. 4-8. FIGURE 4-9 features a Soundcraft 6000 console with an integrated patch bay on the right-hand side.

Switchcraft, Inc. (a Raytheon Co.)

FIG. 4-7. *Switchcraft patch bay.*

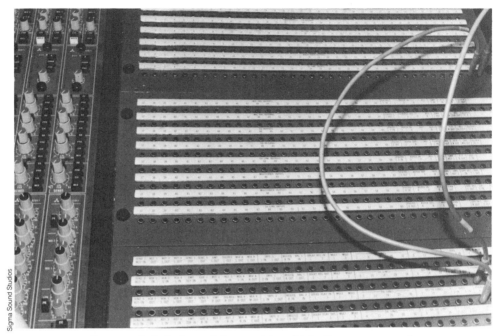

Sigma Sound Studios

FIG. 4-8. *Labeled patch bay on Mitsubishi Superstar console.*

JBL Professional

FIG. 4-9. *Soundcraft 6000 console.*

Patch bays are available with either *balanced* or *unbalanced* patch sockets. Balanced systems are those that consist of two conductors (for signal flow) and a shield for grounding). Unbalanced systems use two conductors in which the shield is a return path. Mating connectors that plug into balanced sockets resemble a stereo 1/4-inch plug with a *tip*, *ring*, and *sleeve* (see FIG. 4-10). Unbalanced patch bays require just a tip and sleeve connector like a 1/4-inch phone plug or RCA phono jack.

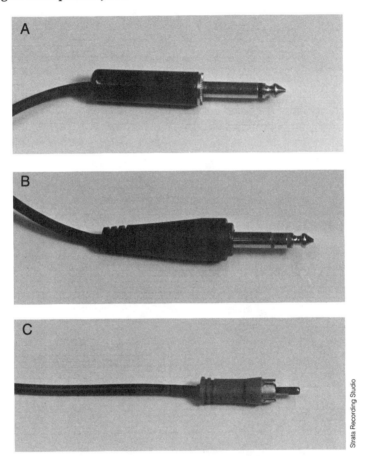

FIG. 4-10. *Patch bay plugs: (A) shows a single-ended, or unbalanced, plug, (B) shows a balanced plug, and (C) shows a single-ended (unbalanced) RCA phono plug.*

FIGURE 4-11 shows an illustration of a *single-ended* (unbalanced) patch bay such as a Tascam PB-64. This is merely a panel with a lot of feed-through connectors. The front side provides a space for labeling to identify inputs and outputs. The back side has the physical wire connections from the patch bay points to the devices.

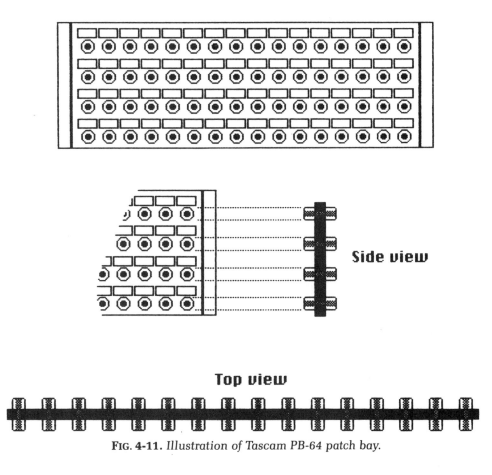

FIG. 4-11. *Illustration of Tascam PB-64 patch bay.*

Let's examine how a patch bay is used for the FIG. 4-6 example of a hook-up from a mike to a compressor to a deck. FIGURE 4-12 shows the physical patch bay connections. The mike is directly connected to the console, but everything else is patch-bay dependent. The connections from the patch bay rear to the equipment are permanent. The connections made on the patch bay front are temporary, using patch cords. The mike signal enters the console, leaves the console via the SEND, and then enters the compressor to be processed. Then it leaves the compressor, re-enters the console at the RCV port, and makes a final exit through the DIRECT OUT port. Its final destination is at the tape deck input to be recorded. The point here is that the patch bay conveniently allows for any type of equipment-to-equipment hook-up at a central location. This kind of flexibility is important to a production.

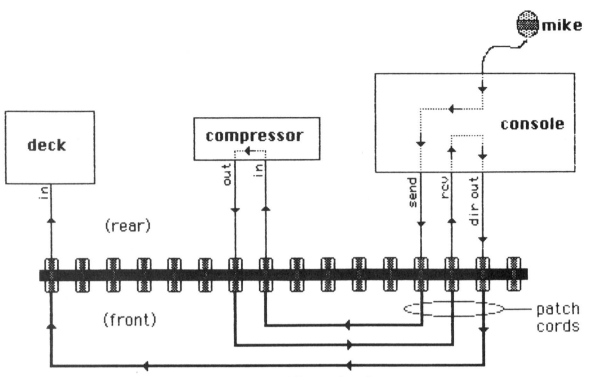

FIG. 4-12. *Patch bay signal flow path with compressor.*

FIGURE 4-13 shows the patch configuration if the compressor was omitted. Note that a jumper has to be in place to maintain the continuity from SEND to RCV; otherwise the signal will be interrupted. Some patch bays are normally closed or "normalled" such that the absence of a patchcord internally jumps the send and receive points via a "make-and-break" circuit. FIGURE 4-14 shows how continuity is maintained between two single-ended points in the absence of a plug and how that continuity is interrupted when plugs are inserted (the inserted plug separates the internal contacts). FIGURE 4-15 illustrates the arrangement for a balanced patch bay. FIGURE 4-16 shows a "half-normalled" configuration for both unbalanced and balanced points. The TAPE OUT connection to the LINE IN is not interrupted by a plug insertion into the TAPE OUT socket, however, it is interrupted when a plug is inserted in the LINE IN socket. This arrangement is very common on patch bays because many consoles only have a channel LINE/MIC select switch where LINE acts as a tape return unless there is a patch bay plug insertion interruption.

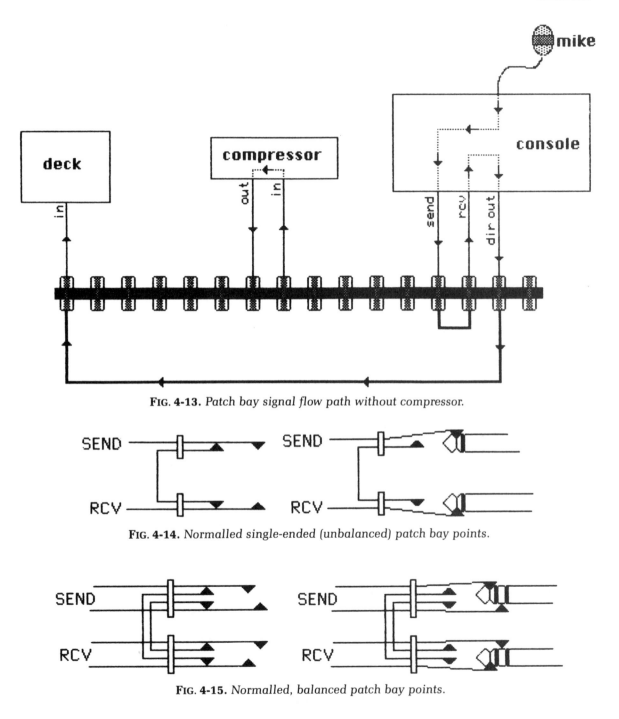

FIG. 4-13. *Patch bay signal flow path without compressor.*

FIG. 4-14. *Normalled single-ended (unbalanced) patch bay points.*

FIG. 4-15. *Normalled, balanced patch bay points.*

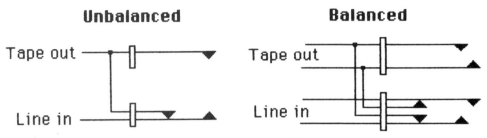

FIG. **4-16.** *Half-normalled points.*

SUBGROUP SECTION

Those are just a few of the application examples. Let's change the situation to introduce a *submaster* application. In the console, there are eight subgroups (submasters) located at the bottom right of the console (FIG. 4-17). Each of the channel inputs (1 through 20) have pushbuttons to select one or more of the eight subs (FIG. 4-18). Thus, signals can be merged from several channels and be used as a single output. A typical situation would be to put three vocalists together on one track. If microphones are in channels #3, #4, and #5 and each has its ASSIGN 1 sub pushed in, then all three signals would be combined and exit the console at the SUB 1 output. FIGURE 4-19 shows the physical arrangement of the pushbuttons on each input module. The shading indicates a depressed button.

FIG. **4-17.** *Tascam M-520 subgroup.*

FIG. 4-18. *Tascam M-520 channel sub assignment pushbuttons.*

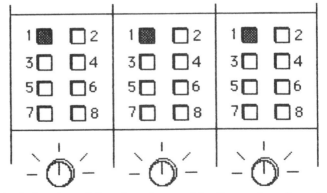

FIG. 4-19. *Input module sub assignment for three microphone inputs.*

FIGURE 4-20 shows schematically what is happening. Instead of using any of the DIRECT OUTs, the sum of the signals was used. Each of the channel faders is used to make gain (volume) adjustments in order to get the proper balance, but then the submaster fader is used to adjust the proper signal level delivered to the deck. FIGURE 4-21 shows the patch bay configuration, but in addition,

83

note that a compressor has been applied in the submaster path. Also note that the submaster output is now driving the tape deck input. Therefore, the call for a submaster application is when two or more sources must be combined. Other situations could be submixing several drums or several synthesizers on a single track.

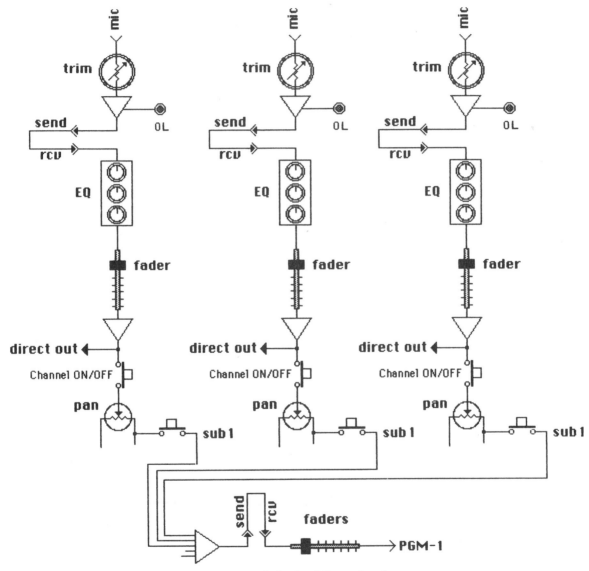

FIG. 4-20. *Submix of three signals.*

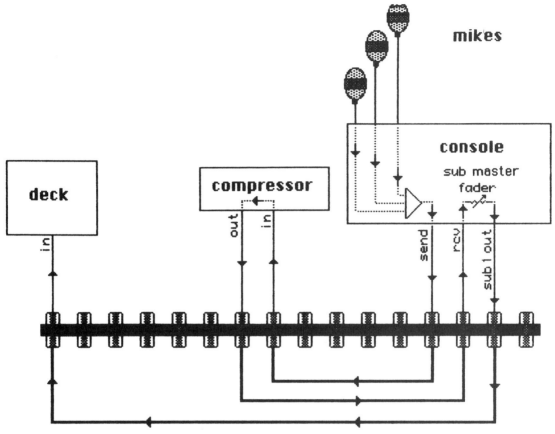

FIG. 4-21. *Patch bay signal flow path for submix.*

Here is another interesting example. Suppose you want to submix a cow-bell, tambourine, a crash cymbal, a ride cymbal, and congas onto two tracks. There are five items to distribute over two tracks. Assume for the moment the instruments are miked, using five input channels on the board. The proper thing to do is to press sub buttons 1 and 2 for each channel (FIG. 4-22) which delivers each signal to both submasters. The sub outputs are connected to two tape inputs. Locate the panning dial below the eight sub assignment buttons. If the dial is in the 12 o'clock position, the signal equally distributes to subs 1 and 2. Rotating the dial left (counterclockwise) increases the signal at SUB 1 and decreases it at SUB 2; rotating the dial right produces the opposite effect. Thus, coming up with a panning scheme for these instruments—putting some left, some right, and others "down the middle"—creates a stereo image. It is important to create the desirable balance among the instruments during this process, for once they are recorded, you cannot change the ratio. Unlike other sources that were recorded on their own tracks, the balance of the submix cannot be changed. It is very important to keep the most essential parts of the whole recording on their own tracks to allow for future adjustment if necessary. It is only wise to submix the least significant parts. For example, do not submix a lead vocal with something else. Put as many elements as possible on its own track, which means that in most sessions, you will be using channel DIRECT OUTs. Having a limited number of tracks often forces the issue of a submix routine.

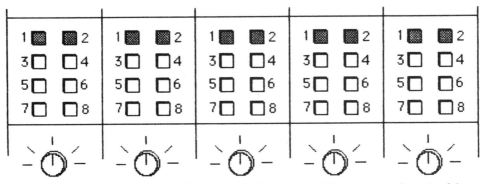

FIG. 4-22. *Sub assignments 1 and 2 are pressed for each of five inputs to be mixed for a stereo output via each channel's pan control.*

The diagram in FIG. 4-23 schematically shows this console setup involving the cowbell, tambourine, congas, and crash and ride cymbals. All the signals are assigned to subs #1 and #2. These signals are summed and brought out as two signals to drive two tape deck inputs. Also, there is a display of the patch bay scheme in FIG. 4-24. This is the patch bay configuration that represents these five percussion inputs submixed through subs #1 and #2. Bear in mind that in almost every console, odd and even sub numbers are panning combinations, where odd is intended for panning left and even for the right. This implies that when using a single sub, be sure that the panning dial is "down the middle" (centered in the 12 o'clock position).

Now look at FIG. 4-25 to see how the subgroup ties in with the input module. Notice how the odd numbers are all connected to the left bus and the even ones are connected to the right panning bus. Note that there are four auxiliary sends and that the driving point is determined by the selector switch position. You can tap the signal flow from the main path after the fader POST position, before the equalizer PRE position, or from the tape return TAPE position. These auxiliaries are usually referred to as *effect sends*. A piece of the signal going through is accessed by the send dial and delivered to a signal processor such as a digital reverb, digital delay (echo), etc. The signal going down the main path

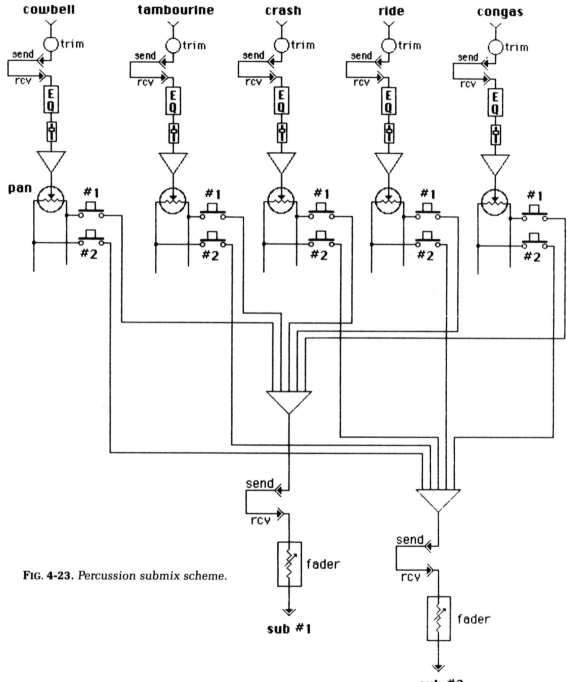

FIG. 4-23. *Percussion submix scheme.*

is usually referred to as the *dry signal* because the signal is unaltered by any effect devices. The signal sent to an effect device such as a reverb becomes a *wet* signal after it passes through the reverb.

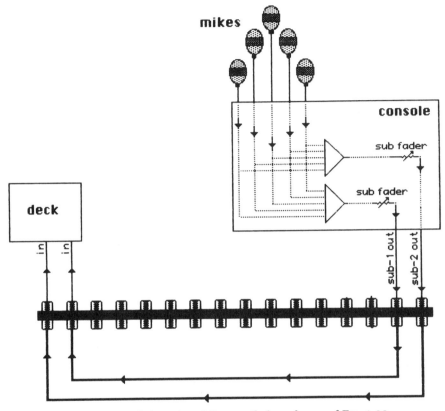

FIG. 4-24. *Patch bay signal flow path for scheme of FIG. 4-23.*

Before leaving the discussion on input modules, focus on the various types of inputs. So far, only mike inputs have been used in the examples. Referring back to FIG. 4-25, there is a table describing the different options for input x. An input module usually has three input selections. The MIC inputs are common in all 20 modules, however, the second and third input positions vary. The first two channels can receive instrument levels directly (see FIG. 4-26). Channels #3 and #4 have impedances for magnetic cartridge signals from turntables (FIG. 4-28). Channels #5 through #20 require stronger signal levels like those on active sources such as synthesizers or tape deck outputs (FIG. 4-28). Channels #17 through #20 are dedicated to the stereo outputs of two mastering decks, although these can also be used as line inputs (FIG. 4-29). The TAPE input, which is common to the first sixteen channels, is the return from the tape deck.

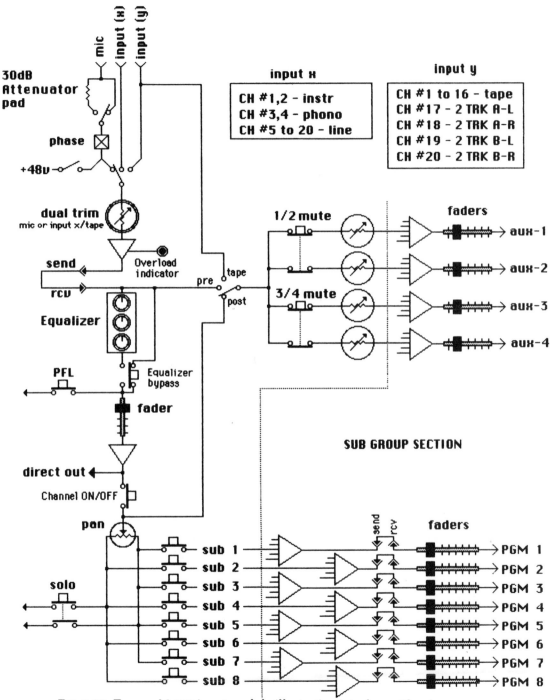

30dB Attenuator pad

mic
input (x)
input (y)

phase

+48v

dual trim
mic or input x/tape

send

Overload indicator

rcv

pre   tape
post

Equalizer

PFL

Equalizer bypass

fader

direct out

Channel ON/OFF

pan

solo

sub 1
sub 2
sub 3
sub 4
sub 5
sub 6
sub 7
sub 8

input x

| CH #1,2 – instr |
| CH #3,4 – phono |
| CH #5 to 20 – line |

input y

| CH #1 to 16 – tape |
| CH #17 – 2 TRK A–L |
| CH #18 – 2 TRK A–R |
| CH #19 – 2 TRK B–L |
| CH #20 – 2 TRK B–R |

1/2 mute

3/4 mute

faders

aux-1
aux-2
aux-3
aux-4

SUB GROUP SECTION

send rcv

faders

PGM 1
PGM 2
PGM 3
PGM 4
PGM 5
PGM 6
PGM 7
PGM 8

FIG. 4-25. *Tascam M-520 input module illustrating interface with subgroup.*

89

Strata Recording Studio

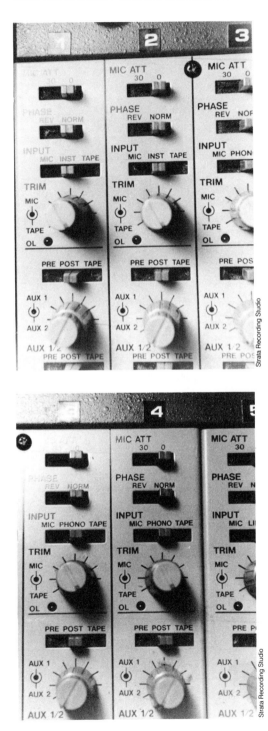

FIG. 4-26. *M-520 channels 1 and 2.*

Strata Recording Studio

FIG. 4-27. *M-520 channels 3 and 4.*

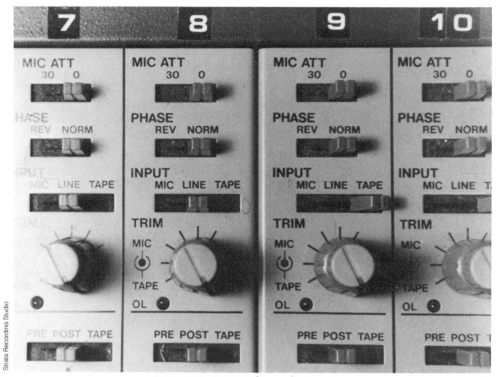

FIG. 4-28. *M-520 channels 5 to 16.*

FIG. 4-29. *M-520 channels 17 to 20.*

91

MONITORING SECTION

The monitoring section controls what you actually hear and is usually located on the right-hand side of the console (FIG. 4-30). What you usually hear during a session are the signals coming back from the multitrack recorder (MTR). The 16 outputs from the recorder feed the first 16 channel tape inputs and are routed internally to the monitoring section. The left half of the 16-track mix monitor is illustrated in FIG. 4-31. Each track has a three-position selector switch, a gain control, and a panning control. The middle switch position is the ''off'' position. Throwing the switch to the right to TAPE permits listening to that track and to the left to BUSS permits listening to a subgroup output signal that corresponds to that switch. The gain control determines how loud that track is. The pan control positions a sound left, right, or somewhere in between.

Pressing the MON button activates the 16-track monitor mix. The BUSS positions on all tracks access signal traffic on subs #1 through #8. (Tracks 9 through 16 are redundant at this setting because they duplicate the BUSS position functions of tracks 1 through 8.) The monitor select buttons are used to select the desired source for listening by monitoring either of the two-track mastering decks (A and B) or one of the auxiliary outputs 1/2 or 3/4. The SPARE can be used for another input such as a cassette deck.

STEREO MASTERs A and B (FIG. 4-32) drive the power amps for the control room and studio respectively. To the right, the T/B button, *talkback*, is used by the engineer to talk to the musicians. This communication is applied to STEREO MASTER B only (the studio amp drive). The three buttons above the T/B (BUSS, AUX 1/2, AUX 3/4) select the outputs where the user can place a test tone (40 Hz, 1 kHz, and 10 kHz). The 40 Hz is a ''slate'' tone that is used for tape cueing and also permits recording a T/B message via the subs or auxilliary sends. It cannot be heard at normal speed but is audible when monitored during fast-forward or rewind tape speeds. The SLATE and T/B dials control the perceived volume.

The Tascam M-520 was used as an example to understand console architecture. Other consoles, for example, the Soundcraft 6000 console (FIG. 4-9) has the integral patch bay, featuring a 28-input mainframe with 24 subs and up to 32-track monitoring. Other frame options can accommodate more channel inputs. The input module section of the Soundcraft 6000 features two sweepable midband parametric equalizers and two shelving types to cover the high and low end of the spectrum (equalization is covered in detail in Chapter 6). There are six effect sends. The monitor tape returns have high and low shelving equalization and two effect sends. The Trident Series 65 pictured in FIG. 4-33 has a similar configuration with 28 inputs, 24 subs, and 24-track monitoring with some equalization and effect sends. The channel inputs have eight effect sends. This console is available with an integral patch bay.

FIG. 4-30. *M-520 monitoring and subgroup sections.*

Tascam Teac Corp. of America

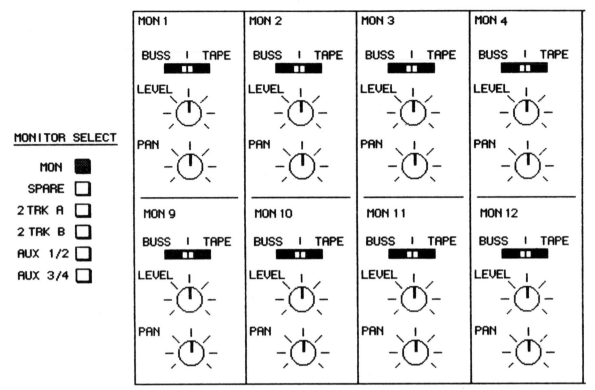

FIG. 4-31. *The left half of the monitor section of Tascam M-520.*

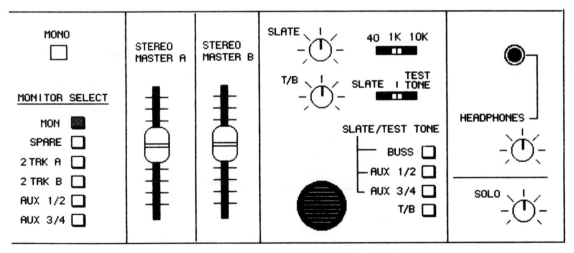

FIG. 4-32. *Tascam M-520 monitor control.*

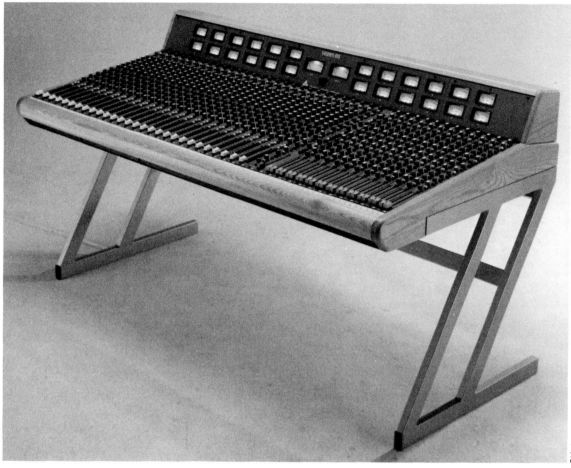

FIG. 4-33. *Trident Series 65 consoles are available in 24-, 28-, and 36-input standard frame sizes. Patch bay option is offered on the latter frame sizes.*

CONSOLE AUTOMATION

The console pictured in FIG. 4-34 is a TAC (Total Audio Concepts) Matchless with automation. Automation is a computer link to the console in which console controls can be substituted with a software interface. A console that is automation-ready requires digital components called *voltage-controlled amplifiers* (VCAs). A VCA can electronically simulate a fader movement. An applied independent voltage source regulates the signal strength. If a computer signal is doing this, then a *digital-to-analog (D/A)* converter is needed to convert the computer's binary code into an analog voltage level. The diagram in FIG. 4-35 shows this relationship, which exists for each fader and rotary control. Thus, computer signals can substitute physical manual operation of console controls.

95

FIG. **4-34.** The TAC Matchless console uses computerized automation.

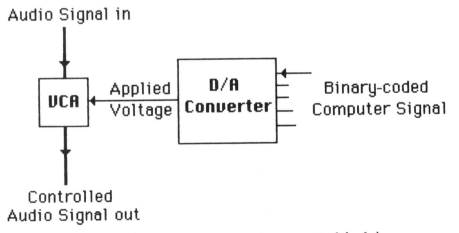

FIG. **4-35.** The VCA replaces manual movement of the fader.

Automation is most valuable for mixdowns where numerous variables are exercised.

Imagine that when all the tracks are recorded, they feed into the console, one input channel per track, for processing. One of the recorded tracks is a SMPTE time code that feeds into the computer. This time code sequences the computer so that its programming coordinates with the tape's recorded events. FIGURE 4-36 shows the system loop. The computer can address the controls in each channel, making the necessary fader, equalizer, and effect send changes during the course of the song. The computer might be able to address signal-processing devices to make control changes as well. When programming the computer, a manual fader movement can be read into the computer. As the tape is being played, the computer registers the fader setting at that moment corresponding to the time code. This requires an analog-to-digital (A/D) converter. A control voltage from the fader is the analog signal that is converted into a digital code for the computer to read as shown in FIG. 4-37. The computer does this when in the "learn" mode. It then duplicates these movements when in the "execute" or "run" mode. The SMPTE (Society of Motion Picture and Television Engineers) time code is covered in Chapter 8, Tape Transports.

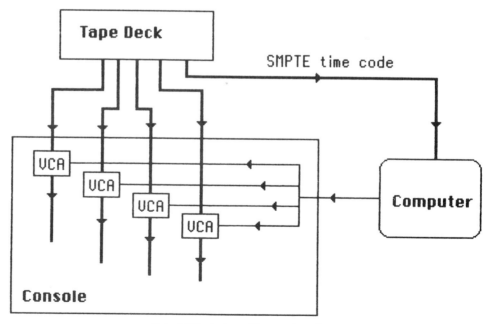

FIG. 4-36. *Automation system loop.*

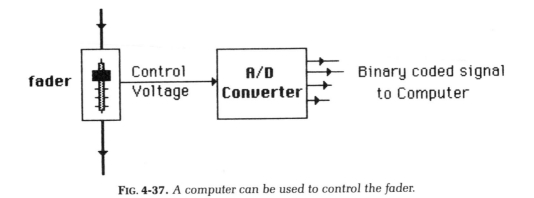

FIG. 4-37. *A computer can be used to control the fader.*

5

System Integration

SYSTEM INTEGRATION IS THE BUSINESS OF MAKING A SYSTEM PLAN IN which all of the devices work effectively as a team. In the previous chapter the compressor was integrated into the console, making it part of the system. Defining a system means first defining each piece of equipment in the control room.

DRY AND WET SIGNAL PROCESSORS

Signal-processing devices can be separated into two categories—*channel patch* or ''dry'' and *effect* or ''wet.'' A compressor is an example of a channel patch signal processor because it is used to treat the dry signal. The dry signal that goes in the compressor is still dry when it leaves. This device is applied as part of the dry signal path using the SEND and RCV ports of the console input module as shown in FIG. 5-1.

A reverb is an example of an effect signal processor that produces a wet signal to be added with the dry signal. A reverb unit typically is not used in the dry signal path like the compressor. By use of an auxiliary send function, the dry signal is ''tapped'' from the main path. This portion of the dry signal can then be routed to the reverb unit to be converted into a wet signal. This wet reverberated signal leaves the unit and re-enters the console to be merged with the original dry signal as shown in FIG. 5-2. Therefore, the major difference between channel patch and effect processors is that channel patch devices just modify the dry signal where effect devices create an additional signal.

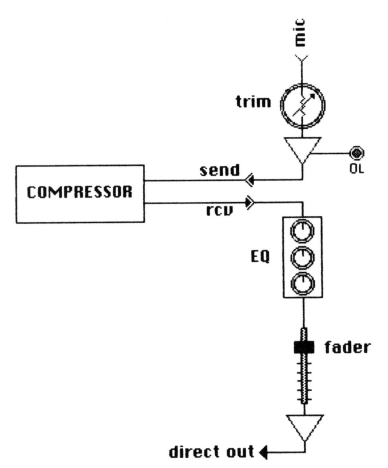

FIG. 5-1. *Compressor in dry signal path.*

The question is, what kind of processors does a studio need?

Channel Patch Devices
    Compressors
    Noise Gates
    Equalizers
    De-essers

Effect Devices
    Reverbs (digital/analog)
    Digital delays (echo devices)
    Multi-effect processors (flanging, phasing, pitch shift, etc.)
    Exciters

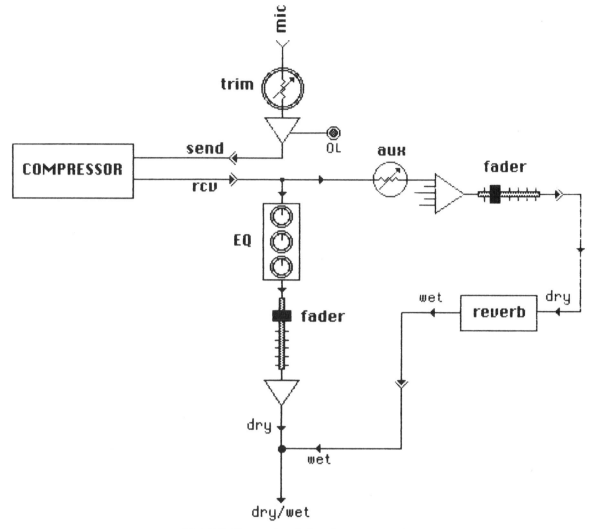

FIG. 5-2. *Dry and wet signals are merged.*

Well-equipped studios usually have multiples of each of these devices in their equipment rack. The standard width dimension for a device is 19 inches. The equipment can thus be mounted on the vertical metal strips in the rack. Later chapters cover operation and application of these devices, but for now let's just concentrate on plugging them into the system.

In the previous diagram, the application of both a compressor and a reverb was demonstrated. There is a need for a noise gate to *squelch* unwanted signals as part of the channel patch. Let's also apply a flanger effect. The diagram in

FIG. 5-3 shows the system configuration to achieve this setup. Note that the noise gate has been serially added to the dry path. As for the flanger, a second auxiliary "tap" is provided to drive it. Now there are two wet signals that merge with the dry signal. The auxiliary send dials control the relative signal strength that drives the effect device. This example focuses on just one channel. Each channel has its own set of auxiliaries, which means the signal coming from these channels can drive the effect units also. The triangle symbol in the effect path represents a summing amplifier that merges any signals from other channels. The fader in the effect path becomes the master send for the effect unit.

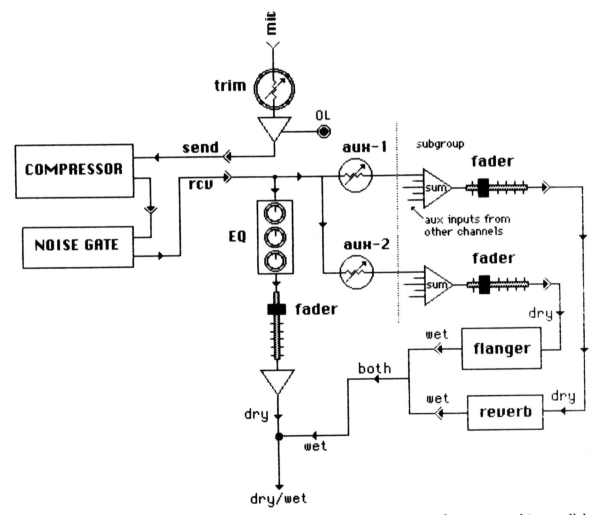

FIG. 5-3. *Channel patch devices are connected serially, and effects are merged or connected in parallel.*

The Tascam M-520 console has up to four auxiliary sends per channel, which means that two more effect units could be added to the diagram. Also, another channel patch device can be added to the serial chain. An important thing to note is that channel patch devices apply only to signals in that path. Effect devices are more accessible. Where only one channel input can use the compressor or noise gate, all input channels can use the reverb or flanger at the same time because all the auxiliaries from every channel can tie in to the summing amp.

INPUTS AND OUTPUTS

The previous chapter showed that the patch bay is the fundamental hardware that pieces together all of the production equipment. The patch bay should therefore accommodate all the necessary inputs and outputs of the mixing console, signal processors, and tape decks. The first duty in organizing a system's integration plan is to itemize the inputs and outputs used in the system. Organize a patch bay starting with the console inputs and outputs, as shown in TABLE 5-1.

TABLE 5-1. Console Patch Bay Assignments Example

		Channels 1 – 20	Qty.	Subs 1 – 8	Qty.	Aux.s 1 – 4	Qty.	Osc.	Qty.
inputs	{	ch. 1: instrument	1	in { rcv.	8	out	4	out	1
		ch. 2: instrument	1	out { out	8		4		1
		ch. 3: phono	1	out { send	8				
		ch. 4: phono	1		24				
		ch.s 5 – 20: line in	16						
		rcv.	20						
outputs	{	direct out	20						
		send	20						
			80					Total = 109	

There are only three ways (per channel) to route signals to the console: mike input, line input, and tape return input. All mike inputs go directly into the console, so there is no patch bay assignment required for these. The same applies to tape return inputs. But the line inputs require patch bay assignment. The first four channels' line inputs are special. Channels 1 and 2 have instrument inputs for transducer levels found on electric guitars. Channels #3 and 4 have phono inputs for magnetic cartridge transducers found on turntables. The rest of the channels' line inputs require the type of levels that come from active sources such as synthesizers or signal processors. The reason for these different types of inputs is to accommodate the nature or characteristic of the source. If you try to plug in a guitar into channel #5 line input, the signal coming from the guitar will not be strong enough to effectively drive the input. On the other hand, synthesizer outputs would be too hot for any of the first four channel inputs. Hence, as a start, that accounts for 20 patch bay assignments.

Now that all of the console inputs are accounted for, what console outputs are needed? Every channel has a DIRECT OUT, which therefore requires 20 patch bay assignments. There are eight subgroub outputs and four auxiliary sends. Each channel has a SEND and RCV port and so do the subgroups.

As you can see, it adds up pretty fast, and this is only for the console. Before leaving the console, there is just one more output—an oscillator output used as a reference tone.

A studio needs at least three tape decks: a multi-track recorder (MTR) (in this case a 16-track transport) and two 2-track mastering decks for stereo mixes. The MTR has 16 inputs and outputs. Each mastering deck has two inputs and two outputs. This makes a total of 40 patch bay assignments for all tape machines (see TABLE 5-2).

TABLE 5-2. Tape Deck Patch Bay Assignments Example

MTR (ch.s 1 – 16)	Qty.	Stereo Deck A	Qty.	Stereo Deck B	Qty.
tape in	16	left in	1	left in	1
tape out	16	right in	1	right in	1
	—	left out	1	left out	1
	32	right out	1	right out	1
			—		—
			4		4
Total = 40					

The only detail now is to account for all the inputs and outputs of the signal processing gear in the equipment rack. By the time it's over, there could be over 300 patch bay points. Plus, for every input and output there must be a cable from the device to the patch bay.

MONITORING

There are a few other items associated with the console hookup. The equipment rack is not complete until power amplifiers are provided to drive the control room and studio speakers. The speakers in both rooms are located overhead.

The console has stereo outputs to drive these amps. There is a fader control in the monitoring section on the console to regulate the drive signals for each amplifier. The diagram in FIG. 5-4 shows this configuration. Note that the studio signals also drive the headset amplifiers that the musicians use during the session. A bank of cassette decks is driven by the studio stereo buses.

The important concept to remember is that the signals heard from the monitors are solely those that have been accessed by the console. Therefore, it is important to study how the console makes provisions for this access.

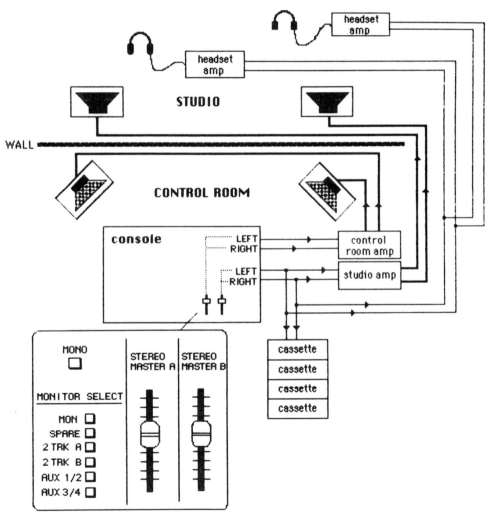

FIG. 5-4. *Control room and studio monitoring system.*

SIGNAL ROUTING

When the MON button is depressed (FIG. 5-5), the 16 tape return/subgroup outputs access both the subgroup busses and tape returns. The middle position is "off." Bear in mind that tape return signals are applied to input modules 1 to 16, and internally, these 16 signals are routed from the modules to this monitoring section. Assume for now that the selector switches are all in the tape return (TAPE) position. The signal flow diagram in FIG. 5-6 models this arrangement. This diagram shows 3 of the 16 monitor sections. Note that the selector switch is in the TAPE return position. Because the MON button is in, the tape signals coming from the deck can be heard (monitored). Observe the left and right summing amplifiers. There's a pair for the control room (STEREO MASTER A) and a pair for the studio (STEREO MASTER B). Even though there is one fader for each, the fader controls both left and right outputs. These outputs drive the power amps in the rack. Also note that all the labeling on the summing amp inputs corresponds to all the push buttons on the board. You would push in AUX 1/2 to hear and verify (monitor) the signals going to the effect devices. To reinforce this understanding, the diagram in FIG. 5-7 should be helpful.

It should be clear how these push buttons make the connection to a source. The same applies for AUX 3/4. Push in both and hear all the signal traffic from all the sends. During a session, it is very common to use AUX 1/2 to drive a reverb and use AUX 3/4 to monitor the wet returns. This is a special application, however. To make this all clear, the following discussion describes the system loop for an actual session.

Examine a case where we are recording a vocal track and the singer makes a request for reverb in the monitor. The objective as an engineer is to let the *vocalist* hear the reverb but not to record this wet signal (that is something that should be done in the "mixdown" phase of the production; in fact, all tracks are usually recorded dry).

Now trace the signal path in the system starting with the microphone. The diagram in FIG. 5-8 shows the system loop. Here is a situation in which the mike signal is going to channel #3, to the compressor, out of the compressor back through the board, and then out of the board and to the tape deck input track #5. The tape return drives console tape input #5. The AUX 1 send for channel #5 drives the reverb unit. The wet signal from the reverb enters channel #20 line input and is placed on AUX 3 and 4 for monitoring purposes. Therefore, in the monitor section, pushing MON permits listening to the tape return, and pushing AUX 3/4 plays the wet signal. Note that only the dry signal is being recorded.

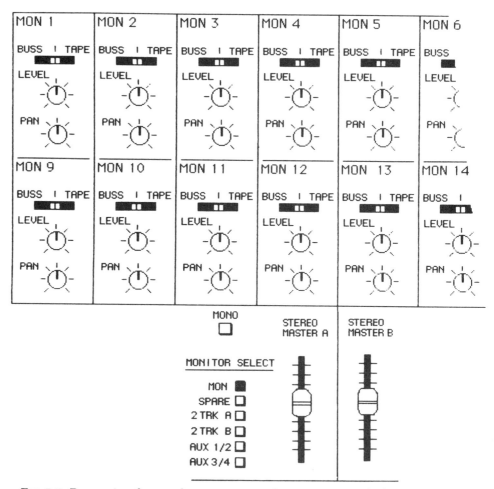

FIG. 5-5. *Depressing the* MON *button accesses the 16 tape return/subgroup outputs.*

In the figure, the channel #5 AUX 1 is set for the TAPE position. This means that the AUX 1 dial accesses the tape return input. For channel #20, AUX 3 and 4 are set in the PRE position. Because a signal is coming in at the line input, the only choices are POST or PRE. The PRE position is a little more convenient since it does not involve the fader. To make this clear, examine the diagram of the input module in FIG. 5-9, which shows where the TAPE, POST and PRE positions actually tap the signal. If the position is used for fader operation, the channel ON/OFF push button must be ON.

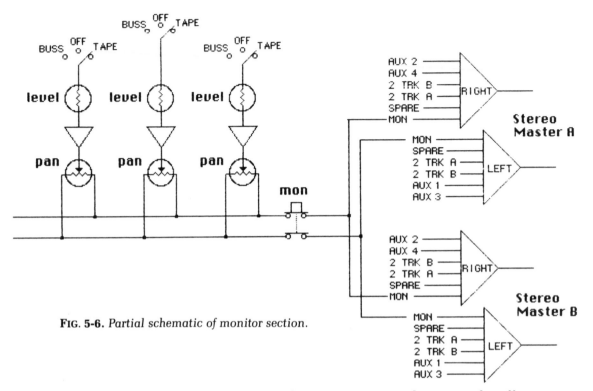

FIG. 5-6. *Partial schematic of monitor section.*

It is generally convenient to use the tape returns as the source for effect sends because you can still hear the effect on the playback. But you might not want to hear the vocal playback with the reverb so as not to interfere with critical listening. In this case, do not use the tape return for a source. Instead, drive the reverb using channel #3 AUX 1. When recording, the signal is there to drive the reverb, but not for playback.

Examine the system loop in FIG. 5-10 and compare it to the previous diagram in FIG. 5-8. Note that the channel #3 AUX 1 is set for PRE position. The reverb drive signal is part of the present incoming vocal. Now suppose the singer says, ''In spite of your recommendation, I want to record with reverb.'' How is this done? From the present system diagram, only the dry signal is applied to the deck. Both dry and wet signals must now be applied. You now must resort to using a submaster (subgroup)—remember that two signals are placed on one track by merging them via a sub. Right now, the wet signal is coming in on channel #20. Pass this signal all the way through and choose a sub common to both channel #3 and #20 (any number from 1 to 8). As an example, if you choose sub #5, push in sub button #5 for both channels (3 and 20). Make a patch bay change also—sub #5 should go to the tape deck input. The diagram in FIG. 5-11 reflects this system change.

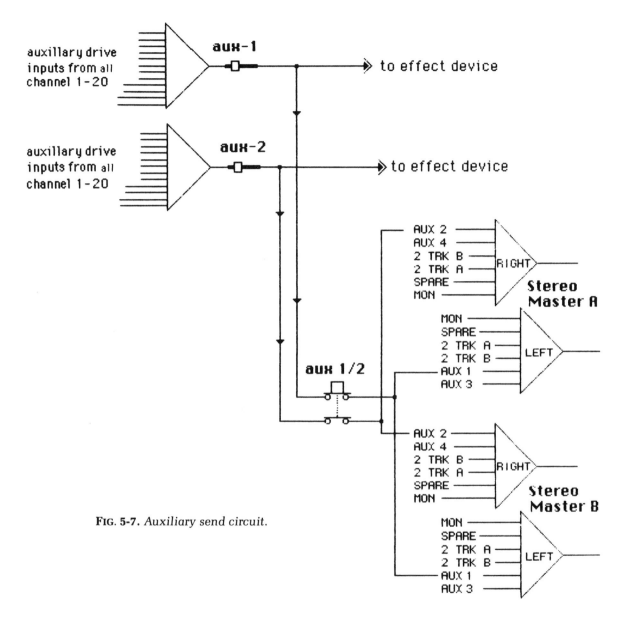

FIG. 5-7. *Auxiliary send circuit.*

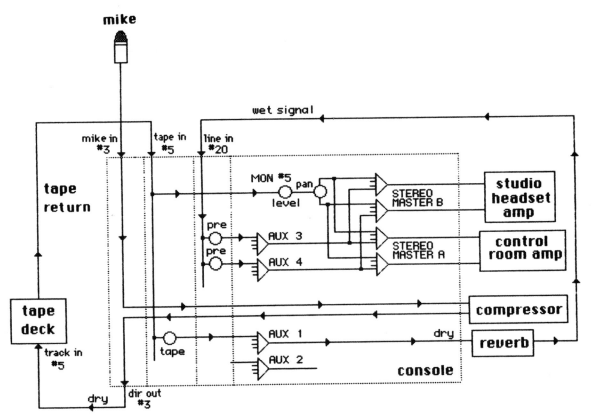

FIG. 5-8. *System loop monitoring reverb from tape return.*

Recording on track #5 has nothing to do with selecting sub #5. Any sub will do the same job. Note that the channel #3 AUX 1 is now in the POST position. Any channel #3 fader changes keep the wet signal in proportion to the dry signal. If the auxiliary was set to PRE, the drive signal would stay the same in spite of fader changes. When the fader is lowered, the reverb would start to sound stronger in relation to the decreased dry signal.

In this chapter, three practical situations have been reviewed that apply to sessions. FIGURE 5-12 is a system diagram that is not wired. Make copies of this to practice system connections to test your understanding. Try using different color codes for the dry and wet signals.

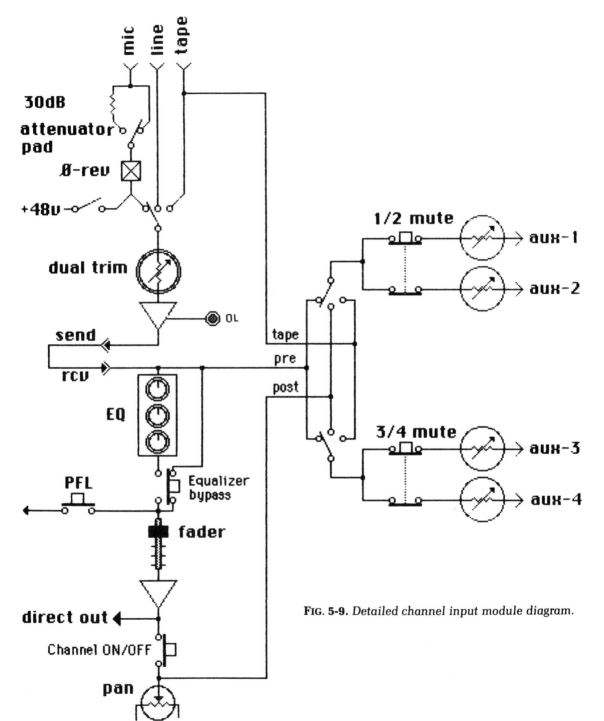

FIG. 5-9. *Detailed channel input module diagram.*

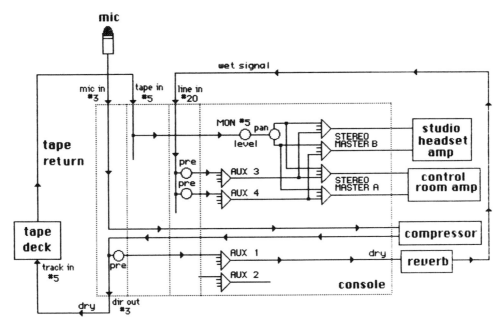

FIG. 5-10. *System loop monitoring reverb from mike input signal.*

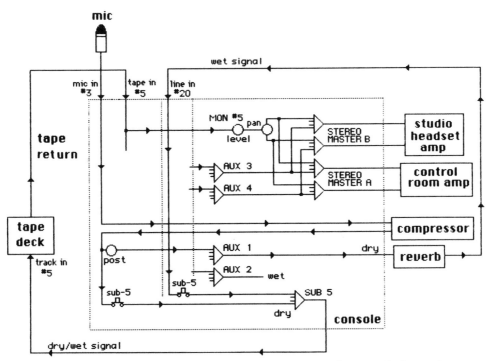

FIG. 5-11. *System loop recording with reverb via a submaster (subgroup).*

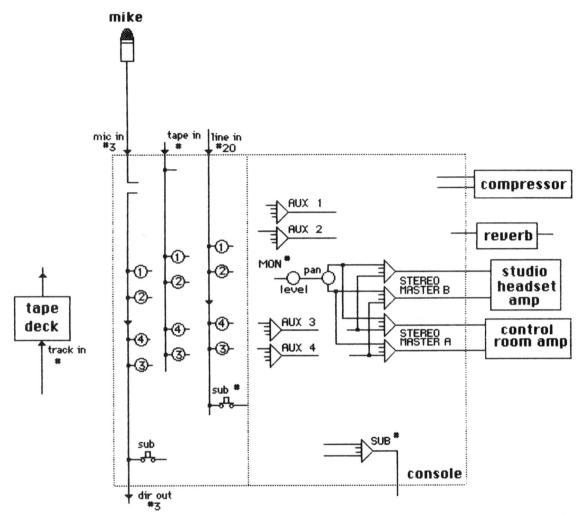

FIG. 5-12. *System loop connection template.*

6

Channel Patch
Signal Processors

THIS CHAPTER EXPLORES THE PROPER USE OF THE VARIOUS CONTROLS AND indicators on signal-processing devices. But before talking about any of these processors, a little information on the properties of sound should first be helpful in order to better understand processor functions.

PROPERTIES OF SOUND

Sound is something perceived as the result of molecular, mechanical vibrations. The molecular composition of air is the medium that couples the sound source to our ears to register intensity and pitch. It is actually the coordination of both intensity and pitch that characterizes the differences in what you hear. There are basically two characteristics that determine what something sounds like: the dynamic profile called the *envelope* and the *harmonic* content.

The word *dynamics* pertains to changes in sound intensity or loudness. Intensity is the *sound pressure level* (SPL), defined in decibels (dB). Because sound is a vibration, it is a physical force applied over the area of an ear drum. Using a piano as the first example, when a player strikes a key, there is a rather instantaneous sound and then it fades away. This dynamic profile can be drawn graphically, where intensity versus time, as shown in Fig. 6-1. Note that the sound reached a maximum intensity and then decayed down to nothing. The first time period, from t_0 to t_1, is the *rise time* it took to reach maximum intensity, which happens in a split second. The *decay* or *fall time*, from t_1 to t_2, is much longer. This entire profile is the envelope.

Another example is the envelope of a flute, shown in FIG. 6-2. A wind instrument can sustain a peak intensity as long as the breath is there. The first time period $_0$ to t_1, is the *rise time*. The period t_1 to t_2 is the note sustained, and

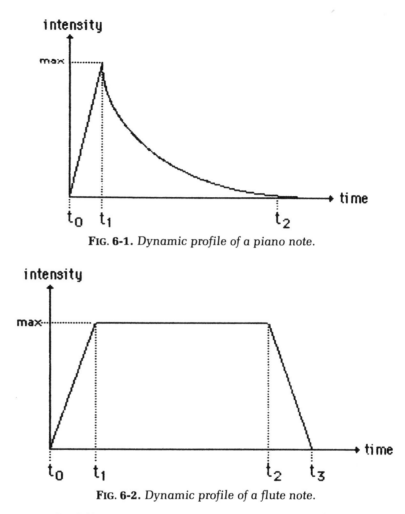

FIG. 6-1. *Dynamic profile of a piano note.*

FIG. 6-2. *Dynamic profile of a flute note.*

finally t_2 to t_3 is the fall time. Bear in mind that the rise and fall times are very rapid. In reality, envelopes can take on many shapes, especially in programmable synthesizers. In recording, dynamic range must be considered because a singer can go from a whisper to a shout. Nearly everything can influence the rise and fall dynamics and everything in between.

The envelope is not the only signature of sound. The harmonic content is the other aspect. Consider the simplest sound waveform. It can be described as a trigonometric function called a *sine wave*. A plucked string vibrates the air as the string oscillates back and forth. This oscillating movement is sinusoidal, and its displacement can be described graphically as displacement versus time, as shown in FIG. 6-3. This is the mechanical profile of simple harmonic motion.

115

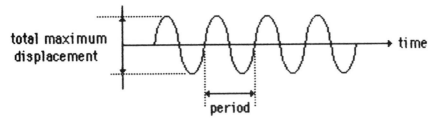

FIG. 6-3. *Acoustic oscillation (sinusoidal waveform).*

The peaks represent the maximum motion or deviation from the still position of the string. The period is the time it takes the string to go from its still position, up to its maximum peak, "down" to its "minimum" peak or other extreme, and return to the still position. This is defined as a *cycle*. Frequency is defined as *cycles per second*, and one cycle per second is represented as *one hertz*. The higher the frequency, the more cycles that occur in the same time frame. By the same token, a loudspeaker communicates sound because of the back- and-forth motion of the speaker cone (FIG. 6-4).

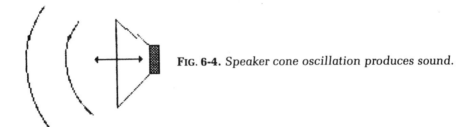

FIG. 6-4. *Speaker cone oscillation produces sound.*

This is a simple case of one fundamental sinusoidal tone, but actually sounds are much more complex than that. Sounds are composed of a multiplicity of sinusoids called *harmonics*. Harmonics are also sine waves, but their frequencies are integral multiples of the fundamental frequency. The most audible pitch is the fundamental frequency, which has the largest displacement or amplitude. The harmonics are the higher frequencies that have varying amplitudes, but they are much lower than that of the fundamental frequency.

The frequency spectrum of a sound can be displayed graphically in terms of amplitude and frequency. A violin has about five significant harmonics in addition to the fundamental as shown in FIG. 6-5. The fundamental f_1 has the highest amplitude. The second harmonic, f_2, is twice the frequency but less than half the amplitude of f_1. The third harmonic is three times the fundamental frequency but less than a quarter of its amplitude. The rest of the harmonics drop off quickly. Harmonics are also called *overtones*. It is these overtones that allow recognition of sound.

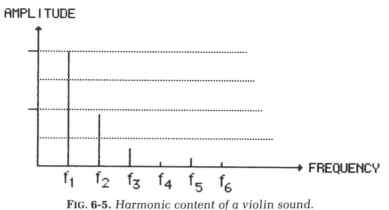

FIG. 6-5. *Harmonic content of a violin sound.*

Another interesting example is that of a square wave, which is among the waveforms that synthesizers use. A square wave is composed of all the odd-ordered harmonics out to infinity, but again the amplitude drops off considerably after the first few. FIGURE 6-6 is the spectral display for a square wave. If all the harmonics are summed, it will result in a square wave. For example, FIG. 6-7 shows the sum of the first three sinusoidal waveforms. The more harmonics that are added, the squarer the waveform looks (see FIG. 6-8).

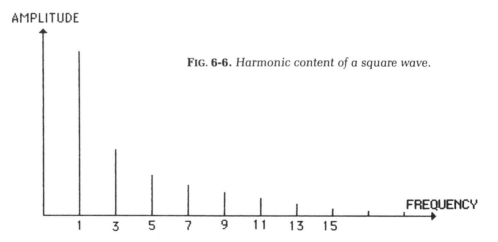

FIG. 6-6. *Harmonic content of a square wave.*

In summary, sound is described in terms of the envelope and harmonics that make it up. Bear this information in mind in understanding signal processors, such as compressors/limiters, de-essers, noise gates, expanders, and equalizers.

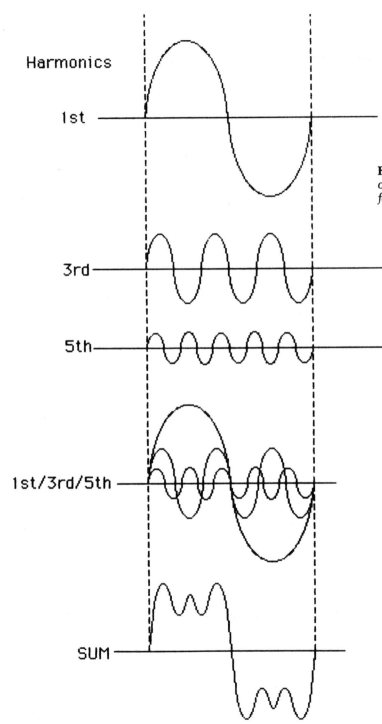

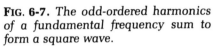

FIG. 6-7. *The odd-ordered harmonics of a fundamental frequency sum to form a square wave.*

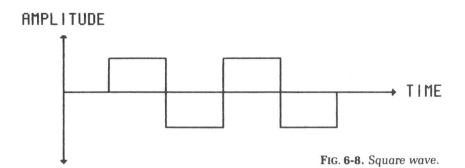

FIG. **6-8.** *Square wave.*

COMPRESSORS/LIMITERS

The task for the compressor is to regulate the dynamic range of a signal, which affects its envelope. Since acoustical signals translate to electronic ones in such a manner that the higher the amplitude, the higher the electronic signal, there is a need to limit how large this amplitude can get. If the tape deck is over-driven, the result is *tape saturation*, which to our ears means *distortion*.

The typical controls found on compressors are:
- Attack
- Release
- Threshold
- Compression ratio
- Gain

Not all compressors have attack and release controls; these settings are sometimes fixed internally. The *attack* is a time-related setting that determines how long the unit waits after being triggered to start compressing the signal. The value of this setting is to allow the initial rise time to go through without being affected. This signal transient is very important to the signature or identi-fication of the sound, although tampering with the rise time can create interest-ing effects. The *release* time determines how long the compressor stays in effect after the signal drops below the threshold level. Too long a release interferes with the rise time transient.

The most vital settings are the threshold level and compression ratio. The *threshold* setting determines what minimum signal level is required to start the compression mode (any signal below this level passes through the compressor untouched). The *compression ratio* is defined as the change of input level over the change in output level. The curve in FIG. 6-9 shows how this works. Any input signals below the threshold level do not experience compression. The 45-degree line is a 1:1 ratio. However, input levels beyond this point become atten-uated on the output in accordance with the compression ratio chosen. Examine

119

a curve using a compression ratio 2:1 as an example. Reference the threshold setting as the 0 line on the scale (see FIG. 6-10). Prior to compression, an input signal of − 2 yields an output level of − 2 on the output. But an input level of 4 is reduced to a level of 2 on the output as shown by the curve. Mathematically, compression ratio is defined as the change of input over the change or output:

$$\text{compression ratio} = \frac{\Delta \text{ input}}{\Delta \text{ output}}$$

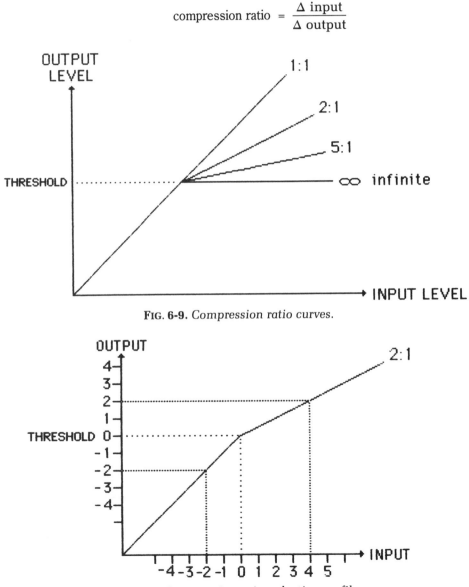

FIG. **6-9**. *Compression ratio curves.*

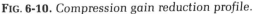

FIG. **6-10**. *Compression gain reduction profile.*

A compressor that is set to have infinite compression is defined as a *limiter*. This is the case when there is no change of output level regardless of how much input level is applied (see FIG. 6-11). The output is the same no matter how high the input level is. So in the mathematical expression for compression ratio, there is a zero in the denominator, and any number divided by zero is undefined, or infinite.

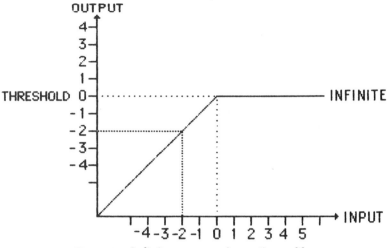

FIG. **6-11.** *Infinite compression ratio profile.*

Most compressors have LED (light-emitting-diode) bar metering, which indicates how much energy is being absorbed by the compressor. The amount of reduction is expressed in decibels (dB). This is not to be confused with acoustical SPL decibels. Though similar, it is somewhat different for electronic signals. In electronics, a decibel is defined as the logarithmic ratio of two power levels. In this case, it's the logarithmic ratio of output power over input power.

$$\text{gain (dB)} = 10 \log (P_{out}/P_{in})$$

Plug in a few numbers to get a feel for what this expression means. If the power out is the same as the power in, the ratio is one.

$$dB = 10 \log (1)$$

This relationship is referred to as *unity gain*. Solving the above equation, the log (1) = 0, and if 10 × 0 = 0, then dB = 0. So remember that if dB = 0, it means unity gain.

121

Take another case in which the output power is twice the input power. That means $P_{out}/P_{in} = 2$, so:

$$dB = 10 \log (2) = 3$$

What about a compressor that reduces the signal such that the power out is half of that going in?

$$dB = 10 \log (^1/_2) = -3$$

The point is that power ratios (P_{out}/P_{in}) greater than 1 yield positive numbers, and those less than 1 yield negative numbers. Since a compressor is a device that has negative gain, meaning that it reduces input signals, the LED meter has gain reduction numbers on it. Recall that a log is an exponent raised to the base number 10. The relationship is such that if

$$10 \log (x) = dB$$

then

$$\log (x) = dB/10$$

and

$$x = 10^{(dB/10)}$$

If 0 dB means unity gain, then $x = 10^{(0/10)} = 10^{(0)} = 1$. So a gain of 20 dB means what?

$$x = 10^{(20/10)} = 10^2 = 100$$

This says that a gain of 20 dB means that the power out is 100 times greater than the power in. If a compressor has a gain reduction of 20 dB (-20 dB), then the ratio is $x = 10^{(-20/10)} = 10^{-2} = ^1/_{100} = .01$. This means that the power going in the threshold level is 100 times smaller at the output. As a matter of fact, all the metering on recording equipment is expressed in dB. Consoles and tape machines have VU meters that register decibels. (However, VU meter decibels have a slightly different implication and are covered in Chapter 8.)

Here is the setup procedure for a compressor in the recording studio. Assume that a compressor has already been patched in. The first thing to look for on the compressor is the bypass switch. When activated, this switch allows the signal to pass through unaffected. The point here is to see what the signal is doing on its own. In the bypass condition, adjust the console fader to register about 0 dB on the tape deck VU meter. Now release the bypass switch and adjust the threshold so that the first LED flickers when the VU needle crosses 0 dB. Now set the compression ratio enough to limit the hottest signals from exceeding +2 dB (in the red). If the needle goes a little into the red, it doesn't mean trouble; it's just a warning. Adjusting the attack and release controls is done by trial and error. Trust your ears on these settings. Experiment if something sounds unnatural. Vocals are usually the toughest adjustments because of the wide dynamic range. Setting a threshold at a −2 dB VU metering point and reducing the compression ratio could work out better. Your ears will be the ultimate gauge to judge performance. In summary, follow these steps in sequence:

    Ⓐ Adjust signal level with compressor bypassed.
    Ⓐ Adjust threshold for some VU tape deck reference.
    Ⓐ Adjust compression ratio to avoid ''pegging the meter.''
    Ⓐ Experiment with attack and release.

Some compressors have a gain control. Initially, set this for 0 dB before making a threshold setting.

DE-ESSER

A *de-esser* is part of the limiter family, but its mission is solely to attack overbearing ''s'' sounds in vocals. The de-esser is supposed to soften the ''s'' sound on words like *see* or *kiss*, without deteriorating the fidelity of the track. Assuming that explosive ''s'' sounds are a nuisance at the high end of the spectrum, high-frequency limiting is done to reduce it. Usually, there is a gain reduction control and a bandwidth control to cover the range of operation. Once again trial and error is the best adjustment technique.

NOISE GATES

A noise gate is a squelching device. It suppresses unwanted signals (*noise*) in the absence of the desired signal. Suppose it's a hot summer day and you are at home relaxing with the air conditioner on. All you hear is the purr, or noise, from the air conditioner. You now feel like playing your stereo. You turn on some music at a moderate level. You listen to the music, but you still hear the air conditioner. The more you turn up the stereo, the less aware you are of the air conditioner. If you turn it up loud enough, you won't even be aware of the noise at all. If the desired signal, in this case the stereo, is well above the noise, the noise doesn't matter anymore. In technical terms, if the *signal-to-noise ratio* (S/N) is high enough, the presence of noise is acceptable. If you shut off the stereo, once again you can hear the noisy air conditioner.

In a recording application, noise is acceptable when the desired signal *is* there, but no one wants to hear it when the signal is *not* there. So the purpose of a noise gate is to squelch the noise when the desired signal is not there to cover it up. A typical situation like this happens in the studio when miking a guitar amplifier. "Hiss" or electronic noise is almost always apparent, when the guitarist is not playing. What can be done about this hiss when the guitarist is idle?

The graph in FIG. 6-12 shows the desired signal level versus frequency. The signal, comprised of numerous harmonics, has a bandwidth that occupies a portion of the audio frequency spectrum. Noise is usually broadband (spread throughout the whole spectrum). To comprehend how a noise gate works, first think of it as an on/off switch in which the decision to be on or off depends on some input level. The strategy is to set the triggering level such that only the noise level is too weak to trigger the gate on, so the gate is off because the dB noise level is insufficient and no noise will pass through. But when the desired signal is present, the squelch threshold is broken and both signal and noise pass through. The diagram in FIG. 6-13 graphically compares the input to the output.

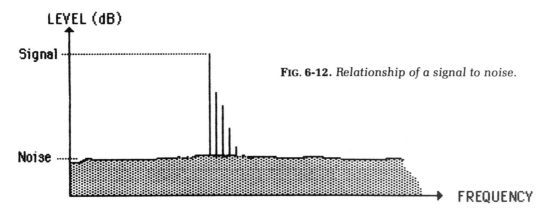

FIG. 6-12. *Relationship of a signal to noise.*

It should now be apparent that a noise gate is a level detection device that uses this information to make a yes/no decision. But that is not all there is to it. As always, a signal has rise and fall characteristics that need some attention. Recall that a signal's rise time is the period it takes to build up to its maximum level. If the triggering level of the noise gate is set at too high a dB level, it could chop the attack of the signal noticeably. Look at the previous graph microscopically depicted in FIG. 6-14. Observe how the triggering level can interfere with the rise and fall times of the signal. In most cases it is more noticeable in the decay cycle than in the rise time. A clear-cut example of a slow rise time is when a person says a word like "hot." It is very easy to chop off the rise time of the "h" and make it sound like "ot." Therefore, triggering levels should be conservative and set close to the noise threshold. A chopped decay pattern is even more obvious. Thus, there is an attack and release setting for a noise gate. The attack provides a rise time when triggering occurs. This is useful if the noise floor is unusually high. The attack control introduces the signal with a smooth transition. The release control provides a smooth transition to exit the signal. There is also another feature called *hold time* that extends the gate's "on time" after the signal level decays past the triggering level. This enables the natural decay pattern to be heard going through the noise floor before being released. FIGURE 6-15 shows the chopped front and back of an envelope in comparison to one treated with attack and release to correct any "snap action." The purpose of these controls is to make the gating action transparent or inaudible. When using this processor, start with the minimum triggering level, letting the "noise only" pass. Advance the triggering level until noise disappears. Then make the other adjustments by trial and error until the signal entry and exit sounds natural.

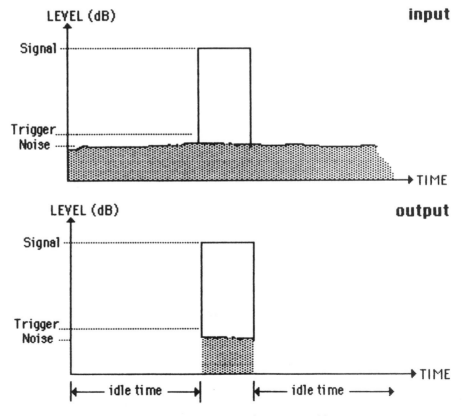

FIG. 6-13. *Noise gate input and output profiles.*

125

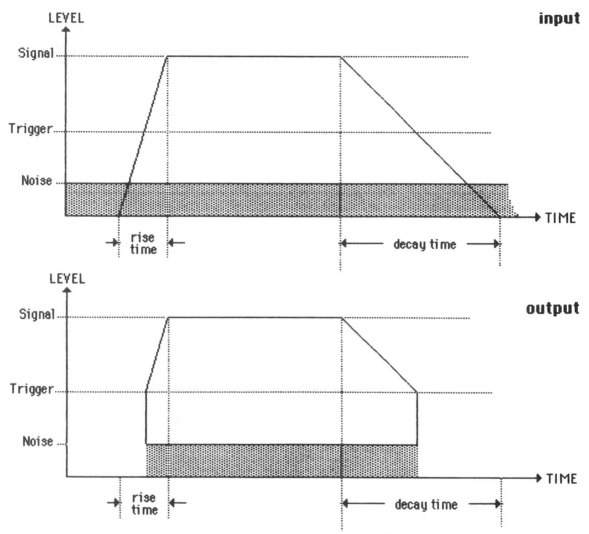

FIG. **6-14.** *Noise gate input and output rise and fall periods.*

Not all noise gates have all of these features. Some units have fixed or preset attack and release times. There are a couple of other features on more sophisticated noise gates. So far, the impression is that a gate is either on or off. However, some gates have a gain reduction control such that a gate is not totally off. There might be some cases where letting some noise through is acceptable in exchange for a fast attack or rise time. Another interesting feature is a "keyed" gate in which an external signal source can be used to do the triggering. A device made by Valley called Gatex (pictured in FIG. 6-16) has four keyed gates in one package, featuring threshold, attenuation range, and release controls.

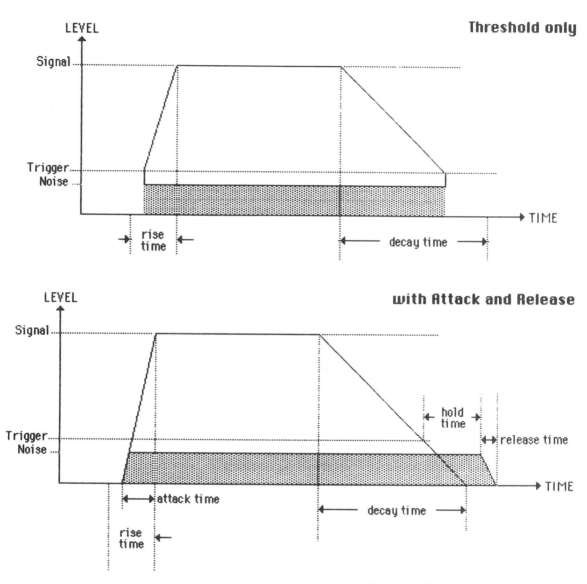

FIG. 6-15. *Noise gate output response.*

Another feature is called a "one shot." This is a function where the signal is initially gated until it first appears breaking the squelch. After that, there is no additional gating and the device is essentially in the bypass mode. A company called dbx makes a gate with this function, the model 904. This is pictured in FIG. 6-17 along with their model 902 de-esser and model 903 compressor.

127

FIG. **6-16.** *The Valley Gatex noise gate has four keyed gates.*

FIG. **6-17.** dbx 900 Series modular signal processing system: (A) Model 902 de-esser; (B) Model 903 compressor; (C) Model 904 noise gate.

These are plug-in units that fit into a mainframe. Other devices combine functions like the Symetrix 525 two-channel or Dual Gated Compressor/Limiter pictured in FIG. 6-18. Noise gates are not to be confused with noise reduction devices. A noise reduction device actually improves the signal-to-noise ratio in the analog recording process. Noise reduction is discussed when tape transports are covered in Chapter 8.

FIG. 6-18. *Symetrix 525 gated compressor.*

EXPANDER

As might be expected, an expander function is somewhat the opposite of a compressor function. However, in essence, an expander is more closely related to a noise gate. For that matter, many devices are identified as "expander/gate" such as the Rane DC24 Dynamic Controller pictured in FIG. 6-19. This unit also features compression. The Valley model 440 is a compressor, limiter, expander, and dynamic sibilance processor (de-esser) in one package (FIG. 6-20). There is an effort made by the expander to intensify the dynamic range of a signal. In general, rising signals are made louder and falling signals are made quieter.

FIG. 6-19. *The Rane DC24 Dynamic Controller is an expander, gate, and compressor.*

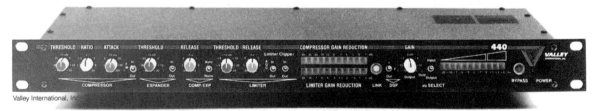

FIG. 6-20. *The Valley 440 dynamic processor is a compressor, limiter, expander, and de-esser.*

DUCKING

Ducking is a gating type of function in which an external signal is used to attenuate the applied signal. This is useful in mixing when a track has to be "pulled down" to let another track "punch through." An example of a device that has multiple functions featuring expanding, gating, compression, and ducking is the Aphex 612 Expander/Gate pictured in FIG. 6-21.

129

FIG. 6-21. *Aphex expander/gate can also do compression and ducking.*

EQUALIZERS

Most people with home stereos are aware of the bass and treble tone controls and their impact on sound reproduction. These controls are actually a form of equalizer. Equalizers deal with boosting or cutting specific regions of the audio frequency spectrum. The human hearing range's definition of the audio spectrum is the bandwidth from 20 to 20,000 hertz. But before various types of equalizers are discussed, some discussion of electronic filter terms is necessary.

Equalizers used in recording are much more complex than the simple operation of common hi-fi tone controls, but as a starting point, what do hi-fi tone controls do? Imagine that a white noise generator was plugged into a system. A white noise generator produces frequencies of equal energy across the audio spectrum. A graphic depiction of what white noise would look like for the human hearing range is in FIG. 6-22. A so-called "bass" control would then boost or cut frequencies at the low end, as shown in FIG. 6-23. Note that in the first case, frequencies at the low end are boosted, and the second graph shows them reduced. Such equalization can be applied at the other end of the spectrum as well (FIG. 6-24). Since the vertical axis is power level and the horizontal axis is frequency, an equalizer (EQ) control is therefore responsible for a spectral boost or cut in power at a certain frequency region. If the boost or cut is at a fixed frequency, this type of control is called *fixed shelving* equalization. If there is a control to choose the frequency range to be boost or cut, this is a *sweep shelving* type of equalizer.

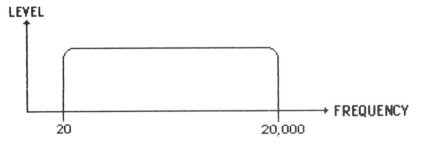

FIG. 6-22. *White noise generated within the human hearing range.*

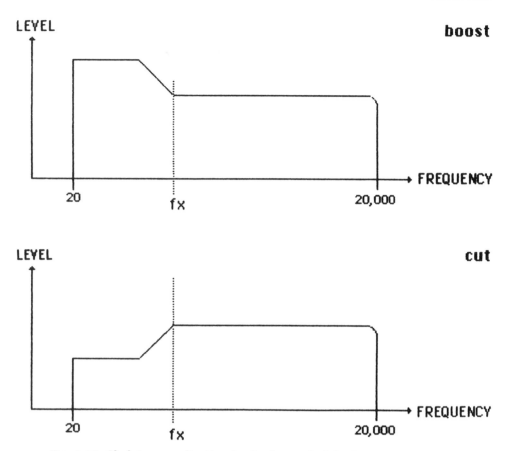

FIG. **6-23.** *Shelving equalization for the low end of the frequency spectrum.*

Because these types of equalizers can boost power, they are called *active filters*. Boost and cut ranges are about +15 dB or −15 dB. On the other hand, there are *passive filters* such as low-pass and high-pass filters that can only cut and not boost power. A low-pass filter cuts the high frequencies allowing the low ones to pass through, and a high-pass filter does the opposite. These two types of filters have fixed "roll-off" or cutoff points as shown in FIG. 6-25. The frequency f_x is the point or frequency at which the attenuation begins. Usually these filters roll off at 12 dB per octave. For example, let's say that the roll-off frequency for the LPF is at 8 kHz. The frequency that is one octave away is 16 kHz. That means that a 16 kHz signal would be 12 dB down in power from 8 kHz, as shown in FIG. 6-26.

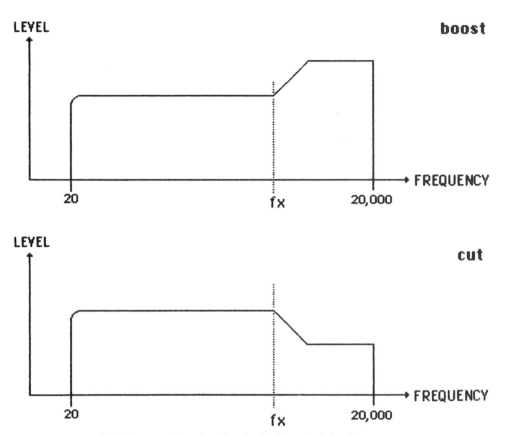

FIG. 6-24. *Shelving equalization for the high end of the frequency spectrum.*

What about the middle portion of the audio spectrum? Equalization controls that affect this part of the spectrum are usually *active bandpass filters*. A bandpass equalizer can boost or cut a band or portion of the spectrum. With a sweepable equalizer, you can select which portion of the spectrum to pass (bandpass) or stop (bandstop), depending on the chosen frequency point, as shown in FIG. 6-27. This type is common to both *graphic* and *parametric* equalizers. A graphic equalizer has several slide controls that can boost or cut frequencies in a bandpass fashion at fixed frequency points. A parametric or sweepable equalizer has fewer controls but has variable center frequency points.

Another characteristic of bandpass filters is the bandwidth or quality factor, simply denoted as Q. Look at a bandpass boost close up (FIG. 6-28). *Bandwidth* is defined as a filter's frequency width at the 3 dB down points. The quality factor Q is defined as the ratio of center frequency (f_c) over the bandwidth (BW).

$$Q = f_c/BW$$

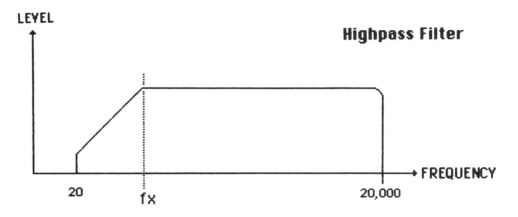

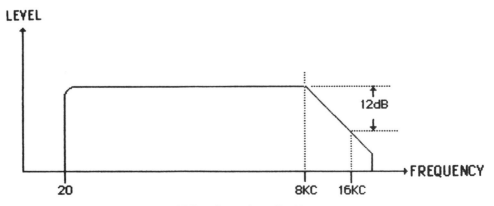

FIG. 6-25. *Passive filters.*

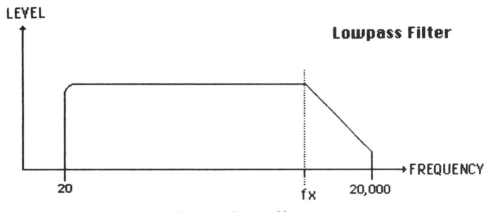

FIG. 6-26. *LPF with 12 dB roll-off per octave.*

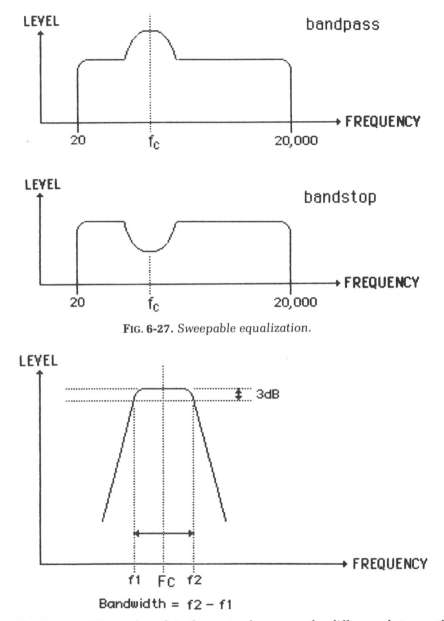

FIG. 6-27. *Sweepable equalization.*

FIG. 6-28. *Bandpass response where f_c is the center frequency, the difference between the 3 dB down points is the bandwidth, and Q is the ratio of f_c to BW.*

Where parametric equalizers control the Q response (the higher the Q, the narrower the shape of the band), graphic equalizers have a fixed Q factor. So the basic difference between graphic and parametric equalizers is that graphic ones boost and cut at fixed center frequency points where parametric ones boost and cut at variable center frequency points. The graphic equalizer has a fixed Q factor where parametric ones have variable Q. Most lower-cost recording consoles have a *quasi-parametric* equalizer, which means it doesn't feature a Q control. The Tascam M-520 has an equalizer configuration that features three sweepable bandpasses that boost or cut 15 dB. The low sweep is from 50 to 500 Hz, the mid is 100 Hz to 5 kHz, and the high is from 2.5 to 15 kHz. If you want a fully parametric equalizer that has a Q control and high- and low-pass filters, such as a Tascam PE-40, it must be channel patched.

An active bandwidth filter used as a boost is a *bandpass* and when used as a cut, it is a *bandstop* filter. When used as a cut or boost with a very high Q (very narrow), it's a *notch* filter. The next question is, how is all this used? Bear in mind that a signal is composed of many frequencies (its fundamental and its harmonics). An engineer can tamper with the relative amplitudes of the harmonics and alter the sound. The usual approach is to first make a decision to either cut or boost, then sweep the band as you listen. Most of what humans hear is concentrated between 100 Hz to 10 kHz. If you were equalizing a violin, it would be a waste of time bothering with the low end of the spectrum where no signals exist. You must experiment to discover where the frequency range is for a given sound.

FIGURE 6-29 shows a parametric equalizer, the dbx model 905. This device has three sweepable bands with frequency, gain, and Q control. The LF (low frequency) and HF (high frequency) bands can be selected to operate as a shelving function. The Rane PE15 pictured in FIG. 6-30 is similar, but it covers five frequency bands. The Orban model 642B pictured in FIG. 6-31 is a two-channel package featuring four sweepable bands with presettable high-pass and low-pass filters. The Yamaha DEQ7 digital equalizer pictured in FIG. 6-32 is very flexible. It can operate as any of the filters discussed in this chapter. It has 30 preset programs including 60 memory locations for user-defined settings.

FIG. **6-29.** *dbx Model 905 parametric equalizer.*

FIG. **6-30.** *Rane PE15 parametric equalizer.*

FIG. 6-31. Orban 642B parametric equalizer/notch filter.

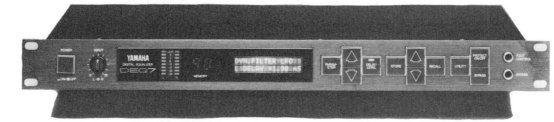

FIG. 6-32. Yamaha DEQ7 digital equalizer.

7

Effects Signal Processors

EFFECTS UNITS ARE DEVICES THAT PRODUCE WET SIGNALS THAT ARE THEN combined with a dry signal. These effects are important to the mix-down. Probably the most important effects are reverb programs. But there are many other effects that have become popular. Most units today are called "multi effect" signal processors because digital technology has made it possible to combine several effects in one unit. Most of these units are address-able through the musical instrument digital interface (MIDI; see Chapter 11) and have programmable parameters.

REVERB

If you have ever been in a gymnasium, church, or any building that has hard walls and a high ceiling, then you have experienced the sonic property called *reverb*. Reverb is the mulitple reflections of a sound bouncing off the walls and ceiling. To make any sense out of using digital reverb devices, you must first understand the parameters that define this acoustical phenomenon. First picture yourself in a field with high grass. There is a person about 30 feet away talking to you. The sound disperses radially in all directions—left, right, forward, up, and down. Since sound travels at about 1100 feet per second, it takes the sound about 27 milliseconds (0.027 sec) to reach you. This is called the direct signal. It is the shortest path (a straight line) between the talker and the listener. The listener hears it only once because there are no surfaces to rebound the signal (the hypothetical tall grass absorbs the signal, preventing it from reflecting off the ground).

Now alter the circumstances and place two people in a room that has a tile floor and plaster walls and ceiling. Imagine the room dimensions to be 20 by 50 feet with a 15-foot ceiling. The two people are placed at each end of the room about 30 feet apart. One person gives a hand clap. The first sound that the listener at the other end of the room hears is the direct signal followed by multiple reflections from the walls, floor and ceiling. The diagram in FIG. 7-1 shows an aerial view of the two people in the room. Note that the direct signal is the shortest path and the reflected signals have longer paths which means they take a little longer to reach the listener. The reflected signals are not as loud as the direct one. Some of the energy is absorbed by the surface and the fact that the travel distance is farther. Only a couple of reflections are shown in the diagram for purposes of discussion, but there are thousands of reflections and collisions reaching the listener the same way a rack of pool balls scatters when struck by a cue ball. So when the hand clap sounds, the reflections continue until all the energy is absorbed. In a real room, the low-frequency content of the sound outlives the higher frequencies because high-frequency content loses momentum faster.

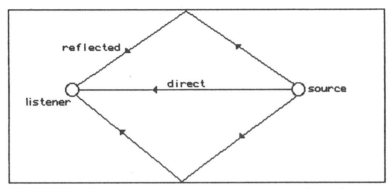

FIG. 7-1. *Relationship between direct and reflected signals.*

Digital reverbs have programmable parameters that simulate the direct signal time, reverb time, and the high-to-low-frequency-ratio dissipation. Most reverbs also provide equalization for this wet signal. Now examine the hand clap pulse graphically in FIG. 7-2. See what happens to the hand clap reflections versus time. The δt is the direct path time and this parameter is expressed in milliseconds. Expect about a millisecond per foot (ms/ft). (Sound travels a little faster than that, about 0.9 ms/ft, but 1.0 ms will do for our purposes.)

The next parameter is *reverb time*. This refers to the entire frequency content that finally diminishes and is expressed in seconds. The next parameter is the *frequency ratio*. Note on the graph that the high-frequency curve times out faster. The higher the frequency, the shorter the time. On digital reverbs, this ratio can be altered. A ratio of 1 means that the high-frequency content lasts just as long as the low frequencies. A ratio of 0.5 means that the high frequency content lasts half as long.

139

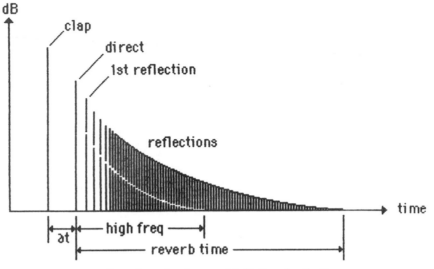

FIG. **7-2.** *Reverberation is a multiplicity of reflections.*

So when making these adjustments, bear in mind that a reverb time setting implies a room size, a delay setting is the time delay of the first reflections following the direct signal heard by the listener, and a ratio setting determines how long you want to hear the highs with respect to the lows. All of these settings become issues of personal taste. Prior to digital technology, reverb devices were mechanical. Spring units were the most affordable but not as desirable as *plate* reverb. Springs simulated reflections by vibrating them mechanically with the dry signal and converting these vibrations to electrical signals. Spring mechanisms had difficulty handling envelopes with fast rise times such as drums. Then plates became popular because it solved the sonic problems found in springs. Plate reverb was a large steel rectangular plate suspended on a frame at each corner with high tension springs, the same way a trampoline canvas is mounted. At one end there was a coil that vibrated the plate with the dry signal and transducers at the other end converted the mechanical plate vibrations to electrical signals. Plates are realistic room simulators, but they took up a lot of space (for example 4 by 6 by 1 feet). But now digital reverbs can outperform plates with all of the programmable features plus they use less space. Digital reverbs did to plates what the calculator did to slide rules.

ECHO

This acoustical phenomenon, like reverb, is a collection of reflections, but they are fewer and more widely time-spaced. Echo is often associated with canyons, valleys, or mountains—environments where reflection surfaces are very far apart. Talking to a wall 550 feet away would produce a repeated signal one second later. Standing between two parallel walls, there would be repeats until the vibration decayed. Echo units simulate this effect. They have parameters to define the time delay between repeats and the amount of repeats. Echo devices are usually referred to as *digital delay*. The diagram in FIG. 7-3 is a graphical representation of the echo envelope. Note that all the repeats are mutually spaced by a time of δt. This can range anywhere from a few milliseconds to seconds. Also note that each repeat has a lower dB level than the previous one. For most devices, the number of repeat settings automatically determines the damping factor (how fast it decays). In real life, each echo or repeat loses more of its highs faster than its lows just like the way reverb reflections do. Remember that increased distance of sound travel decreases high-frequency content more. Have you ever listened to a band outdoors and wondered why the bass seemed to dominate the overall sound? Now you know.

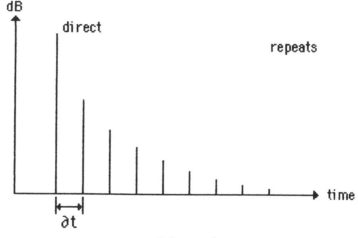

FIG. 7-3. *Echo envelope.*

There are usually three settings for echo. There is a setting for the number of repeats, referred to as the *feedback*. The δt setting is the delay, or time lapse, between repeats, and the third is an output level control. When making the delay setting, think in terms of 1 millisecond per foot. It doesn't take much distance to perceive a repeat. Have you ever been in a room with a TV tuned to the same station as another TV in the next room or listened to the radio in the car and someone in a convertible pulls up next to you blasting the same station? Our ears can discriminate fractional time differences. A very common application in pop music is "slap" echo, which is one repeat with a delay of about 10 to 20 milliseconds.

CHORUSING

This effect simulates the illusion of several instruments playing at once. If you were asked, "can you tell the difference if one person is playing a violin or that six people are playing, even if they are all playing the same note?" Yes you can, but why? That is because of the random pitch, amplitude, and phase relationships of each player. A chorus effect typically addresses amplitude and phasing relationships. When a dry signal is applied, this effect produces several signals with varying delays (phase) and amplitude (decibels).

Consider a real-life situation. Picture yourself listening to four violins playing the same part. Since no one can occupy the same place or sit in the same seat, the direct path distance to your ear varies and therefore so does the volume. Four signals are heard, one from each player, and like reverb or echo reflections, these four signals arrive at your ears at slightly different times. Refer to FIG. 7-4. You would hear the closest player first and the furthest player last.

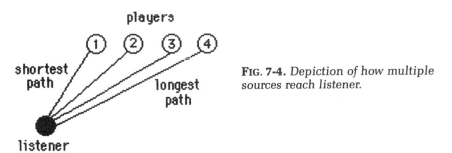

FIG. 7-4. *Depiction of how multiple sources reach listener.*

Even though the delay involved here is a very small fraction of time, observe from the graph in FIG. 7-5 that the listener registers four signals at various dB amplitudes and time delays. This is why you can tell there is more than one player and even when you are listening to a recording. The delays are so close that they are not perceived as echo or reverb but as "more than one." Chorusing is effective in giving a single source the embodiment of several.

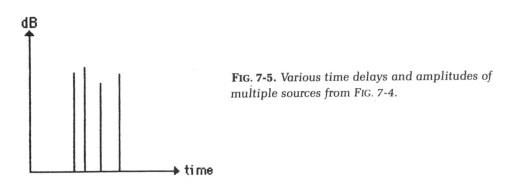

FIG. 7-5. *Various time delays and amplitudes of multiple sources from FIG. 7-4.*

Chorus parameters are not fixed settings but random. The amplitude and phase relationships are modulated. There is usually a *delay modulation* setting that regulates the range of delay imposed on the signals and an *amplitude modulation* setting to regulate the range of the random amplitude changes. Because programmable parameters are so broad in range, most chorus applications are used to make it sound unnatural deliberately.

PHASING

Signal delays that make up reverb, echo, and chorusing effects have thus far been discussed. But when time delays among similar frequencies become very small, another kind of acoustical phenomenon occurs: *phase shift*. Consider a single frequency, a component of sound. One cycle or hertz is 360 degrees, as shown in FIG. 7-6. But for purposes of simplicity, think in terms of 360 degrees.

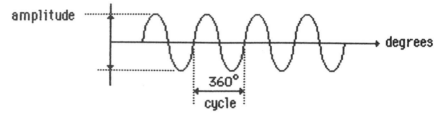

FIG. 7-6. *One cycle, or hertz, equals 360 degrees.*

The diagram in FIG. 7-7 is an example of two identical signals that are *in phase*, meaning that their maximum and minimum points are time coincident (no delay with respect to each other). If these two signals coexist, they superimpose (add up) to make a signal that is now twice the amplitude, as shown in FIG. 7-8. The frequency is still the same—just the magnitude has doubled.

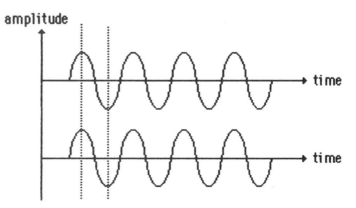

FIG. 7-7. *Two signals that are in phase.*

143

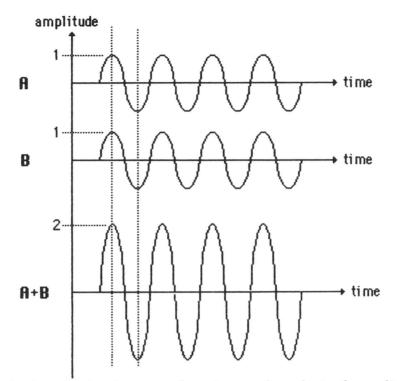

FIG. 7-8. *In phase signals, when summed, create a waveform of twice the amplitude but unchanged in phase.*

Now let's introduce a phase shift. What happens if signal B lags behind A? *Lag* is another expression for delay or phase shift. Consider the case where B is shifted ¹/₄ of a cycle (90 degrees) to the right of signal A (B lags A by 90°). The result is a signal with an amplitude 1.4 times that of either of the originals and a 45-degree phase shift is imposed, as shown in FIG. 7-9. Again, the frequency is still the same. The magnitude of the sum has fallen to 1.4 as opposed to the in-phase signal sum magnitude of 2. If the phase shift keeps increasing, the magnitude will keep decreasing. As a matter of fact, a 180-degree shift (one half cycle) yields zero because both signals would be opposite in phase, cancelling each other out. See FIG. 7-10. Continuing to phase shift beyond 180 degrees causes the signal sum magnitude to increase. A 360-degree shift puts both signals back in phase again.

A half-cycle phase shift (180 degrees out of phase) is the underlying principle of a *vocal eliminator* device. Assuming that the vocal is equal on the left and right on a tape or record, one side is shifted 180 degrees to get a cancellation. However, a problem is that anything else "down the middle" cancels also.

144

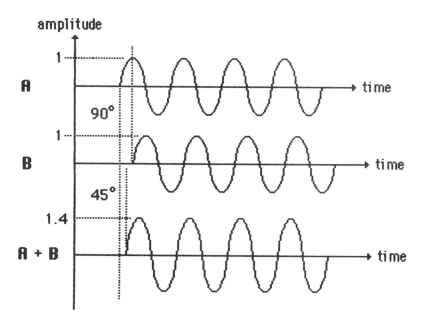

FIG. 7-9. *If signal B lags signal A by 90 degrees, their sum (A + B) would be lower in amplitude (1.4 rather than 2) and have a 45-degree lag.*

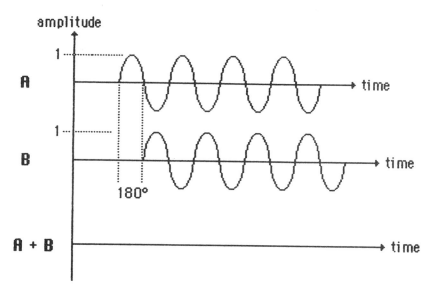

FIG. 7-10. *If signal B lags signal A by 180 degrees (half-cycle phase shift), the signals cancel to zero when summed.*

For those of you with an academic interest, the trigonometric expression for adding two signals with the same frequency and amplitude is:

$$A + B = \sin(\omega t) + \sin(\omega t - \theta)$$
$$= 2\cos(\theta/2)\sin(\omega t - \theta/2)$$

where θ is the phase shift, ω is angular velocity (radians/sec), and t is time (sec). When $\theta = 0$, then $A + B = 2\sin(\omega t)$. If $\theta = 90$, then $\cos(\theta/2) = 0.707$ and $A + B = 1.4\sin(\omega t)$. If $\theta = 180$, then $\cos(\theta/2) = 0$ and $A + B = 0$.

If you duplicate a dry signal twice and vary their phase relationship, their sum $(A + B)$ produces amplitude-modulated signals as they sweep back and forth making phase shifts (FIG. 7-11).

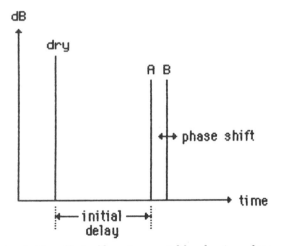

FIG. 7-11. *Chorusing is the effect of hearing variable phasing of two or more signals.*

The programmable parameters usually feature an initial delay so the phased signals don't interfere with the dry signal. Another parameter controls phase modulation depth, or the amount of phase change. Finally, a phase modulation rate parameter regulates how fast these phase shifts occur.

FLANGING

Flanging resembles phasing with the exception that the signal pairs are echoed. The effect is much more sustaining than phasing. It sounds as though a sonic wind is sweeping through as various frequencies are emphasized and de-emphasized. The swelling sound seems to work from one end of the audio spectrum to the other. Listeners experience something in the way of a *doppler effect* as the overtones ripple back and forth past their ears. A doppler effect is a pitch bend (either up or down), or a frequency shift, a phenomenon that occurs when a sound source moves away or toward a listener. Flanging does not actually do this, but the boost-and-cut action of the overtones resembles a shift in pitch. If the phase modulation is extreme enough, then pitch bend would be noticeable.

In comparison to phasing, flanging is sort of an echoed phasing. Flanging is a series of decaying, repeated, phase-shifted signal pairs, as shown in FIG. 7-12. All the programmable parameters resemble phasing except that there is often a feedback or regeneration control to regulate the repeats. Devices vary in features, for example, some have parameters to modulate the initial delay or the distance between echoes.

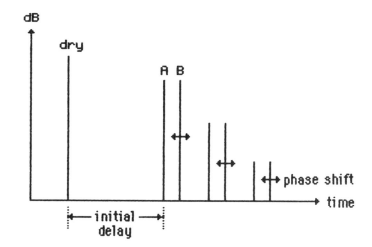

FIG. 7-12. *Flanging is a series of echoed or delayed phased signals.*

EXCITER

An *exciter* is a processor that can restore missing harmonics. A phase cancellation technique is used here as constructive interference. Certain regions of the spectrum most susceptible to distortion can randomly be cancelled or get notched out. These spectral holes are then refilled. The result of this reconstruction process restores the natural presence, clarity, and transparency of a signal. FIGURE 7-13 pictures the Aphex Type C Aural exciter. The overall effect is that it brightens the sound. The wet signal itself sounds shrill, but when this wet signal is combined with the dry, it seems to enhance the high end of the signal. A good reason to apply this effect is when the signal seems to "get lost" in mixdown. This effect can give that edge or "bite" to make it stand out.

FIG. **7-13.** *Aphex exciter.*

PITCH SHIFT

This effect simply alters the frequency of the original sound in the same way a tape deck speed change does, but without changing the time base. A tape deck speed change stretches the time duration to lower the pitch and compresses time passage to raise it. A pitch processor changes pitch without affecting the time. The only penalty is that there is a delay on the output. Time is lost in the process and might sound out of sync with the rest of the material.

SUMMARY

All of these signal processors deal with the parameters that describe sound: frequency, phase, amplitude, time, envelope, and harmonics. Unfortunately, only speaking of these parameters quantitatively does not provide the same benefit as the experience of hearing them in action. However, being acquainted with the theory of operation of these devices should make your attempts and approaches to using these devices more practical. With an understanding of the principles of operation, you can comprehend various concepts, for example *gated reverb* (knowing that a gate can influence a decay time, you can make a dense reverb dampen unnaturally fast). Many of the effects are combinations of the operations for the sake of producing unearthly sounds.

There are many digital devices on the market. FIGURE 7-14 pictures the Yamaha REV5 digital reverb and the SPX9011 multieffects processor is in FIG. 7-15. Lexicon makes the PCM 70 pictured in FIG. 7-16 and the 480L (FIG. 7-17).

FIG. **7-14.** *Yamaha REV5 digital reverberator.*

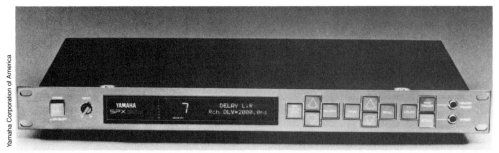

FIG. **7-15.** *Yamaha SPX90II multieffects processor.*

FIG. **7-16.** Lexicon PCM 70 digital effects processor.

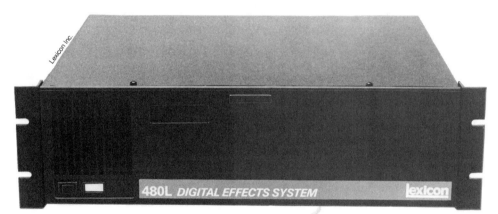

FIG. **7-17.** Lexicon 480L digital effects system.

FIG. **7-18.** *The ART Multiverb was the first processor that could do four effects simultaneously.*

149

Other digital effect processors are the ART multiverb in FIG. 7-18, the Digitech DSP 128 PLUS in FIG. 7-19, and the Dynacord DRP 20 in FIG. 7-20. The Eventide H3000 Ultra-Harmonizer featured in FIG. 7-21 is dedicated mostly to pitch shift effects such as diatonic pitch shifting for doing harmony lines.

FIG. 7-19. *Digitech DSP 128 effects processor.*   DOD Electronics Corp.

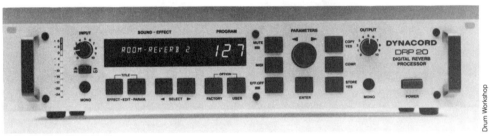

FIG. 7-20. *Dynacord DRP 20 digital reverb processor.*

FIG. 7-21. *Eventide H3000 Ultra Harmonizer.*

150

8

Analog Tape Transports

A TAPE TRANSPORT (OR TAPE DECK) IS A MECHANISM THAT STORES AUDIO signals from the console on magnetic tape via a record head and reproduces these signals via a playback head. For this reason a transport is referred to as a *recorder/reproducer*. This chapter explains its features and functions.

MECHANICAL FEATURES AND CONTROLS

Professional machines have three heads: an erase, record/playback, and playback head. The mechanical portion consists of one *supply* and one *take-up* reel, tape guides, idlers, rollers, a pinch roller, tape lifters, and a capstan as illustrated in FIG. 8-1. The reels move in a counterclockwise direction. The supply reel has some back tension (*reverse torque*) for tape tension to ensure good contact with the heads. The capstan is the drive roller that moves the tape and establishes the tape speed of 15 ips (inches per second). The take-up reel has enough forward torque to prevent tape slack. The idlers are torque sensors in that they move up or down depending on the tape tension. The position of the take-up idler (FIG. 8-2) determines how much torque is applied. Too much take-up reel torque would drive the idler upward, but as this happens, the idler acts as a feedback control to reduce take-up reel torque. If the idler starts to droop as a result of insufficient torque, the feedback information would increase take-up reel motor torque. The same principle is applied to the supply reel in which the motor torque responds with idler position change. As tape transfers from one reel to the other, the torque requirements change.

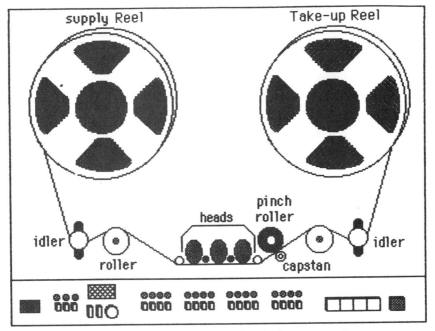

FIG. 8-1. *Tape transport mechanical components.*

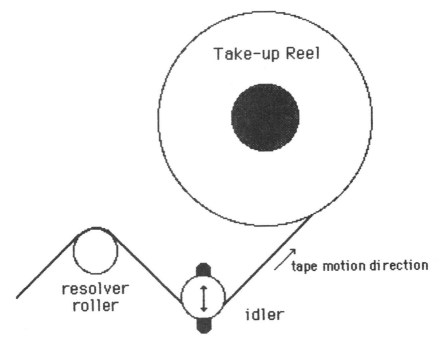

FIG. 8-2. *Each idler arm controls its respective reel torque.*

The capstan is the tape motion shaft that drags the tape across the heads at a steady rate when the pinch roller engages. The supply and take-up reels have nothing to do with tape speed in the PLAY or RECORD mode. The tape is pressed between the capstan and the pinch roller. A relay engages the pinch roller against the rotating capstan and moves the tape like clothes going through a wringer (FIG. 8-3). The roller supporting the tape between the pinch roller and take-up reel idler is a *resolver*, which electronically controls the counter display. The counter indicates tape position from a zero reference by rotating with tape motion in either direction (counting up or down).

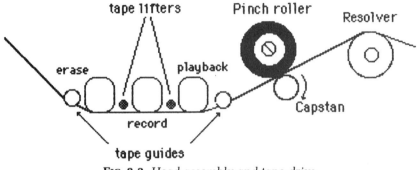

FIG. 8-3. *Head assembly and tape drive.*

There are four pushbuttons that control the transport tape motion, which is just about standard for professional decks; FAST FORWARD, REWIND, PLAY, and STOP (FIG. 8-4). The RECORD button is used with the PLAY when recording. The FAST FORWARD and REWIND functions move tape at high speed, but in many units, pressing the FAST FORWARD or REWIND twice moves tape at a slower speed, called *spooling*, whose purpose is to stack the tape neatly onto the reel because fast winding speeds can cause the tape edges to be exposed and possibly crease or be damaged if mishandled. If this kind of damage occurs, it prevents the tape from making firm contact with the heads when replayed, and *drop outs* can then occur on the tracks during playback. Drop out is when you hear blank spots when listening to a tape. Therefore, it is always good practice to record the most important parts or "busiest" parts on the inner tracks. When in the FORWARD, REWIND, or spooling modes, the tape lifters (FIG. 8-3) move the tape away from the heads to protect them from wearing. Pushing the RECORD button in conjunction with the PLAY button engages the record mode. Pressing STOP once does so for any tape motion, and pressing it twice releases the reel brakes for manual tape shuttling. This is done for editing because the engineer can rock the reels back and forth manually to pinpoint a location for a splice.

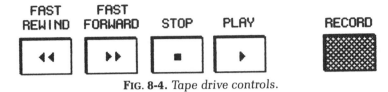

FIG. 8-4. *Tape drive controls.*

The *auto locating* function makes the deck shuttle to a preset counter position. The deck searches for zero or for a cue in accordance with the visual time or counter display. Tape displacement is metered out in counts, or minutes and seconds. These auto location functions are one-pushbutton actions. The reset button zeros the counter. The cue button remembers the count displayed. RTZ means "return to zero" and STC "search to cue." The tape transport then shuttles to the counter position called for.

There should be a rotary type dial for pitch control. This varies the play speed plus or minus several percent. The pitch control comes in handy when dubbing in an instrument that has a pitch offset. The deck can be slowed down or sped up accordingly to make the recorded tracks match up with the instrument pitch. Reduced speed lowers pitch and increased speed raises pitch.

Another manual operation is the cue lever. This releases the tape lifters while in the high speed modes, allowing the tape to make contact with the heads. The purpose of this is to spot check for recorded material.

MULTITRACK TAPE HEADS

There are three heads in a transport assembly (FIG. 8-3). The first (to the left) is the erase head, to the far right is the playback head, and in the center is the record/playback head (a dual function). Each of the heads are segmented in such a way as to divide the tape area into sections (FIG. 8-5). Thus, the tracks are marked off in "layers." It is very important that the tape guides hold the tape's vertical position as it travels past the head. If the tape *skews* (moves up or down), then the tape's track layers will not match up with the head layers. The tape guide (FIG. 8-6) can make the tape buckle and lose contact with the head.

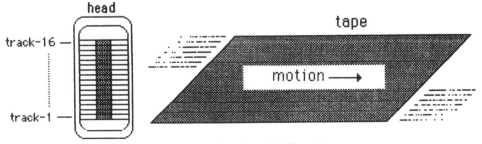

FIG. 8-5. *Tape head track allocation.*

154

Front   Side

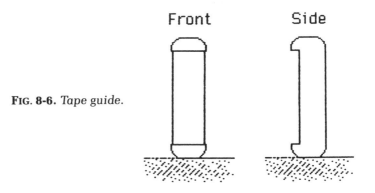

FIG. **8-6.** *Tape guide.*

Tape guides are fixed vertical posts that stabilize the tape when in motion. A maladjustment will cause tape-to-head misalignment and motion anomalies like tape skew.

Let's take a closer look at a dissected head. Observing one segment, or layer, shows that it is a metallic ring with a gap. Wire windings are on each leg (FIG. 8-7). In the record mode, the audio signal goes through the windings and a magnetic field is set up across the gap, polarizing the magnetic ferric oxide coating of the tape. During PLAY, the playback head is polarized by the magnetic tape flux when crossing the gap, reproducing the audio signal in the head windings.

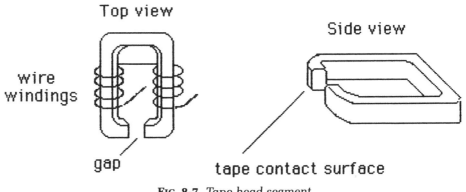

FIG. **8-7.** *Tape head segment.*

In the recording process, the audio signal is mixed with a high-frequency ac *bias* signal because the process of magnetizing tape works more efficiently and practically using these high frequencies. So the audio information needs the help of a bias signal with a frequency in the order of 150 to 200 kHz. The audio signal mixes with the bias signal in such a way that the audio signal *amplitude modulates* the bias signal as illustrated in FIG. 8-8. The bias signal

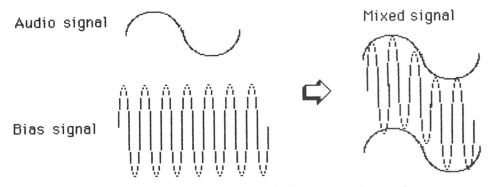

FIG. 8-8. *Audio and bias are recorded as a "mixed" signal.*

level follows the audio signal. In the playback process, the bias signal is removed with a low-pass filter, leaving only the audio signal. Such a filter is called a *bias trap*. When recording, the erase head uses the bias signal to eliminate prerecorded information on the tape. A tape is said to be "erased" by recording this high-frequency bias signal on it. It is not audible on playback because it is filtered out. Note that the tape crosses the erase head first, so when in the record mode, the erase head wipes out any prerecorded signals before recording new ones.

ALIGNMENT AND CALIBRATION

Faithful signal reproduction depends on competent electronic calibration, proper head alignment and uniform tape motion as opposed to irregularities like tape skew. Tape head assemblies have *azimuth* and *zenith* adjustments. The azimuth is the adjustment of the head in the dimensional plane parallel to the tape. The head alignment should be very vertical, forming a right angle with respect to the tape edge. The zenith adjustment pertains to the tilt of the head. If the head surface is not parallel to the tape surface, then head-to-tape contact cannot be uniform. If the tape starts to lose contact with the head, then the high-frequency content suffers. This audible fluctuation or modulation of the highs dropping in and out is referred to as *flutter*. Another possible transport symptom affecting uniform tape motion is speed variations that produce pitch changes in the signals. These audible fluctuations are referred to as *wow*.

The electronic calibration procedure should be performed in accordance with the service manual. This usually requires first to calibrate the VU meters by applying a 1 kHz tone at the proper level for a 0 dB deflection using a signal generator and a calibrated voltmeter to monitor this applied signal. Then use a reference tape in the playback mode. With the meters registering the test tone, tweak the output adjustment for each track for a 0 dB meter deflection. Then test the playback response using other frequencies across the audio band for each track to achieve a flat response. Similarly, make adjustments for the record mode, especially the bias current, which varies depending on the tape used. The objective of the calibration is to achieve a flat response so that signals that go in are faithfully reproduced at all frequencies.

DEGAUSSING

Prior to any calibration, the heads and other metal parts in the tape path should be demagnetized, or *degaussed*. Parts that are in constant contact with magnetic tape can become magnetized themselves. When this happens, it threatens to degrade the high-frequency content of the recorded tracks and even add noise. The remedy is to use a demagnetizer. To use this electrically powered device, begin several feet away before turning the unit on. Then approach the head with the tip of the demagnetizer wand and sweep it back and forth close to, but not touching, the head. Gradually retreat while doing this sweeping motion until several feet away. Then turn the unit off.

MULTITRACK RECORDER OPERATION

With an understanding of the mechanical aspects of the transport and an idea of how signals are recorded and reproduced, this section explains the multitrack control configuration of the Tascam 85-16 16-track transport (FIG. 8-9). There are three monitor pushbuttons: input, sync, and repro. The *input* mode allows the engineer to hear the signals reaching the deck. The *sync* mode allows hearing the signals, in record or playback mode, from the record head. The *repro* mode reproduces signals from the playback head. When recording, select the sync mode. On the Tascam 86-16 deck, there are 16 pushbuttons (one for each track) to select which track or tracks you want to record on. The center head does the recording by activating those head segments corresponding to the tracks selected. You can hear the signal being recorded as well as any prerecorded signals on other tracks. Tracks not selected for recording are in the playback mode. This center head (sync) has this dual function, while the other head (repro) is playback only.

The repro head is really a convenience feature. Let's say you have just recorded on tracks 2,3,9,12,13, and 14 in the sync mode. To hear the playback in the sync mode, you could release all of the track select buttons, but it is easier to just select the repro mode (playback only) and leave the track select buttons where they are. More than likely, another "take" will be necessary anyway, so why not leave the select pushbuttons in? This ensures against accidentally skipping a button or pressing a wrong one for the next take.

FIG. **8-9.** *Tascam 85-16 16-track recorder.*

The process of recording additional tracks with previously recorded tracks is sometimes called *dubbing*. Most studio time is spent dubbing tracks. In modern recording, lead vocals and instruments are usually scheduled in after the basic rhythm tracks are down. When recording, a very useful feature is called *punch-in*. This gives the engineer the flexibility to put a track in a standby record mode while the tape is in the playback mode. When the PLAY and RECORD buttons are pressed simultaneously, this puts the machine in the standby record mode. If no track select buttons are in, the red pilot RECORD button flashes, indicating a record standby condition. As soon as a track button is punched in, the pilot glows continuously, indicating that a record condition is in progress. The advantage of this feature is that a track can have an insert without having to do the whole track over.

VU METERING REFERENCES

There is a VU meter for every track (as shown in FIG. 8-9). The 0 dB reference corresponds to signal level. There are two standards in the industry, a balanced + 4 dBm and an unbalanced – 10 dBV reference. The + 4 dBm reference is a decibel power expression using 1 milliwatt as the 0 dB VU reference. In this case, 1 milliwatt is defined as the power absorbed by a 600-ohm load. Where power is the voltage squared over the resistance:

$$P = V^2/R$$

Solving for V:

$$V = \sqrt{PR}$$

"0 dBm" is defined as the condition when 1 milliwatt of power ($P = 0.001$) drives a 600-ohm load ($R = 600$). Plugging in these numbers for P and R in the above expression yields $V = 0.775$ volts. A $+4$ dBm level is the VU "0" dB. The voltage level into 600 ohms for $+4$ dBM can be determined from the logarithmic expression:

$$10 \log(P/0.001) = dBm$$

For $+4$ dBm (zero VU):

$$
\begin{aligned}
10 \log(P/0.001) &= 4 \\
\log(P/0.001) &= 0.4 \\
P/0.001 &= 10^{(0.4)} \\
P/0.001 &= 2.5 \\
P &= (0.001)(2.5) \\
P = 0.0025 \text{ W} &= 2.5 \text{ mW}
\end{aligned}
$$

Where $P = 0.0025$ and $R = 600$, then $V = 1.23$ volts for "0" VU ($+4$ dBm).

The -10 dBV standard uses 1 volt as the 0 dB reference where:

$$20 \log(V) = dBV$$

So for a -10 dBV metering reference:

$$
\begin{aligned}
20 \log(V) &= -10 \\
\log(V) &= -0.5 \\
V &= 10^{(-0.5)} \\
V &= 0.316 \text{ V} = 316 \text{ mV}
\end{aligned}
$$

In summary, the required signal strength to make a 0 dB meter deflection is 1.23 volts for a $+4$ dBm system and 0.316 volts for a -10 dBV system. The decibel difference between the two systems can be calculated by the logarithmic

159

ratio of the voltages where:

$$20 \log(1.23/0.316) = 11.8 \text{ dB}$$

In spite of the level difference, the important thing is that it translates to the same flux density tape magnetization.

The Tascam 85-16 is a −10 dBV recorder. Many decks have provision for both systems. FIGURE 8-10 pictures the Otari MX-70 16-track transport in which operation of +4 dBm or −10 dBV is selectable. Like the Tascam 85-16, the Otari MX-70 uses a 1-inch tape format. The MX-70 bias frequency is 192 kHz. The Otari MTR-90-11 pictured in FIG. 8-11 is a 24-track machine using a 2-inch tape format. This deck does not have a pinch roller to advance the tape but depends on a microprocessor-controlled drive system for uniform tape motion and tension. Tascam makes the ATR-80 24-track transport pictured in FIG. 8-12 with its remote control unit. A close-up of this deck's erase, record/playback, and playback heads are shown also. Another 24-track machine with its remote controller is the Studer A820 featured in FIG. 8-13. Finally, FIG. 8-14 shows the Otari MX-80 32-track deck on a 2-inch tape format.

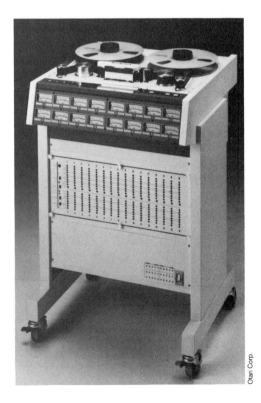

FIG. **8-10.** *Otari MX-70 16-track recorder.*

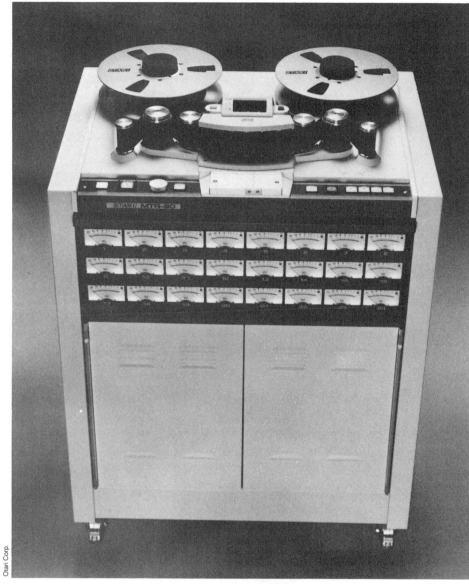

Otari Corp.

FIG. 8-11. *Otari MX-90-II 24-track recorder.*

In cases where a −10 dBV system must be applied to a +4 dBm system, there are devices on the market to make the interface such as the Tascam LA-40, Fostex 5030, or Valley HH2X2B Level Matching Interface pictured in FIG. 8-15.

161

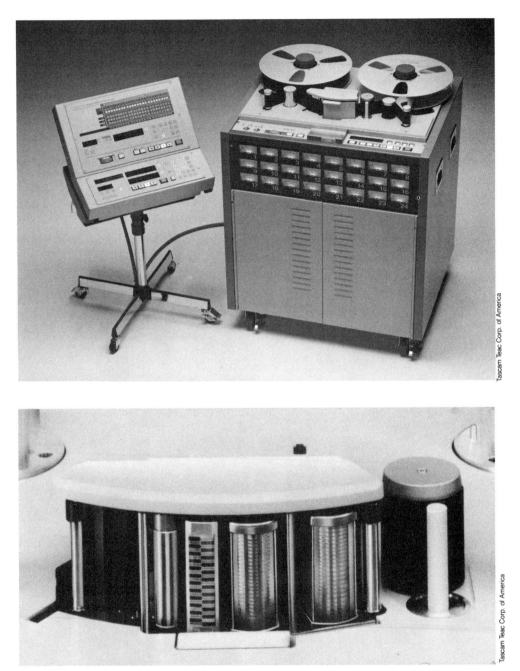

FIG. 8-12. *Tascam ATR-80 24-track recorder and its remote control panel (top) and a close-up view of the ATR-80's head system.*

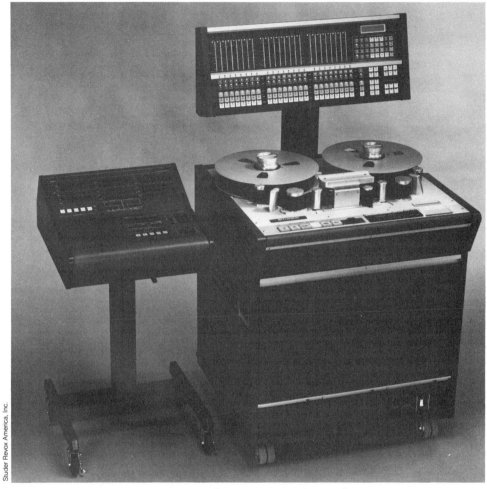

FIG. **8-13.** *Studer A820 24-track recorder.*

STEREO MASTERING DECKS

A two-track stereo deck is functionally similar to a multitrack deck. The expression ''half track stereo'' implies that one track occupies about half the tape width. You can only record on one side of the tape, or in other words, one direction. This is the standard in professional applications. High-fidelity open-reel consumer decks are usually quarter track stereo, meaning that one track occupies about one fourth of the tape width. Therefore, the stereo head covers half the width of the tape and it is possible to record on both sides (both directions). FIGURE 8-16 shows the track allocation for both of these stereo formats. Track layers 1 and 3 comprise one stereo pair for the first side and layers 2 and 4 are the stereo pair for the other side.

163

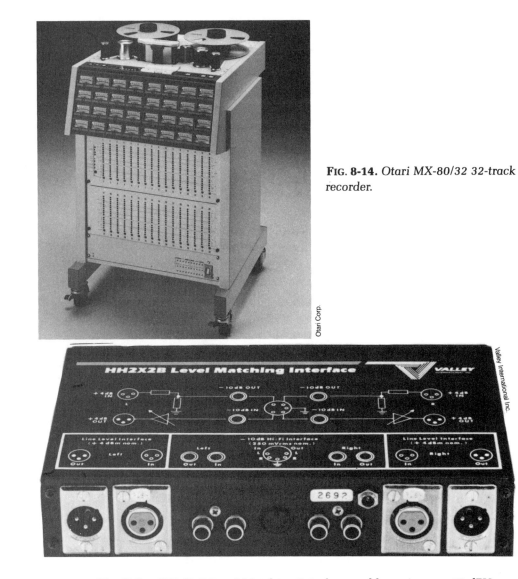

FIG. 8-14. *Otari MX-80/32 32-track recorder.*

FIG. 8-15. *The Valley HH2X2B Level Matching Interface enables using a −10 dBV system with a +4 dBm system.*

Regardless of the electrical systems used (+4 dBm/−10 dBV), a 0 dB meter reference is based on the same tape fluxivity. There are two references commonly used: 250 nWb/m or 320 nWb/m (nanowebers/meter). The 250 nWb/m reference offers more "headroom" prior to tape saturation but worse signal-to-noise ratio; the 320 nWb/m reference has these pros and cons reversed. Headroom refers to the maximum signal level prior to distortion.

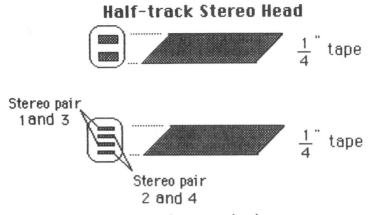

Half-track Stereo Head

$\frac{1}{4}$" tape

Stereo pair 1 and 3

Stereo pair 2 and 4

$\frac{1}{4}$" tape

FIG. 8-16. *Stereo tape heads.*

FIGURE 8-17 pictures the Otari MX-55TM two-channel deck. This is a half track recorder format on 1/4-inch tape, featuring a center track SMPTE time code, a three-point memory locator, selectable + 4 dBm or – 10 dBV level, selectable 185/250/370 or 250/320/514 nWb/m reference fluxivity, ± 20 percent variable speed control, and Dolby HX-Pro bias optimization circuitry for increased headroom at high frequencies.

FIG. 8-17. *Otari MX-55M two-track recorder.*

Otari Corp.

SMPTE TIME CODE

The Society of Motion Picture and Television Engineers (SMPTE) time code is applicable to both multitrack and two-channel decks. On multitrack recorders, a track is dedicated to a time code signature for synchronization to another device or recorder. A two-channel deck cannot afford to use a whole track for time code, so an additional center track is used. SMPTE was developed as a means to synchronize video with sound. This application has been extended to synchronizing two tape machines to work together or any other time-code-based devices. This sort of synchronization depends on an additional device called a *synchronizer* to interface, for example, two 24-track recorders. If you ''stripe'' a time code on each deck, that would leave 23 tracks open on each for a total of 46 tracks for recording. The job of the time-coded tracks and the synchronizer is to electronically interlock the two recorders so that recorded tracks on one deck stay in sync with the tracks on the other. FIGURE 8-18 shows the Tascam ES-50/501 synchronizer. FIGURE 8-19 shows the relationship between the decks and the synchronizer.

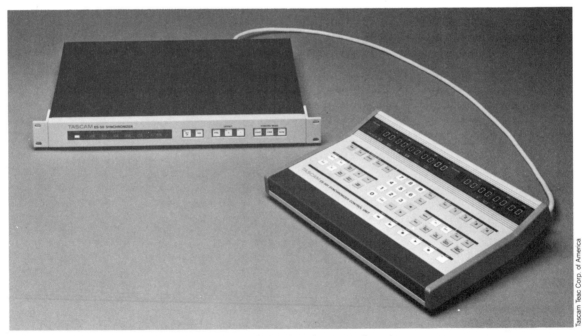

FIG. 8-18. *Tascam ES-50/501 synchronizer.*

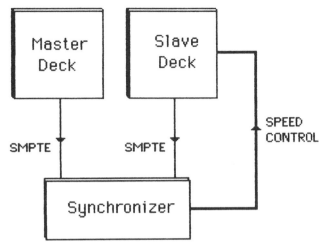

Fig. 8-19. *Interlocking two recorders.*

For now, think of the time code as a counter to index time intervals on the tape called *frames*. The synchronizer reads the time code on both decks and processes these readings to make a comparison. One deck serves as a fixed reference called the *master* and is compared with the other deck, the *slave*. If the time code count of the slave is less than the master, the synchronizer speeds the slave up until the time codes match and vice versa. The master deck speed is not controlled. The condition where the slave deck "chases" the master is referred to as *chase-lock* synchronization or *phase-locked* operation. In order for this to be successful, both decks should be cued up at a similar position so that the chase won't be too radical. A half minute or so lead-in prior to the start of a recording is necessary to give the chase-lock time to capture and stabilize.

SMPTE time code mechanism registers counts in terms of hours, minutes, seconds, and frames. There are 30 frames per second. The synchronizer has a visual time display for both decks. Each count is composed of an 80-bit digital word made up of ones and zeros. This is a serial transmission using a format called *biphase mark*. Figure 8-20 shows a section of the transmission showing how ones and zeros are encoded. Any time there is a transition in a bit cell interval—whether it's a positive- or negative-going transition—it is construed as a one. Figure 8-21 shows the entire 80-bit-stream frame. Certain portions of the bit stream are reserved as frames, seconds, minutes, and hours. The last 16 bits is a sync code that marks the end of one frame and starts the beginning of another.

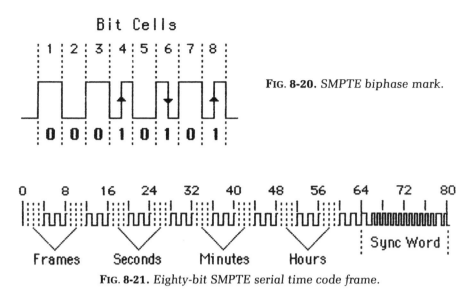

FIG. 8-20. *SMPTE biphase mark.*

FIG. 8-21. *Eighty-bit SMPTE serial time code frame.*

SMPTE is useful for applications other than chase-lock operation. It can be used for more accurate editing or tape location as opposed to counting done by the deck's resolver. A resolver can slip because its accuracy is solely dependent on tape motion contact. Critical punch-ins and punch-outs are more reliable when programmed and controlled with a fixed time code instead of manual attempts.

PRINT THROUGH

Since tape is magnetized, it has the potential to partially transfer information to an adjacent concentric layer on the reel during storage, known as *print through*. If transferred to an unrecorded area, it might be audible and could interfere with a fade-in or fade-out of a song.

Tapes can be spooled and stored either on the take-up reel or the supply reel. When stored on the take-up reel, the tape is said to be stored "tails out." When stored on the supply reel, the tape is stored "heads out." The advantage of storing a tape tails out is that any print through will be at the beginning of the tape and can be edited out. However, some better grade tapes such as Ampex 456 are back-coated to prevent print through.

NOISE REDUCTION

In the recording process, noise or "hiss" is inevitably added to the signal and is audible in the playback. Most professional decks have a signal-to-noise ratio of about 60 to 65 dB. Noise reduction units improve the ratio about another 30 dB, making S/N ratio about 90 to 95 dB. Understand that noise reduction systems do not remove noise from the original signal, but they prevent the potential noise from being added in the recording process.

The illustration in FIG. 8-22 shows the applied signal to the deck with some noise and the signal reproduced in the playback (without noise reduction). Note that the noise level increased on the playback output. With noise reduction, the noise level of the input signal will not get any worse in playback.

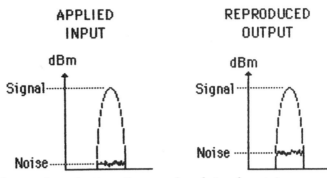

FIG. **8-22.** *With no noise reduction, the reproduced signal contains more noise than the original signal.*

Tape speed, track width, and tape quality are variables that determine the potential post-record noise floor. That is why recording with a normal-bias cassette without noise reduction is a disaster. Cassettes have very slow tape speed and narrow track width. The playback noise is much higher with a cassette as opposed to a deck that has a tape speed ten times faster and with more than twice the tape width. Typical open-reel machines have a tape speed of 15 ips. Some decks can pace at 30 ips to improve the signal-to-noise ratio.

In the recording industry, there are three types of noise reduction that have become popular for professional applications: dbx Type 1, Dolby A, and Dolby SR. Consumer types are dbx Type 2, Dolby B, and Dolby C.

dbx Type 1 Noise Reduction

FIGURE 8-23 pictures a dbx 150X Type 1 module. Prior to the record phase, the dbx puts preemphasis to the signal, boosting the high-frequency content much higher than the low end. This disproportioned signal is compressed, or *encoded*, to avoid tape saturation. When the signal is played back, the inherent noise is added, but the boosted high end is still well above the total noise floor.

FIG. **8-23.** *dbx 150X Type 1 noise reduction unit.*

This playback signal must then be decoded where the signal is expanded, followed by post-emphasis that reduces the high end. The strategy is that the low end is suppressed so that the high end could benefit the better S/N ratio. If the low end is not sacrificed, then tape saturation would occur in an attempt to accommodate the boosted high end. There is only so much energy a signal can have. Less lows make more ''headroom'' for the highs.

Dolby A

This noise reduction (NR) system resembles dbx in the sense that they both use compression and expansion. Dolby A has the disposition that if the signal is strong enough, the noise is not audible. So the performance of this system depends on signal level. The lower the signal, the more processing it does. If a signal is down more than -30 dB, gain is added to the input signal to encode it with a hotter level for the sake of an improved S/N ratio. But when the signal exceeds -30 dB, compression begins to reduce the gain. By the time the signal reaches -10 dB, the encoding action has no effect and lets the signal go on to tape normally. Now, even the low-level signals have been recorded as though they were high-level signals. Somehow the decoding process has to know what signals are supposed to be of a low level in the playback. The decode process must reduce playback signals that are intended to be dynamically below -30 dB, expand signals that are supposed to normally be heard in the -10 to -30 dB range, and do nothing to signals above -10 dB. A negative feedback mechanism is used to control the amount of signal to be subtracted from the playback output. There must be information about the playback signal that regulates the proper feedback for the signal. This encoding and decoding operates over four frequency bands: 80 Hz (low pass), 80 Hz to 3 kHz, 3 to 9 kHz, and 9 kHz (high pass). FIGURE 8-24 shows the Dolby XP Series that houses 24 channels of Dolby A.

FIG. 8-24. *XP Series 24-channel Dolby A noise reduction system.*

Dolby SR

Spectral recording (SR) is analog's countermeasure to digital recording technology. It can provide a dynamic range of 90 to 96 dB as opposed to the usual 70 dB found in analog machines. Even Dolby A improves the dynamic range to only about 75 to 80 dB. FIGURE 8-25 shows the Dolby Model 363 with two SR/A cards. These plug-in cards are selectable allowing the user to choose Dolby SR or Dolby A operation.

Dolby Labs

FIG. **8-25.** *Model 363 Dolby SR/A noise reduction unit.*

9

Digital Audio Recording

CHAPTER 8 EXPLAINED THE METHOD OF RECORDING AND REPRODUCING signals in an analog fashion, where audio signals are described in terms of amplitude versus time. An analog recording can be considered an infinite series of discrete amplitudes. This analog recording process is satisfactory, but the issue of noise in the process is a nuisance. Another imposing limitation is tape saturation, which limits the available dynamic range to about 70 dB. However, today's digital techniques greatly overcome these limitations. The digital encoding and decoding process is insensitive to noise, and the recording level is constant, requiring no dynamic performance.

PULSE CODE MODULATION

Pulse code modulation (PCM) is the name for this digital processing. It is described in terms of *sampling rate* and *bit resolution*. Sampling rate refers to how often a signal's amplitude is tested. Since the amplitude varies with time, sampling results in a collection of amplitudes corresponding to a series of time intervals. If a sampling rate means how often amplitude is read, it stands to reason that the more often a signal is sampled, the bigger the collection of amplitude data is for a given time period. More information implies more accuracy or detail about the signal. The diagram in FIG. 9-1 shows the impact of two sampling rates applied to the same signal. The higher sampling rate offers a larger collection of data points.

With each sampling interval, there is a change in amplitude. These sampled amplitudes are converted into a binary code that represents this analog value. Each sample has a binary word (data byte) to represent its amplitude, each of which is recorded sequentially. This recording process is the PCM encoding. In the decoding or playback process, these binary words are translated back into analog signals in the same order, reconstructing the original signal. The diagram in FIG. 9-2 shows the coarse reconstruction of the previous signal using the same two sampling rates.

Just as a higher sampling rate offers more accuracy for signal reconstruction, the amplitude *bit resolution* also affects accuracy of the signal reconstruction in the decode process. Bit resolution has to do with the scale a sampled amplitude is placed on. The more counts or bits that are used to describe a signal level, the more accurate the encoding. In the encoding phase, an amplitude is converted to a binary code electronically using a device called an analog-to-digital converter. The binary code is strictly an integer representation. Ones and zeros are used to represent these integers, as shown in FIG. 9-3.

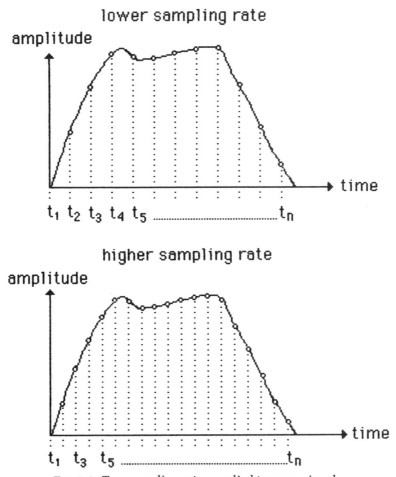

FIG. **9-1.** *Two sampling rates applied to same signal.*

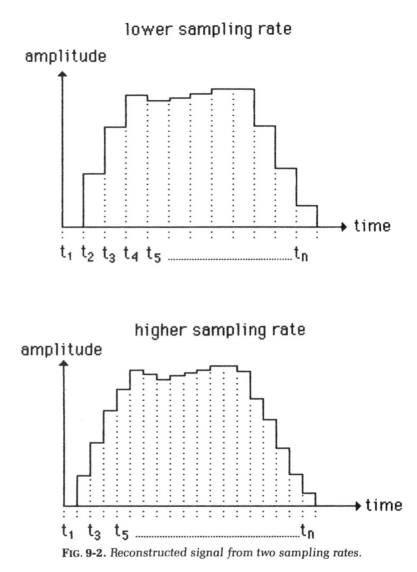

FIG. 9-2. *Reconstructed signal from two sampling rates.*

A four-bit resolution implies a scale from 0 to 15, which is a total of 2^4 or 16 discrete levels to represent amplitude. A 12-bit resolution implies $2^{12} = 4096$ discrete levels, and 16-bit resolution has $2^{16} = 65,536$. FIGURES 9-4 and 9-5 are a graphic comparison of 3-bit resolution against 4-bit resolution with the same sampling quantization. FIGURE 9-4 shows the 3-bit resolution (levels 0 through 7), and the appearance of its reconstructed signal; below that, FIG. 9-5 shows the 4-bit resolution (levels 0 through 15), with its reconstructed signal.

$$0 = 0$$
$$1 = 1$$
$$10 = 2$$
$$11 = 3$$
$$100 = 4$$
$$101 = 5$$
$$110 = 6$$
$$111 = 7$$
$$1000 = 8$$
$$1001 = 9$$
$$1010 = 10$$
$$1011 = 11$$
$$1100 = 12$$
$$1101 = 13$$
$$1110 = 14$$
$$1111 = 15$$

$$\vdots$$

etc.

FIG. 9-3. *Decimal-to-binary code conversion.*

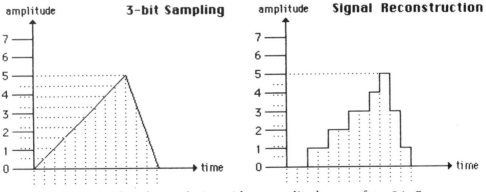

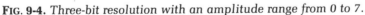

FIG. 9-4. *Three-bit resolution with an amplitude range from 0 to 7.*

In the sampling process, the A/D converter rounds off to the lowest integer. The sampled amplitude must reach a quantized threshold for a particular integer encoding. Note, for example, in the 4-bit signal reconstruction diagram (FIG. 9-5) that the sampled amplitude of 7.8 was encoded as a 7. Clearly, the higher the bit resolution, the more accurate the encoded binary representation.

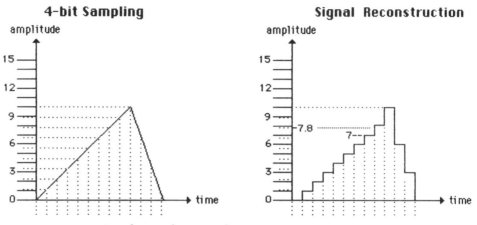

FIG. **9-5.** *Four-bit resolution with an amplitude range from 0 to 15.*

When a signal is encoded, the bits are serially recorded onto the tape. The decode or playback process reverses this, converting the digital 1s and 0s back to amplitudes reconstructing the signal via a D/A converter (digital-to-analog converter). The block diagram in FIG. 9-6 represents this record/playback cycle.

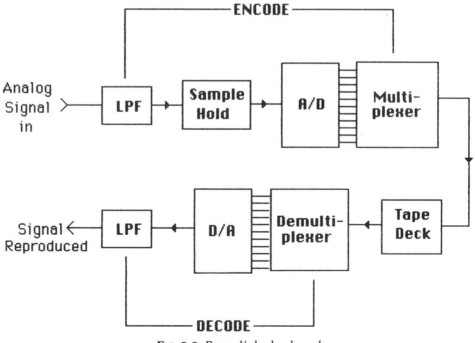

FIG. **9-6.** *Record/playback cycle.*

Initially, the incoming analog signal goes through a low-pass filter (LPF) to screen out unwanted high-frequency content above one-half the sampling rate. The *Nyquist criterion* for sampling states that the sampling frequency (f_s) must be twice the maximum (highest) audio frequency (f_m); $f_s = 2f_m$. However there is an undesirable phenomenon that happens when frequencies are sampled in excess of the maximum audio frequency $(f_m = f_s/2)$. A frequency sampled beyond f_m produces an "alias" frequency f_a, which equals $f_x - f_m$ (where $f_x > f_m$). As an example, if $f_s = 50$ kHz, then the maximum allowable audio frequency is $f_m = 25$ kHz. An attempt to sample 27 kHz would produce an alias frequency $f_a = 27 - 25 = 2$ kHz. Therefore, the low-pass filter must roll off sharply to reject frequencies above f_m. This usually calls for a Cauer-parameter (elliptical) filter design.

The *sample hold* stage reads an amplitude periodically in accordance with the sampling rate. This amplitude value is held until the next reading. Each reading is fed to the A/D converter. Here the analog signal is converted into a binary value. This must be done before the next sample appears. If the sampling rate is 44.1 kHz, then the time interval for encoding must be done within $1/44.1$ kHz = 22.68 μs. The A/D converter delivers the binary configuration as a parallel output, meaning the 1s and 0s appear simultaneously, an output for each bit. Following the A/D converter, a multiplexer manipulates the parallel bit configuration for a serial transmission, one at a time to the tape deck. In the playback mode, the serial transmission is fed into the demultiplexer and re-arranges the bits for a parallel feed to the D/A converter. This reconstructs the analog signal by reproducing and integrating the amplitudes at the sampling rate it was disintegrated at. Sampling rates used are at least twice the highest frequency of interest. Since our hearing range is about 20 kHz, sampling rates are typically well over 40 kHz.

Sampling rates commonly used are 44.1 kHz and 48 kHz at 16-bit resolution. You can calculate how many bits are encoded per second. As an example, a sampling rate of 48 kHz means that 48,000 samples occur per second. Every sample is 16 bits. The total number of bits per second is $48,000 \times 16 = 768,000$ bits/second (768 kb/s). The taping mechanism must have the bandwidth to accommodate this data rate. There are two common taping mechanisms: *stationary* and *rotary* head types.

STATIONARY HEAD RECORDERS

Stationary head PCM recorders are open reel-to-reel machines that resemble analog decks. The transport drags the tape across stationary heads in the same manner. There are special bandwidth requirements for these PCM decks.

Understanding these requirements requires explanation of the serial bit transmission delivered to the record head. The job of the multiplexer is to make a serial transmission of 1s and 0s in which a 1 is represented by a logic voltage level and a 0 is represented by a lower logic level, usually zero or ground potential. The timing diagram in FIG. 9-7 shows a serial representation of a 16-bit binary word called NRZ (nonreturn to zero).

FIG. 9-7. *NRZ encoding.*

Note that if there is a series of consecutive 1s or 0s, a voltage level can appear as dc (no voltage transitions), which is not suitable for magnetic recording. All 1s would look like a dc battery, and all 0s would look like a short circuit. This NRZ bit stream should be translated into another form in which transitions occur all the time. A technique used by some manufacturers is *biphase encoding*. In this type of encoding, there is a positive-going transition for a 1 and a negative-going transition for a 0. The diagram in FIG. 9-8 shows NRZ translated into biphase. The transitions are made in the middle of a bit cell; bit cells are defined by the vertical dotted lines. In the playback mode, these biphase bit streams can be decoded by sampling every $3/4$-bit cell as shown in FIG. 9-9.

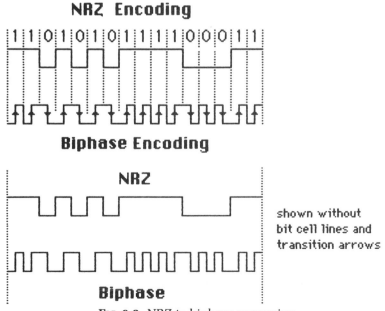

FIG. 9-8. *NRZ to biphase conversion.*

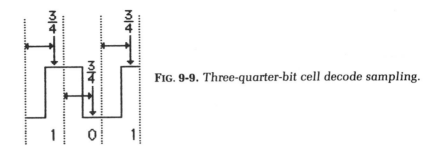

FIG. **9-9.** *Three-quarter-bit cell decode sampling.*

Using biphase encoding, the maximum frequency recorded is when there are consecutive 1s or 0s in the bit stream. The minimum frequency is alternating 1s and 0s (10101...), shown in FIG. 9-10. The required bandwidth of the PCM tape deck must accommodate these maximum and minimum frequencies. In this case, the maximum frequency is twice the minimum.

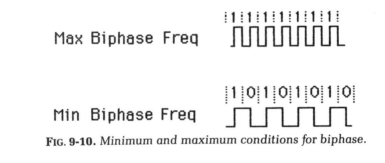

FIG. **9-10.** *Minimum and maximum conditions for biphase.*

Frequency is defined by the width of one cycle, which is the time interval between two positive-going transitions. The maximum frequency pulse width is equivalent to a bit cell interval, and the minimum frequency pulse width is equivalent to two bit cells. If t is the time period for a cycle, then frequency $f = 1/t$, shown in FIG. 9-11.

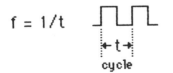

FIG. **9-11.** *One data cycle is represented by t; its reciprocal (1/t) gives the frequency.*

So far, the impression created is that 16-bit bytes transmit serially to the record head at the sampling rate. If this were the case, the decoder, in the reproduction phase, would not be able to tell where one byte begins or another ends. There is a call for a *preamble or sync* code in front of each 16-bit byte, which is an unambiguous code comprised of 1s and 0s. Typical codes are 8 bits, which means that most samples are made up of a total of 16 + 8 = 24 bits. If the sampling frequency is 50 kHz at 16-bit resolution with an 8-bit sync code, then the bit rate is:

$$50,000 \text{ samples/sec} \times 24 \text{ bits/sample} = 1200 \text{ kb/s}$$

A bit cell time period is $t = 1/1200 \text{ kb/s} = 0.833 \text{ } \mu\text{s/bit cell}$. Another way to look at it is to realize that a sample period is $1/50,000 = 20 \text{ } \mu\text{s}$. This means that 24 bits have to fit in this time frame. Therefore, a bit cell must be at the most 20 $\mu\text{s}/24$ bits = 0.833 $\mu\text{s/b}$.

If biphase encoding is used, then the maximum frequency is 1200 kb/s and the minimum frequency is 600 kb/s. The period for f_{max} is $t_{min} = 0.833 \text{ } \mu\text{s}$ and for f_{min}, $t_{max} = 1/600 \text{ kb/s} = 1.66 \text{ } \mu\text{s/b}$. If the tape speed is 38 cm/s (15 ips), then one f_{max} period occupies 0.38 m/s $\times$ 0.833 $\mu\text{s} = 0.317 \text{ } \mu\text{m}$. At a tape speed of 76 cm/s (30 ips), it would be 0.633 μm. For reliable reproduction, a minimum of 1.5 μm displacement is required, which in terms of frequency is $f = 0.38$ m/s $\times$ 1 cycle/1.5 $\mu\text{m} \approx 250$ kHz, for 15 ips. Consequently, 30 ips can handle about 500 kHz data rates.

Obviously, these conventional tape speeds are not adequate for 1200 kHz and 600 kHz data rates. However, a technique in which a serial data bit stream can be shared or allocated to several tracks can effectively reduce the frequency per track. To accommodate 1200 kHz, six tracks would have to be considered where the effective frequency per track would be 200 kHz, which should be acceptable for 15 ips. At 30 ips, maybe only three tracks would be needed.

Biphase encoding has been used by some manufacturers for stereo machines, but it is not as popular as other encoding methods. Apparently, the track requirements consume too much tape width. One of the more popular encoding techniques has been *modified frequency modulation* (MFM), sometimes referred to as *Miller modulation*. MFM is merely biphase, filtered by a flip-flop in the *divide-by-two* mode. A *flip-flop* is a digital device whose output changes state with each consecutive positive-going transition. FIGURE 9-12 shows the progression of data conversion from NRZ to biphase to MFM. Note from the diagram that a change occurs for every biphase positive transition only. Also note that in an MFM encoding, a binary 1 has a transition in the bit cell whereas there is no transition for a 0 unless there are consecutive 0s, and these transitions occur on the bit cell boundary. The advantage of doing this is because the maximum MFM frequency, a condition of consecutive 1s or 0s, is equivalent to the biphase minimum frequency. Thus, only half as much track allocation is required.

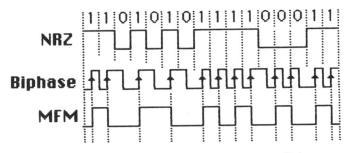

FIG. 9-12. *Data conversion from NRZ to MFM.*

There are many other encoding techniques used, but as an example of a manufacturer that uses MFM, here are some actual specifications. Matsushita uses a sampling rate of 50.4 kHz and 16-bit resolution. The MFM serial transmission is distributed over four tracks using a tape speed of 15 ips. Assuming an 8-bit sync code, the data rate is:

$$50.4 \text{ kb/s} \times 24 \text{ bits/sample} = 1209.6 \text{ kb/s}$$

On a per track basis:

$$1209.6/4 = 302.4 \text{ kb/s/trk}$$

If biphase was used, this track frequency would be too high, but MFM cuts it in half to an effective recorded frequency of about 150 kb/s, which is adequate for 15 ips. The recording density is:

$$\delta = 302.4 \text{ kb/15 in}$$
$$= 20.16 \text{ kb/in}$$

As you might imagine, a 24-track machine requires a head format with multiples of digital tracks. A typical 24-track format is for 1-inch tape. In the case where four digital tracks are required per bit stream, a 24-track deck requires a head format with $24 \times 4 = 96$ digital tracks. That means that each track width is about 260 μm. In comparison to 24-track analog decks that distribute 24 tracks over a 2-inch tape, the track width is about a 1000 μm. With such narrow digital track widths, there is a sizable threat of dropouts and errors. In the digital processing, an error correction scheme must be applied to compensate for reproduction flaws. A popular error detection method is *cyclic redundancy check code* (CRCC). To carry this method out requires some digital processing in the encode stage.

Each byte is divided by a number in which the remainder is encoded at the end of the byte. The result is a sampled byte that has a preamble in front and a check code behind it. In the reproduce stage, bytes are checked for errors by comparing the recorded remainder with the reproduced remainder. If there is a mismatch, then the byte is considered to have an error. A routine is then executed in which a parity byte from the encode stage is manipulated to correct the byte error. A *parity byte* is information tagged at the end of a series of sampled bytes called a *block*. These sampled bytes are added in such a way as to generate the parity byte with the same amount of bits as a sampled byte. FIGURE 9-13 shows a block with a parity byte at the end.

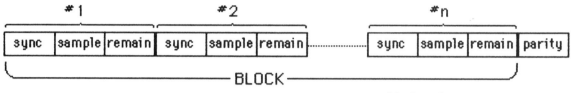

FIG. **9-13.** *Data block with parity byte at the end.*

If an error is detected in the reproduction stage, a new parity byte is generated by this special binary addition using the same group, only now with an error, plus the original parity byte. This new parity byte is recombined with the errored byte to reproduce the correct byte using parity addition once again.

In cases where the remainder byte has an error and falsely accuses a sample of being in error, it turns out mathematically that the error correction attempt is transparent to the byte and won't be altered. An example of how this works using 8-bit bytes is demonstrated in FIG. 9-14. If errors are unusually numerous, then error *concealment* is used, which takes the average of the adjacent error-free samples.

Hence, a versatility has been introduced because manufacturers have developed digital transports of various sampling rates and track formats as opposed to analog decks where a tape is compatible from machine to machine. The professional digital (PD) format is used in the Otari DTR-900B 32-track digital recorder shown in FIG. 9-15. This is accomplished on 1-inch tape. The PD format uses 45 tracks: 32 for music data, 8 for parity codes, 2 for reference analog tracks, 2 auxiliary digital data, and 1 track for the SMPTE/EBU time code. This format is compatible with the Mitsubishi X-850. Sampling frequencies used are 44.1/48 kHz, 16-bit resolution at 30 ips tape speed.

Other manufacturers have jointly agreed to standardize at least a two-track digital recorder using the digital audio stationary head (DASH) format. This format has an analog track for left and right stereo channels and a track dedicated for an independent time code such as SMPTE in addition to the digital tracks.

183

```
Recorded bytes #1 ─→  10010100
              #2 ─→  00100110
              #3 ─→  01100011
                     11010001  Parity byte
```

Case 1: Byte #2 error

```
Reproduced bytes #1 ─→  10010100
                #2 ─→  01100100 (error)
                #3 ─→  01100011
                       11010001  Parity byte
                       01000010  New parity byte
                #2 ─→  01100100  (error)
                       00100110  byte #2 corrected
```

Case 2: Correct byte #2 cited as an error

```
Reproduced bytes #1 ─→  10010100
                #2 ─→  00100110
                #3 ─→  01100011
                       11010001  Parity byte
                       00000000  New parity byte
                #2 ─→  00100110
                       00100110  byte #2 corrected
```

FIG. 9-14. *Cyclic redundancy check code (CRCC). For parity addition, add each column. Two 0s give a 0, a 0 and a 1 give a 1, and two 1s give a 0 with a 1 carry. Therefore, an odd number of 1s added together yields a 1 and an even amount gives a 0.*

The analog tracks serve as a cue for razor blade editing. The DASH format has the following specifications:

Sampling rate: 48 kHz/44.056 kHz/44.1 kHz (selectable)
Bit resolution: 16
Tracks per channel: 4
Tape speeds: $7^1/_2$ ips, 15 ips

Dynamic range and S/N performance go hand in hand. The same mathematical expression is used to calculate both: $6n + 1.76$ dB, where n is the bit resolution. For 16-bit resolution, dynamic range and S/N is 97.76 dB. There is a DASH format that applies to multitrack digital recorders such as the Sony PCM-3348 pictured in FIG. 9-16.

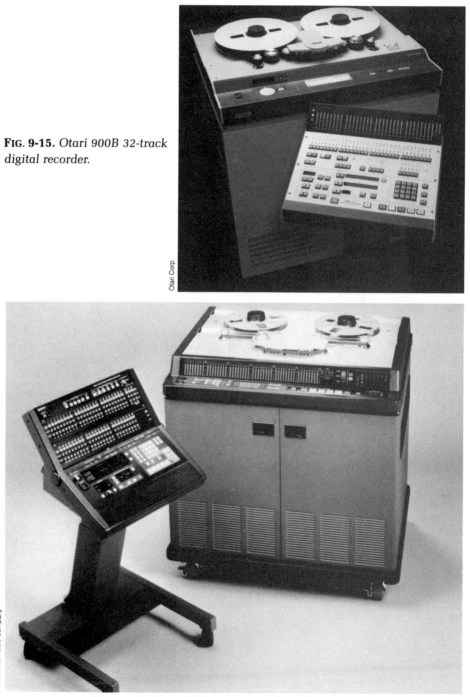

FIG. 9-15. *Otari 900B 32-track digital recorder.*

Otari Corp.

Professional Audio Company

FIG. 9-16. *Sony PCM-3348 48-track digital recorder.*

PCM ROTRY HEADS

In contrast to stationary head recorders, rotary head systems have the advantage of high-density recording, which results in less tape consumption. The basic disadvantage is that encoding and decoding is restricted to stereo recordings, and razor blade editing is not possible because of the nature of the medium.

A cost-effective approach is to use a VCR in conjunction with a digital audio processor such as the Sony PCM-601. The VCR becomes the transport and the digital audio processor provides the encode/decode functions. Since the VCR is a video recorder using helical scanning, the bit-encoded audio samples must be transmitted as a video signal with horizontal sync pulses. This substitutes for a sync preamble on stationary head encoding.

The helical scan mechanism utilizes a rotating drum with two recording heads 180 degrees apart. The drum rotation is counter to the tape motion. The tape arcs around the drum, covering a little more than 50 percent of the perimeter as shown in FIG. 9-17.

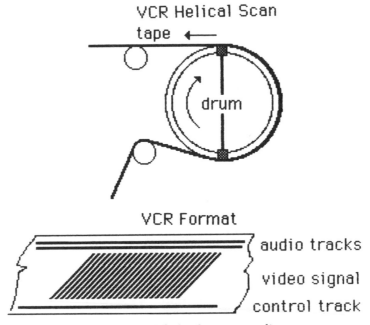

FIG. 9-17. *VCR helical scan recording.*

As one head tracks diagonally across the tape, the other head starts an adjacent trace as the first head is leaving. The tape speed is time coordinated with the rotation of the drum such that each head alternates, making adjacent traces.

The tracks are only about 30 μm wide. This helical scan enables the signal to occupy almost the entire surface area of the tape. But some room is saved along the edges for analog audio and a control track. Since the tape-to-head speed is relatively high, the bandwidth can easily accommodate the high-bit-density encoded video signal

Referring to FIG. 9-18, the encoded serial bit stream is used to frequency modulate an RF carrier in such a manner that a binary 1 raises the frequency and a binary 0 lowers the carrier frequency. Assuming that the carrier is phase locked, any dc data components, such as long consecutive strings of NRZ 1s or 0s, attempt to move the video signal back to the carrier position, which is midway between the maximum and minimum frequency deviations. Frequency modulation (FM) only works if the data transitions are too fast for the phase-locked loop to react. That's why something like a biphase transmission would be suitable. Note the relationship between the bit stream and the modulated carrier. When the bit stream data is high, the carrier contracts to a maximum frequency. When low, the carrier expands for a minimum frequency.

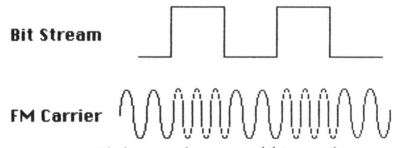

Bit Stream

FM Carrier

FIG. **9-18.** *The bit stream frequency-modulates a carrier.*

Thus, the recorded signal is a modulated carrier. The signal is encoded in both left and right channels. The sampled bytes, left and right, alternate in the serial transmission. When reproduced, the video signal is demodulated and the stereo channels are decoded. The diagram in FIG. 9-19 shows a VCR hooked up to a digital audio processor. The PCM-601 processor, pictured in FIG. 9-20, has a 44.1 kHz sampling rate and 16-bit resolution. This is compatible with CD mastering formats. The diagram in FIG. 9-21 reveals an interesting PCM application involving two VCRs. Here a digitally recorded tape in VCR #1 is remastered with some compression and recorded on VCR #2. The video signal from VCR #1 is decoded into stereo audio signals. These audio signals are processed by the console with compressors patched in. The stereo signal levels leaving the console are monitored by submaster VU meters. The signals are encoded back to a video carrier and recorded on VCR #2.

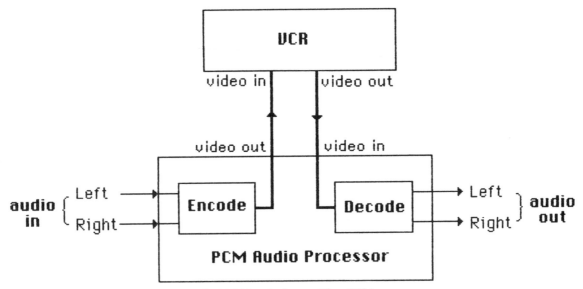

FIG. **9-19.** *Block diagram of a VCR hooked up with a PCM processor.*

FIG. **9-20.** *Sony PCM-601 digital audio encoder/decoder.*

Other machines that work on this principle are *digital audio tape* (DAT) decks. Think of a DAT as a VCR and audio processor combined. The DAT cassette tape is much smaller than standard VHS or BETA formats. Its size resembles a video camcorder tape. The Panasonic SV-3500 DAT deck is featured in FIG. 9-22. It has three selectable sampling rates: 32, 44.1, and 48 kHz. A similar unit is the Sony PCM-2500 DAT recorder pictured in FIG. 9-23.

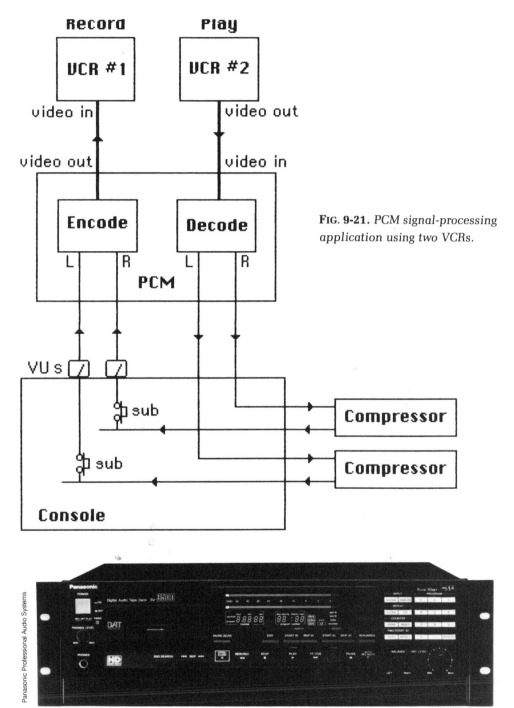

FIG. **9-21.** *PCM signal-processing application using two VCRs.*

FIG. **9-22.** *Panasonic SV-3500 digital audio tape deck.*

FIG. 9-23. Sony PCM-2500 professional digital audio tape recorder.

10

Microphones

A MICROPHONE IS A DEVICE THAT CONVERTS ACOUSTICAL ENERGY INTO AN electrical signal. This involves a moving part such as a coil or ribbon whose mechanical displacement translates into ac voltage. There are basically two types: *dynamic* microphones and *condenser* microphones.

DYNAMIC MOVING-COIL MIKES

FIGURE 10-1 shows a cross section of a microphone capsule. Fine wire is coiled onto a diaphragm and housed over a magnet. FIGURE 10-2 shows the intangible magnetic lines of force stretched between the magnetic poles. FIGURE 10-3 reveals that the diaphragm is a delicate disc with windings. When sound vibrates this diaphragm, the coil cuts through the magnetic field force between the poles, generating an electrical signal in the coil.

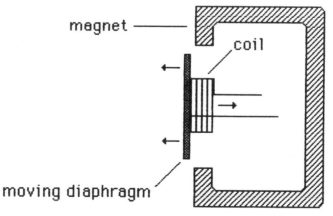

FIG. **10-1.** *Dynamic microphone cross section.*

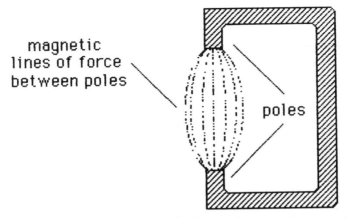

FIG. **10-2.** *An intangible magnetic field exists between the two poles.*

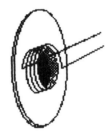

FIG. **10-3.** *The diaphragm is a delicate, pressure-sensitive device.*

DYNAMIC RIBBON MIKES

The dynamic ribbon type works the same way as a moving coil except a filament called the *ribbon* is the moving part rather than a diaphragm. FIGURE 10-4 shows that the ribbon is a thin, metallic, corrugated strip suspended between the magnetic poles. Sound vibrations move this ribbon through the magnetic lines of force, generating a signal. A ribbon microphone is sometimes called a *pressure gradient* or *velocity* mike.

CONDENSER MIKES

In electronics, *condenser* is another word for *capacitor* because physically a condenser is two spaced metallic surfaces that work on electrostatic principle instead of a magnetic one (FIG. 10-5). The spacing and surface area determine a specific electrical property called *capacitance*. When one of the surfaces or plates is charged, it creates a voltage potential across the plates. As the spacing between the plates varies with sound vibration, the capacitance changes, causing voltage fluctuations. The charge on the fixed plate travels back and forth through the resistor, producing a voltage-generated signal.

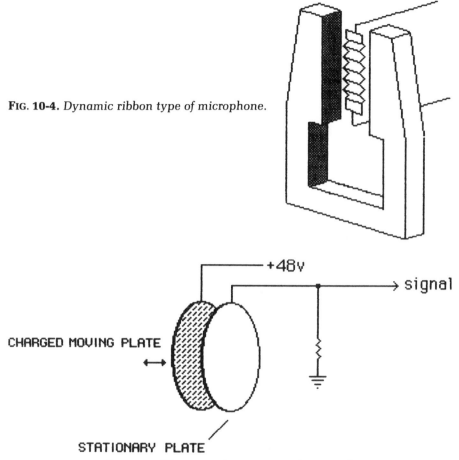

FIG. **10-4.** *Dynamic ribbon type of microphone.*

FIG. **10-5.** *How a condenser microphone works.*

The voltage-generated signal is then amplified by the internal electronics in the microphone encasement, which require a ''phantom'' power supply (an external source). A + 48 dc supply is usually used to power the preamplifier in the mike casing and also place the charge on, or *polarize*, the condenser plates. Phantom power is usually a feature built into recording consoles. Since dc power does not interfere with the audio information transduced, the dc power is applied to the mike cable directly and sent down the audio signal path. Professional microphones are low impedance (about 150 ohms), and have three-pin XLR connectors. The transduced signal has a balanced output, meaning that there are two signal conductors to drive the console and a common ground or shield as shown in FIG. 10-6.

193

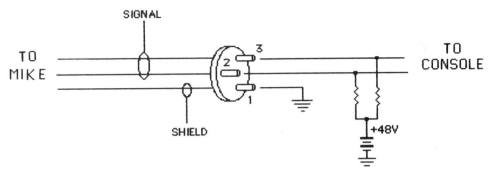

FIG. 10-6. *Phantom power applied to balanced line.*

ELECTRET CONDENSER MIKES

This type of condenser operates on the same principle aforementioned. The major difference here is that the plates are permanently polarized by the manufacturer. The plates do not depend on the phantom power, only the mike preamp does. As shown in FIG. 10-7, the transformer isolates the phantom +48 Vdc power from the output of the mike's preamp because dc cannot transfer from the secondary winding to the primary winding like ac signals can. The secondary winding is tapped, and +48 Vdc is applied to the proper place internally. The transduced ac audio signals are transferable from the transformer's primary to secondary windings and propagate down the balanced signal paths.

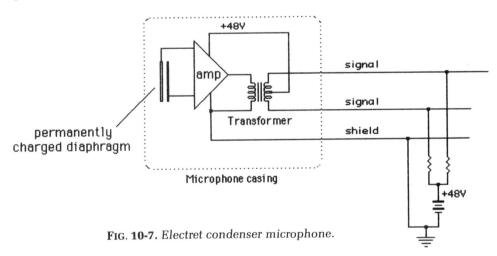

FIG. 10-7. *Electret condenser microphone.*

BALANCED LINES

Balanced lines are important for the purpose of noise immunity. Bear in mind that a voltage transduced by a microphone is very small and any noise can result in a poor S/N ratio. The shielding encompassing the cable helps immensely to keep out radio signal noise. After all, a mike cable is potentially an antenna. The diagram in FIG. 10-8 is a model of how a microphone with a balanced line electrically interfaces with a console with active inputs.

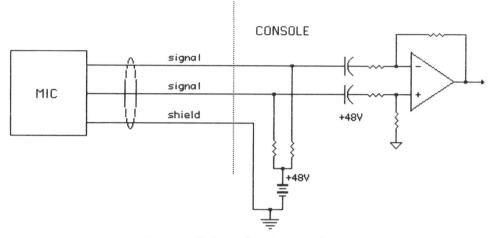

FIG. **10-8.** *Balanced active console input.*

FIGURE 10-9 shows an unbalanced configuration using a coaxial cable. In this case, the shield acts as a signal return path. As long as they are short, these conductors can be considered to have no resistance. But with long mike cables, resistance becomes significant. The shield in long cables acts ''lossy'' (resistive), provoking a condition called *ground loop*. A shield should act as a ground (zero impedance) in order to reject radio frequency interference. For this reason, the balanced line technique is used because the balanced line shield is not involved in carrying any signal. Typically, unbalanced lines are used by high-impedance microphones and instrument transducers.

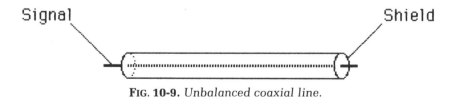

FIG. **10-9.** *Unbalanced coaxial line.*

DIRECTIONAL CHARACTERISTICS

Microphones are also classified by their directional sensitivity to sound sources. There are basically three types: omnidirectional, unidirectional, and bidirectional microphones.

Omnidirectional

This type of microphone perceives sound mutually from all directions—front, rear, sides, top, and bottom. On this kind of mike, sound pressure acts on the diaphragm on just one side as shown in FIG. 10-10. However, there is some masking of sounds originating directly behind the capsule.

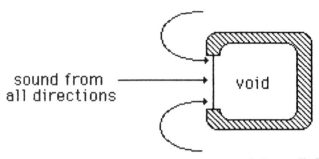

sound from
all directions ——→ void

FIG. 10-10. *An omnidirectional microphone perceives sound from all directions but the sound pressure acts on only one side of the diaphragm.*

Some microphones use a dual, back-to-back capsule that can eliminate any masking problems. Such a mike is the AKG C414B/ULS pictured in FIG. 10-11.

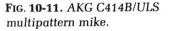

FIG. 10-11. *AKG C414B/ULS multipattern mike.*

Both sides of the microphone are shown. On the front (pictured left) is a pattern select switch. This condenser microphone is capable of several directional characteristics such as a figure eight (bidirectional), cardioid (heart-shaped), and hypercardioid (all of which are discussed later in this chapter). A close examination of FIG. 10-11 shows that the omnidirectional pattern is the third switch position. On the reverse side (pictured right) are selectable attenuation and low-frequency roll-off switches. For hot SPL levels, 10 or 20 dB attenuation can be used to reduce output level to the console. If other than a flat frequency response is desired, a selectable roll-off at 75 or 150 Hz is also selectable.

Unidirectional

Unidirectional mikes tend to perceive sound mostly from one direction. Sound becomes less and less perceptible as the sound source is directed more and more to the rear of the mike. This directionality is achieved by allowing sound pressure to act on both sides of the diaphragm as shown in FIG. 10-12. Most of the sound acts on the front side, but only a portion coming from the rear acts on the inner side. This is how sounds coming from the rear are rejected. Back pressure opposes the front pressure, and the net pressure is reduced. Assume that sounds originating from the rear are unwanted signals. Since the distance of sound travel is farther and therefore longer to reach the front, an acoustical phase shift network is built into the mike to delay the signal entering through the capsule rear. Without the phase shift network, the rear signal would arrive first. Instead, the front and rear signals are in phase, but the force vectors oppose each other to cancel the signal.

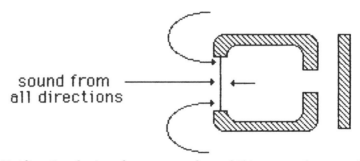

sound from
all directions

FIG. 10-12. *Unidirectional microphones use a phase-shifting network to cancel unwanted signals.*

FIGURE 10-13 pictures the Sennheiser MD421 cardioid (unidirectional) dynamic microphone. The word *cardioid* is used to describe a certain type of heart-shaped directional characteristic. The Neumann U47 FET is a condenser cardioid, pictured in FIG. 10-14. Note the cardioid symbol in the middle of the mike. FIGURE 10-15 shows a multipattern Neumann U89. Its selector switch is set to cardioid and displays the cardioid symbol. Another example of a condenser cardioid is the AKG C 460 B with the CK 61-ULS capsule in FIG. 10-16. A unidirectional cardioid type can be either a dynamic or condenser mike.

197

FIG. **10-13.** *Sennheiser MD421 cardioid mike.*

Sennheiser Electronics Corp.

Gotham Audio Corp.

FIG. **10-14.** *Neumann U47 FET cardioid mike.*

FIG. 10-15. *Neumann U89 multipattern mike in the cardioid mode (note symbol).*

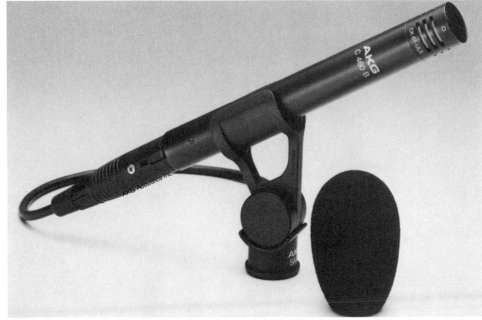

FIG. 10-16. *AKG C460/B cardioid mike.*

Another type of unidirectional microphone is the supercardioid pattern. This has a higher degree of rejection of off-axis sound directed toward the sides. As the name implies, this type of microphone is more directional. FIGURE 10-17 shows a Beyer M400S dynamic supercardioid microphone. The next step up is the hypercardioid unidirectional mike, which has even more side rejection but the penalty for this extra performance is poorer rear rejection. Examples of this kind of microphone are the Beyer M88 dynamic hypercardioid displayed in FIG. 10-18 and the AKG D 330 BT pictured in FIG. 10-19. An extremely directional mike is the ''shotgun'' or ''lobe'' type like the AKG D900 pictured in FIG. 10-20. This type of mike is commonly used in uncontrolled environments to isolate surrounding interference and noise found, for example, in film and television studios or when broadcasting sporting events.

FIG. **10-17.** *Beyer M400S supercardioid mike.*

FIG. 10-18. *Beyer M88 hypercardioid mike.*

FIG. 10-19. *AKG D330/BT hypercardioid mike.*

FIG. **10-20.** *AKG D900 "shotgun" mike.*

Bidirectional

Bidirectional microphones favor sounds coming from opposite directions (front and rear) and tend to reject sounds coming from either side, as depicted in FIG. 10-21 (left). Both faces of the diaphragm are exposed. Sound sources directed perpendicularly to either surface, front or rear, are optimum. Sound pressures are phase shifted with respect to front and rear such that the forces complement each other and superimpose instead of cancel. Sound forces coming in from the sides act mutually on both faces and cancel as shown in FIG. 10-21 (right). Bidirectional microphones are usually ribbon types like the Beyer M 130 N featured in FIG. 10-22. Many selectable multipattern microphones have a bidirectional position such as the condenser Neumann U87 shown in FIG. 10-23; note the figure eight symbol in the view slot.

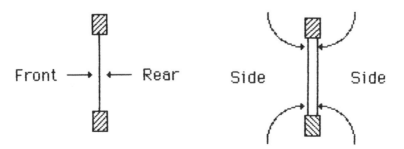

FIG. **10-21.** *Bidirectional microphone.*

FIG. **10-22.** *Beyer M130N bidirectional ribbon mike.*

FIG. **10-23.** *Neumann U87 multipattern mike.*

POLAR PATTERNS

The last section showed that directional sensitivity has to do with diaphragm exposure. This sensitivity can be quanitized graphically. These graphical representations are called *polar patterns*. To understand their significance, picture an aerial view of a microphone placed in the center of an imaginary circle as illustrated in FIG. 10-24. This is a 360-degree circle marked off in quadrants. Imagine a sound source with constant volume at some frequency is present on the circle's perimeter. If testing a unidirectional mike, the sound is best perceived on the 0-degree axis because the sound is aimed directly at the diaphragm surface. Here the sound is on-axis and anywhere else is off-axis. In the control room, set the on-axis response for 0 dB meter deflection. As the sound source moves more and more off-axis, the meter level drops until reaching the lowest point when the source is positioned directly behind the mike (180 degrees). So a polar pattern is a collection of points that can be graphed in terms of degrees and dB attenuation. The attenuation is represented by concentric circles and degrees by radial lines. Distance from the mike is not a factor except that the distance at which the radial SPL measurements were made was consistent. Therefore, polar pattern graphs represent the relative sound pressure sensitivity of the mike with regard to the direction from which the sound source is coming.

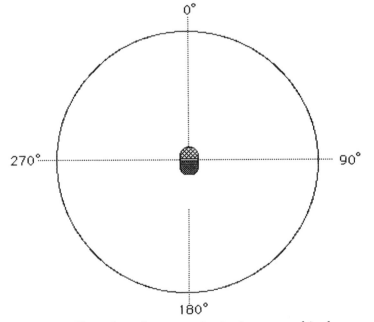

FIG. **10-24.** *The polar reference perimeter is measured in degrees.*

FIGURE 10-25 shows the basic polar pattern of a unidirectional cardioid microphone. Picture the mike at the center. Note that the frontal arc from 60 degrees to 300 degrees falls on the 0 dB circle. This means that the mike has 120 degrees (plus and minus 60 degrees) of off-axis performance that is just as good as its on-axis performance. But notice that at 90 and 270 degrees, the level drops off about 3 dB. On the 180-degree axis (rear), the level drops by 20 dB. The collection of points resembles a heart shape and therefore is called a cardioid mike.

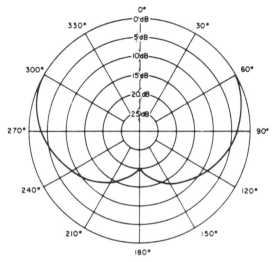

FIG. 10-25. *Unidirectional cardioid polar pattern.*

FIGURE 10-26 features the Shure SM7 dynamic cardioid microphone showing its polar pattern and frequency response diagrams. The pattern varies a little depending on frequency. The cardioid pattern shrinks for higher frequencies. The semilog frequency response graph shows the flatness of the mike over the audio spectrum. A selector switch can alter the nominal flat response as shown. In comparison, the Electro-Voice RE20 dynamic cardioid is displayed in FIG. 10-27. The SM7 seems to have a little more rear rejection. The frequency response graph shows two curves for the RE20, the 0-degree on-axis and the 180-degree rear rejection axis. In general, the response at the rear is about 15 dB down across the band.

The Shure SM81 in FIG. 10-28 is a condenser cardioid. Note that the polar pattern's high-frequency cardioid response at 10 kHz doesn't shrink, giving it consistent off-axis performance. Also note that the response curve is very flat across the audio band. Another popular cardioid mike is the Shure SM57 in FIG. 10-29. Note that it has a midrange peak at about 5 kHz on the graph.

Polar Pattern

Cardioid (unidirectional) — uniform with frequency, symmetrical about axis (see Figure 2)

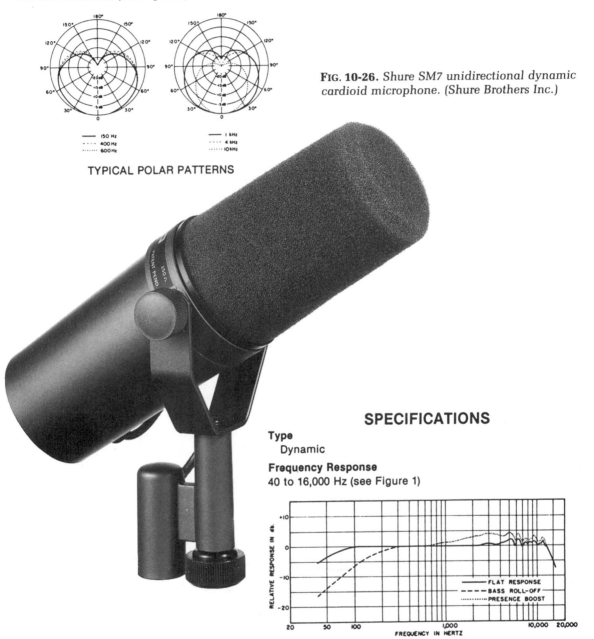

TYPICAL POLAR PATTERNS

FIG. 10-26. *Shure SM7 unidirectional dynamic cardioid microphone. (Shure Brothers Inc.)*

SPECIFICATIONS

Type
Dynamic

Frequency Response
40 to 16,000 Hz (see Figure 1)

TYPICAL FREQUENCY RESPONSE

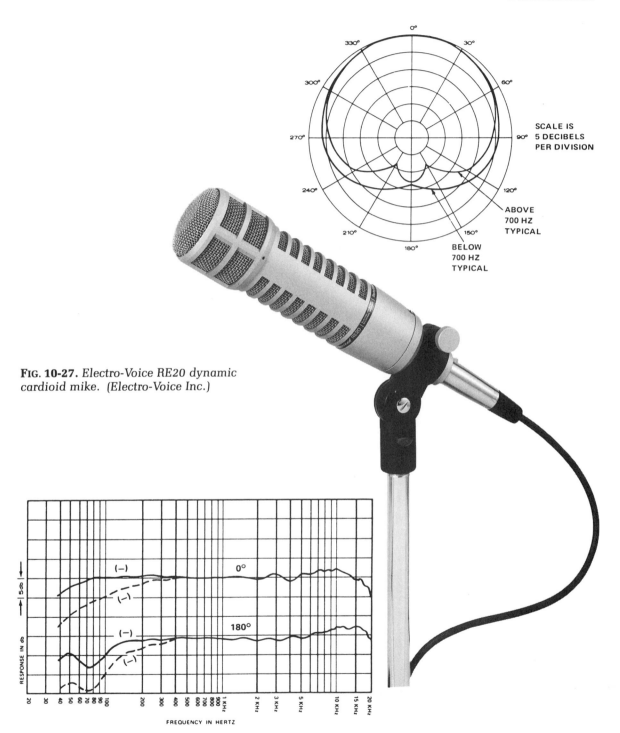

SCALE IS
5 DECIBELS
PER DIVISION

ABOVE
700 HZ
TYPICAL

BELOW
700 HZ
TYPICAL

Fig. 10-27. *Electro-Voice RE20 dynamic cardioid mike. (Electro-Voice Inc.)*

207

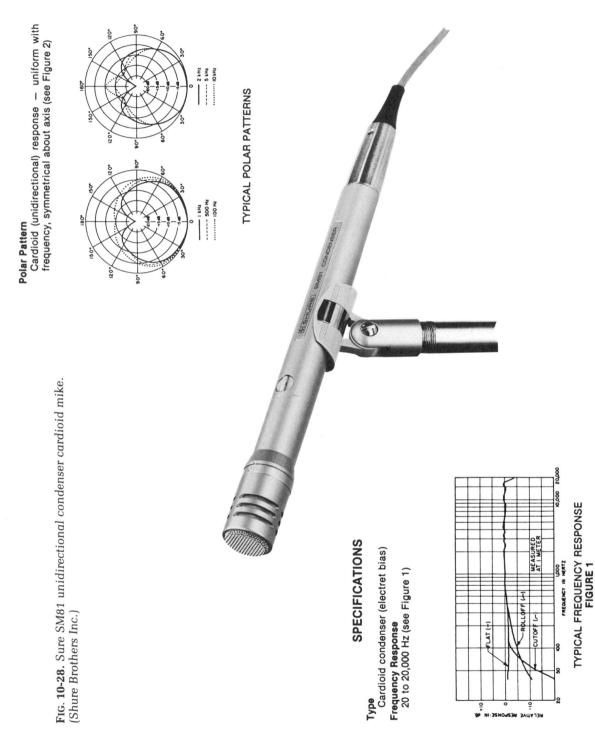

Polar Pattern
Cardioid (unidirectional) response — uniform with frequency, symmetrical about axis (see Figure 2)

TYPICAL POLAR PATTERNS

FIG. **10-28.** *Sure SM81 unidirectional condenser cardioid mike.* (*Shure Brothers Inc.*)

SPECIFICATIONS

Type
Cardioid condenser (electret bias)

Frequency Response
20 to 20,000 Hz (see Figure 1)

TYPICAL FREQUENCY RESPONSE
FIGURE 1

Polar Pattern
Cardioid (unidirectional)—effective rejection of sound at rear of microphone uniform at all frequencies—front pickup characteristics symmetrical about axis (see Figure 2)

FIG. 10-29. *Shure SM57 unidirectional dynamic cardioid mike. (Shure Brothers Inc.)*

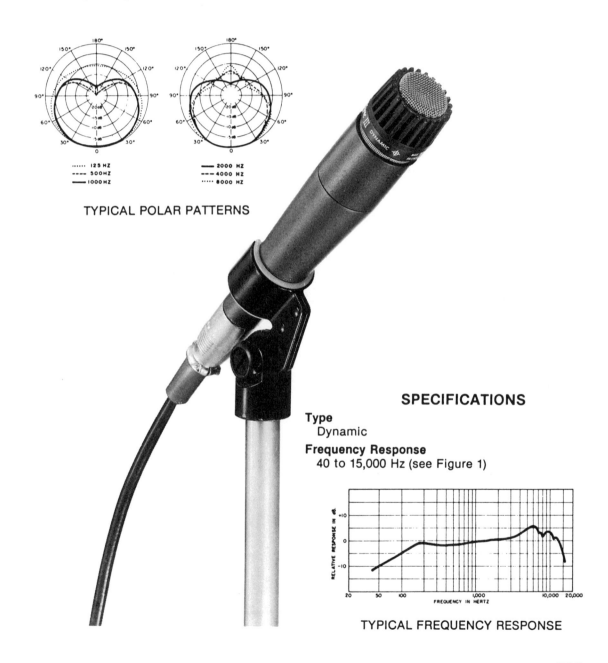

...... 125 HZ
---- 500 HZ
—— 1000 HZ

—— 2000 HZ
--- 4000 HZ
...... 8000 HZ

TYPICAL POLAR PATTERNS

SPECIFICATIONS

Type
Dynamic

Frequency Response
40 to 15,000 Hz (see Figure 1)

TYPICAL FREQUENCY RESPONSE

209

FIGURE 10-30 shows a basic supercardioid polar pattern. Note that at the side angles, 90 and 270 degrees, the attenuation is about 7 dB, as opposed to 3 dB in a regular cardioid. The trade-off is that the supercardioid has worse rear isolation in exchange for a little more side rejection. FIGURE 10-31 shows a Shure SM87 supercardioid condenser microphone. Note that the 10 kHz polar pattern tends to be hyper relative to the low frequencies. Correspondingly, the frequency response curve reveals a boost in this region. The Electro-Voice RE16 supercardioid dynamic mike in FIG. 10-32 has a flatter response. This graph displays the response for three axes, the 0-degree on-axis, the 180-degree rear axis, and the 150-degree (or 210) rear side axis. This is consistent with the polar pattern where the best rejection is at 150 or 210 degrees.

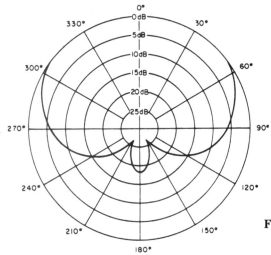

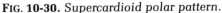

FIG. 10-30. *Supercardioid polar pattern.*

FIGURE 10-33 is a general hypercardioid polar pattern. This side rejection has a better than 10 dB attenuation but a much worse rear rejection than any of the other cardioid types. FIGURE 10-34 shows a Sennheiser MD441 dynamic microphone with a hypercardioid polar pattern and a rather smooth frequency response.

FIGURE 10-35 shows a shotgun pattern. This has the highest all-around rejection and is therefore the most unidirectional. There is not very much margin for off-axis application. FIGURE 10-36 shows the Electro-Voice DL 42 shotgun mike. Note that the higher frequency range is intensely more directional than the lower ones. For this reason, high-fidelity recording is difficult with such off-axis coloration. The Shure SM89 shotgun mike is pictured in FIG. 10-37 with the windscreen and shock mount. The polar pattern response resembles the Electro-Voice DL 42.

Polar Pattern
Supercardioid response—narrower than cardioid for higher directionality, superior rejection of undesirable sounds

FIG. **10-31.** *Shure SM87 supercardioid condenser mike. (Shure Brothers Inc.)*

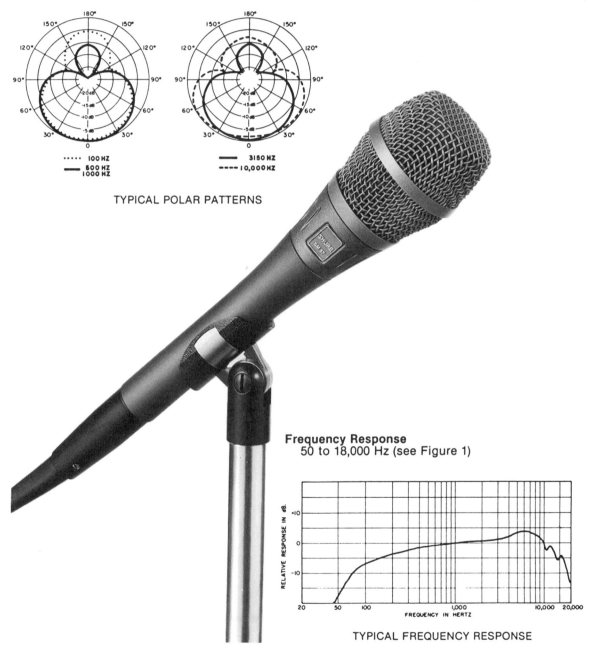

TYPICAL POLAR PATTERNS

····· 100 HZ
— 500 HZ 1000 HZ
— 3150 HZ
---- 10,000 HZ

Frequency Response
50 to 18,000 Hz (see Figure 1)

TYPICAL FREQUENCY RESPONSE

211

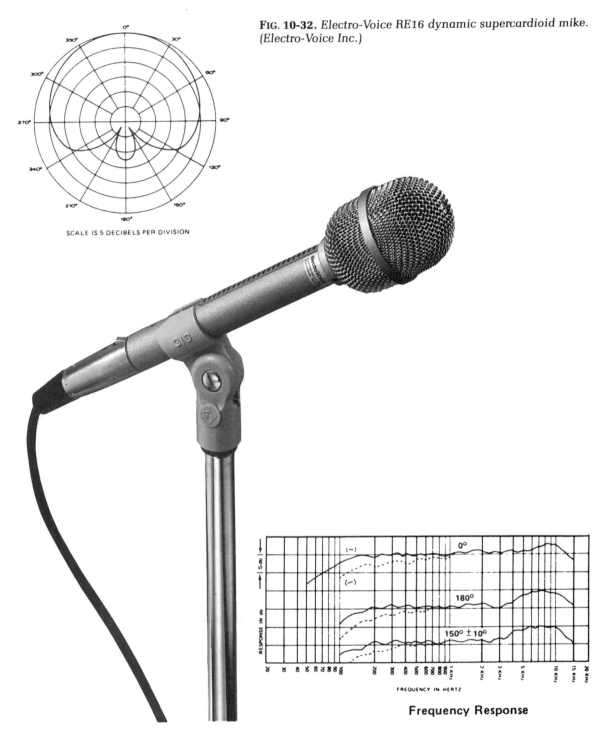

SCALE IS 5 DECIBELS PER DIVISION

FIG. **10-32.** Electro-Voice RE16 dynamic supercardioid mike. (Electro-Voice Inc.)

Frequency Response

212

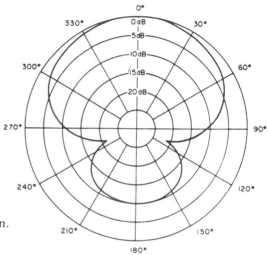

FIG. 10-33. *Hypercardioid polar pattern.*

FIGURE 10-38 represents a bidirectional (figure eight) polar pattern. Rejection is very intense at 90 and 270 degrees. Note that the front and rear lobes are equal. FIGURE 10-39 is the omnidirectional pattern. There is some loss at the rear due to the masking effect of the microphone body for single-diaphragm mikes, but for most practical purposes, this type is mutually sensitive in all directions.

Hence, the range of polar patterns goes from the all-encompassing omnidirectional type to the ultradirectional shotgun type. Earlier in the chapter, dual-diaphragm mikes were mentioned. These combinations make it possible to create various polar patterns via a built-in selector switch. Multipattern capability can be achieved also on a single diaphragm mike by mechanical alterations to the casing.

Polar pattern measurements are made in an *anechoic chamber*. This is a special chamber that is covered with very dense sound-absorbing material, which is usually a deeply convoluted pyramid-shaped sponge-like matter. This material is important for preventing reflections from influencing the off-axis measurements.

The polar patterns might seem as though they are in a two-dimensional plane. When referring to the sides of the mike as being the 90- and 270- degree markings as in FIG. 10-24, this means any point along the perimeter of the intersecting circular plane (FIG. 10-40). This is the unseen third dimension in a polar diagram. For every axis on the polar diagram, there is a perpendicular plane. Anywhere on that circle can be considered a side viewing point. Therefore, for every pair of polar coordinates (30 and 330, 60 and 300, etc.), there is an intersecting circular plane whose perimeter represents a mutual direction

213

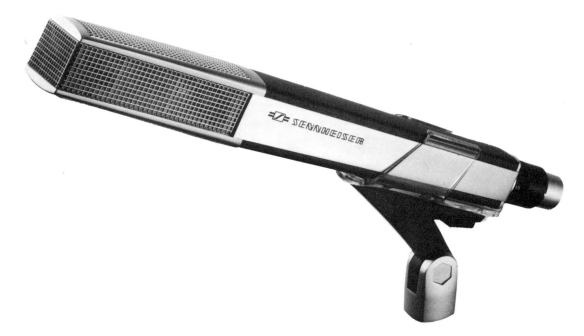

Frequency response

Rated frequency response of the free field no-load
transmission factor
Selector positions:
Bass control: M
presence switch: linear

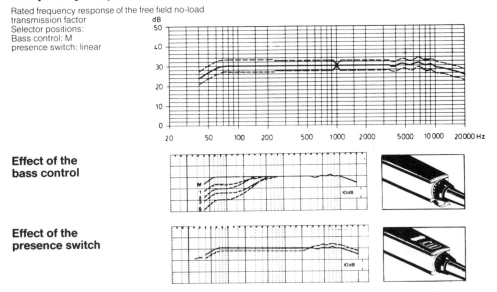

**Effect of the
bass control**

**Effect of the
presence switch**

FIG. 10-34. *Sennheiser MD 441 dynamic hypercardioid mike.* (Sennheiser Electronics
Corp.)

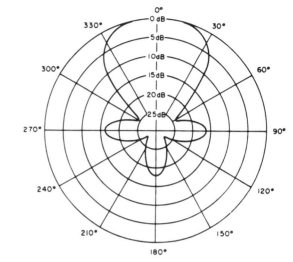

FIG. **10-35**. *Shotgun polar pattern.*

around the mike. Note that every pattern, be it cardioid, bidirectional or whatever, is symmetrical about the 0-180-degree axis. FIGURE 10-41 should help you visualize these patterns.

FREQUENCY RESPONSE AND SENSITIVITY

Polar patterns, frequency response curves, sensitivity, and SPL specs are the basic components that determine the performance of a microphone. There have been numerous demonstrations that a mike's polar pattern is not consistent for all frequencies. The frequency response can be affected by position with respect to the sound source. One of the penalties of off-axis applications is that the high-frequency content attenuates first. Sounds approaching from the rear can sound "muddy." Conversely, on-axis sounds that are close to the diaphragm exaggerate the lows, called a *proximity effect*. The muddy sound is referred to as *off-axis coloration*. Proximity effect might be desirable to embody vocals, but more expensive microphones feature a "roll-off" switch that counteracts this if desired.

The frequency response of a microphone should certainly be of concern, but most professional microphones have sufficient bandwidth to cover any audio application, with is generally 50 Hz to 18 kHz. But equally important is for what dynamic range does this specification apply? It might be difficult for a mike to have a full bandwidth for faint sounds, but more expensive mikes should have better sensitivity and faithfully reproduce faint sounds more efficiently than cheaper mikes. Sensitivity is associated with how much signal output a mike can produce for a given SPL. Condenser mikes have higher sensitivity than dynamic ones, meaning that it will produce a hotter signal (10 to 15 dB more) for the same acoustical power level.

215

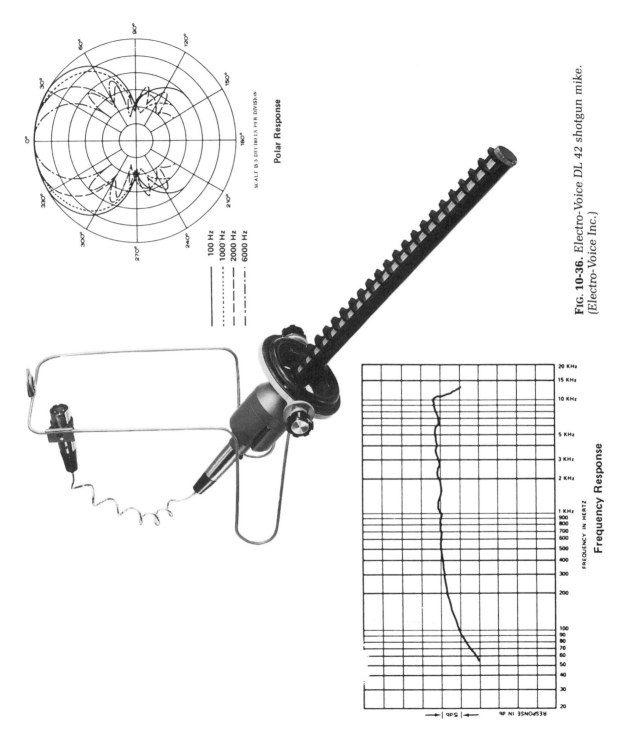

Polar Response

SCALE IS 5 DECIBELS PER DIVISION

—————— 100 Hz
··············· 1000 Hz
— — — 2000 Hz
—·—·— 6000 Hz

FIG. 10-36. *Electro-Voice DL 42 shotgun mike. (Electro-Voice Inc.)*

Frequency Response

FREQUENCY IN HERTZ

RESPONSE IN db

5db

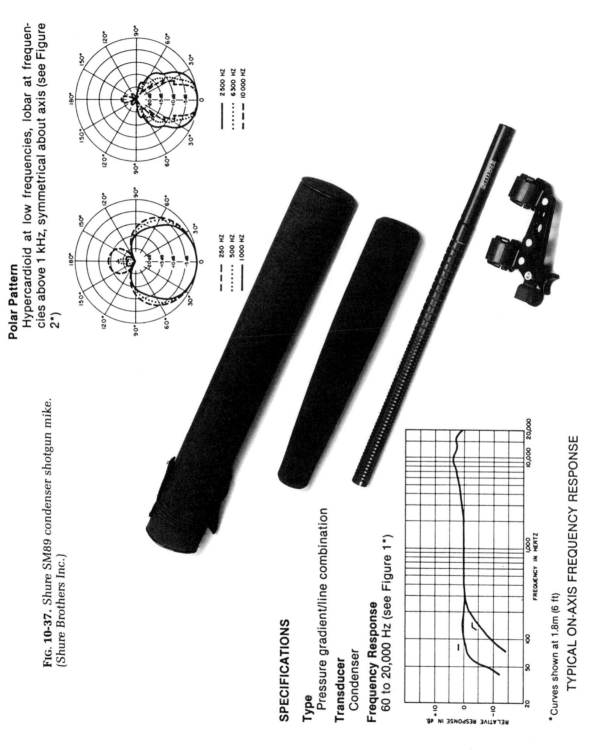

Polar Pattern

Hypercardioid at low frequencies, lobar at frequencies above 1 kHz, symmetrical about axis (see Figure 2*)

2 500 HZ
6 300 HZ
10 000 HZ

250 HZ
500 HZ
1000 HZ

FIG. **10-37.** Shure SM89 condenser shotgun mike. (Shure Brothers Inc.)

SPECIFICATIONS

Type
Pressure gradient/line combination

Transducer
Condenser

Frequency Response
60 to 20,000 Hz (see Figure 1*)

* Curves shown at 1.8m (6 ft)

TYPICAL ON-AXIS FREQUENCY RESPONSE

RELATIVE RESPONSE IN dB.

FREQUENCY IN HERTZ

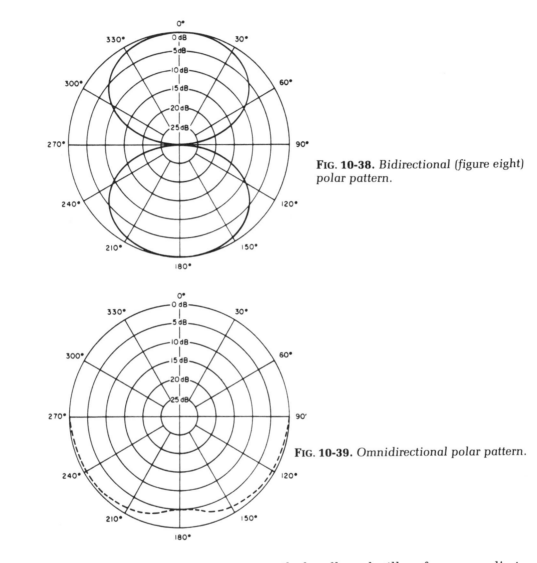

FIG. **10-38.** *Bidirectional (figure eight) polar pattern.*

FIG. **10-39.** *Omnidirectional polar pattern.*

How loud or great an SPL can a mike handle and still perform normally is another concern. Professional condenser microphones can be expected to handle sound pressure levels in the order of 130 to 135 decibels. Dynamic microphones can handle such high sound pressure intensities (greater than 150 decibels) that this specification can be ignored. Because condenser mikes are active devices and have higher sensitivity, these mikes have attenuation switches to pad down the output. Otherwise, a high SPL condition could easily overload the console input.

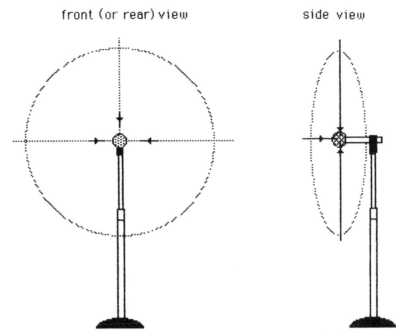

FIG. 10-40. *The 90/270-degree polar plane is perpendicular to the 0/180-degree axis.*

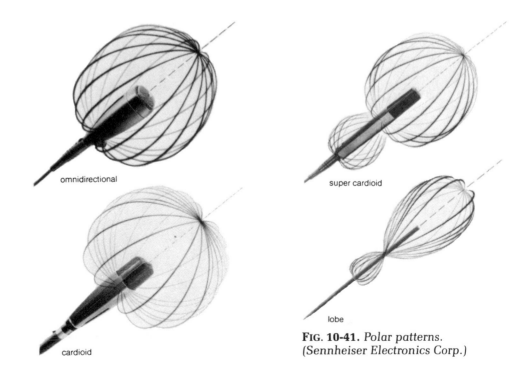

omnidirectional

super cardioid

cardioid

lobe

FIG. 10-41. *Polar patterns. (Sennheiser Electronics Corp.)*

219

WINDSCREENS AND SHOCK MOUNTS

Ambient air movement can detrimentally affect the performance of a diaphragm or ribbon. Surrounding sound vibrations cause small movement in a microphone transducer in proportion to a breath of air directly striking the surface. Such a condition is common when vocalists say words that begin with a p. This air movement creates a vocal "pop" when striking the diaphragm. A windscreen, used to counteract excessive air motion, is a spongy foam jacket placed over the mike's grill.

Another disturbing condition is the presence of very low (subsonic) frequencies. These vibrations can transfer themselves through the mike stand and act on the mike. Shock mounts, devised to absorb these vibrations, are suspension systems in which the mike casing is mechanically decoupled from the solid structure that anchors the mike via rubberized strands. FIGURE 10-42 shows a Neumann U47 in a shock mount.

FIG. **10-42.** *Neumann U47 in shock mount.*

MICROPHONE APPLICATION TECHNIQUES

Understanding polar patterns is the key to mike selection and placement. Since professional microphone performance is rather competitive from manufacturer to manufacturer, those favored are a matter of personal taste. Sometimes the character of a mike behaves differently from console to console or studio to studio, so that could influence your opinion of its performance. In most applications, unidirectional microphones are used to attain optimum control.

Close Miking versus Distant Miking

In spite of the fact that a recording studio is a somewhat controlled and consistent acoustic environment, the character of sound will vary in relationship with microphone placement and the source. A microphone placed at a distance, let's say twelve feet from the source, not only picks up the on-axis sound but also any off-axis reflections from the walls, floor, and ceiling. Capturing these off-axis reflections deliberately is usually referred to as *ambient miking*. On the other hand, close microphone placement registers the on-axis sound mostly. At close range, the direct sound is so overpowering that any reflections are barely perceptible, yielding a sound with a lot of "presence." Sometimes the combination of the two, close and distant miking of a source, is used so that the ambient sound enhances the close-up sound. For this technique, an omnidirectional mike might be used for the ambient recording.

Close miking can mean ranges from about six inches to a couple of feet. There is a potential danger of mike placement that compromises close and distant applications. Referring to the illustration in FIG. 10-43, it is shown that a reflection could be of significant magnitude. Since the reflection path is always longer, the phase relationship with the direct path could result in serious frequency cancellations and consequently deteriorate the tonal quality. These frequency drop-outs give the response a *comb filtering* effect. A remedy for a condition where recording close to a hard surface is unavoidable is to use a *boundary* or *pressure zone* microphone, such as the Crown electret condenser PZM-31S. The polar response for this mike is semi-omni because it is mounted on a large plate. Its physical construction allows for placement on a floor, table, wall, piano lid, or any other surface. Because the diaphragm is so close to the potentially reflective surface, the direct and reflected paths are almost coincident. A pressure zone mike is particularly useful for recording the voice of an individual seated at a table. Due to its semi-omni polar pattern, it can be mounted on a wall and capture a group of vocalists gathered about the mike without any off-axis problems found in unidirectional mikes.

Mike Placement and Tonal Quality

The decision of mike placement depends on the source. For example, an acoustic guitar has a better tonal balance at two feet away than at six inches. A little distance gives the sound a chance to blend. It pays to explore the possibilities with mike placement and make comparisons. The blend changes with location. Close mike placement usually yields a harsher and more percussive sound. On a guitar, finger movement on the fretboard and picking action on the strings are more noticeable at close range.

221

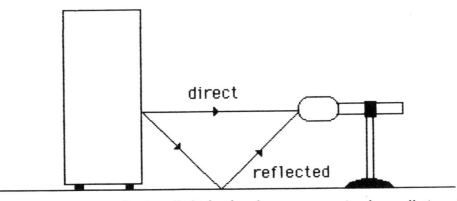

FIG. 10-43. *Destructive reflection off of a hard surface can cause signal cancellation at the mike.*

You are better off trying to achieve good sound with placement before making any equalization attempts. You might discover that miking a tambourine or cowbell at a distance of 10 or 12 feet sounds much nicer than at close range. It might be harder to get a VU meter deflection at these distances, but these kinds of instruments seem to punch through even when recording them at a −5 dB meter deflection. However, an instrument like a flute might call for miking closer to the mouthpiece to capture the breath.

Microphone Colocation

Because of space limitations or other reasons, studios are often forced to use more than one mike in the same area. In this case, unidirectional mikes are necessary to improve isolation, minimizing the bleed from one mike to another. A good example of a colocated microphone application is the multiple miking of a drum set where you are forced to have mike placement in the same vicinity.

The rule is to use the least number of mikes possible to do the job. Minimizing the number allows for greater placement spacing between the mikes and less bleed. Because of the distance between microphones, a phase difference is introduced between the direct signal registered by one mike and the same signal spilled over to an adjacent mike. Placing a mike with each adjacent tom will do more damage than good, and you won't get the isolation it was intended for either. The "3 to 1" principle can be helpful in placement strategy. This principle asserts that the distance between two microphones should be at least three times as great as the mike-to-source distance to achieve acceptable isolation as shown in FIG. 10-44. Miking drums can get tricky because placement might be dimensionally awkward. With an unusual number of mikes being this close, the channel phase-reversal switches on the console can counter some destructive phase cancelling. Exercise trial and error.

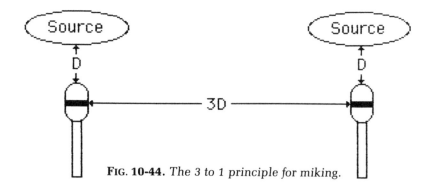

FIG. **10-44.** *The 3 to 1 principle for miking.*

When working with vocalists, the engineer has the luxury of spreading them out a little to make the "3 to 1" rule more practical, but you should still use the least number of microphones to do the job. Sometimes mikes can be co-located for the purpose of broadening reception as opposed to isolation reasons. FIGURE 10-45 shows an example of a pair of mikes colocated to capture a wide angle source, say a group of vocalists in a semicircle or maybe an ensemble.

FIG. **10-45.** *Stereo miking.*

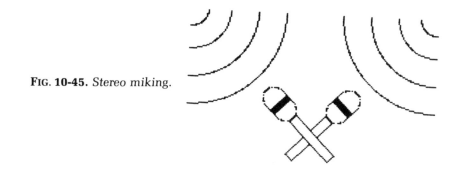

Because the mikes are so close, the phase relationships coincide. Therefore, spillover would not be disastrous. However, the angled on-axis relationships tend to create a stereo image. A microphone like the AKG C422 is a stereo condenser type that could be used for such an application.

11

MIDI Applications

MIDI IS AN ABBREVIATION FOR MUSICAL INSTRUMENT DIGITAL INTERFACE. An instrument such as a keyboard synthesizer that has such an interface is considered to be an *addressable* device because it can be controlled or operated by an external source. This source would have to be a compatible device that can transmit and receive digital control information that the synthesizer could "understand."

ADDRESSABILITY

Most MIDI devices can receive information as well as send it. Therefore, expect to find at least one MIDI IN and one MIDI OUT connector on a synthesizer. Most synthesizers, except for the oldest ones, have a MIDI THRU connector also, which is an output that "folds back" the same information it receives at the MIDI IN port. This way, the same information can be relayed from synth to synth using one source. For example, a keyboard can be the source to operate, or "slave," several keyboards as demonstrated in FIG. 11-1. Synth #1 is the source, or *controller*, transmitting MIDI messages to synth #2. Synth #2 then relays the same MIDI data it received to synth #3, and synth #3 relays it to synth #4, etc. Using MIDI, a musician playing synth #1 can trigger these additional synthesizers and get four sound programs at once.

MIDI terminals are the 5-pin DIN connector type, which is a German industrial standard (*deutsche industrie normen*). The MIDI terminals like those on a synthesizer are depicted in FIG. 11-2. The terminals are female and the cable connectors are male. Only the middle three pins are actually used. Two paths are for the actual data traffic and one is for the cable shield that is grounded. The MIDI OUT terminal does the shield grounding. The MIDI IN only sees the two data connections (see FIG. 11-3.)

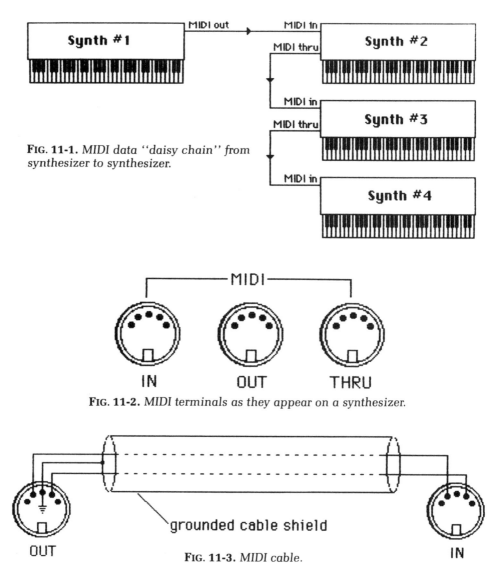

FIG. **11-1.** *MIDI data "daisy chain" from synthesizer to synthesizer.*

FIG. **11-2.** *MIDI terminals as they appear on a synthesizer.*

FIG. **11-3.** *MIDI cable.*

BINARY CODING

MIDI digital messages are in binary form. These messages are binary words called bytes. Recall from Chapter 9 that a *byte* is a group of bits. Combinations of 0s and 1s (bits) make up binary *words* (a byte or group of bytes). This makes up a digital vocabulary that serves as instructions for addressable devices. As a small example, how many 4-bit words can be made with 0s and 1s? The answer is 2^4 or 16, as demonstrated in FIG. 11-4.

(0) 0000   (8) 1000
(1) 0001   (9) 1001
(2) 0010   (10) 1010
(3) 0011   (11) 1011
(4) 0100   (12) 1100
(5) 0101   (13) 1101
(6) 0110   (14) 1110
(7) 0111   (15) 1111

FIG. 11-4. For a 4-bit number, there are 16 possible combinations: $2^4 = 2 \times 2 \times 2 \times 2$ = 16.

If a word is eight bits long, then there are 256 (2^8) possible combinations of 0s and 1s. With this many words, there are many possibilities or instructions to tell a synth what to do. In MIDI applications, 8-bit words are used. Technically, a 0 is zero volts and a 1 is represented by + 5 volts. The serial data rate is 31.25 kilobaud, which means that 31,250 bits are transmitted per second. That also implies that a bit time is 32 microseconds (1/31,250), or in other words, 32 millionths of a second. For example, if a binary word is 10010110, the transmission looks like the one in FIG. 11-5. Pulse widths of 32 μs at + 5 volts determine the presence of 1s and 32 μs time durations at 0 volts determine the presence of 0s. Each word is introduced with a start bit, which is always a 0 and ends with a stop bit that is always a 1. Therefore, an 8-bit word is a 10-bit byte (FIG. 11-6).

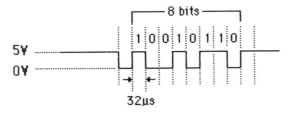

FIG. 11-5. An 8-bit word has 256 possible combinations.

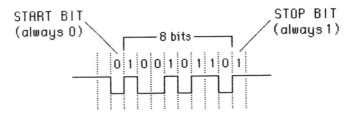

FIG. 11-6. A 10-bit byte results from adding a start and stop bit to each 8-bit word.

MIDI MESSAGES

To demonstrate the various MIDI commands, examine a setup where a computer is addressing three synthesizers. Refer to FIG. 11-7. Anytime the computer sends a command, all three synths get the message but a coding system determines if one or more of these synths actually executes the command. This coding is called *MIDI receive channel number.* There are 16 receive channels that a synthesizer can be set to. The synthesizer only responds to messages sent on its channel in the same sense that a TV or radio can only pick up signals that it is tuned to.

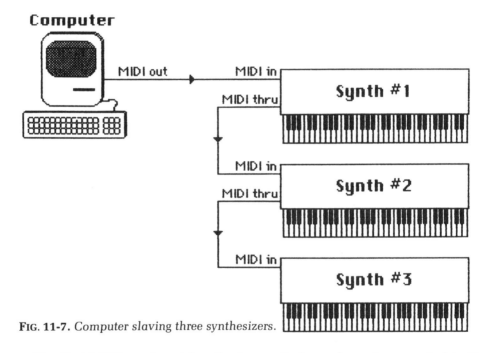

FIG. 11-7. *Computer slaving three synthesizers.*

The first MIDI word sent has the transmit channel number encoded in it. As an example, if the command from the computer is to play a middle C note on a synth that is set on MIDI receive channel #5, the transmit word from the computer would appear as shown in FIG. 11-8. The first four bits is the ''note on'' command and the last four bits is the channel number. The second word is the *pitch,* or note that is to be played. The third word is a volume code in which maximum loudness is 01111111, and minimum or no volume is 00000000. There are 127 volume increments possible. The final event is a ''note off,'' 4-bit command and 4-bit channel code. This completes the sequence necessary to actually hear a sound.

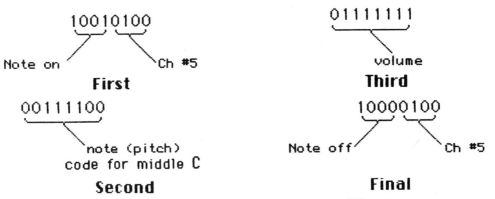

FIG. 11-8. *Each word in a MIDI data packet serves a different purpose.*

The four-word sequence is a serial data packet. The pulsed data stream is in FIG. 11-9. The first three bytes take 960 μs of time (less than a thousandth of a second) to clock in. The time t is how long the note is heard, which is enormously longer than the MIDI words. The split (/ /) implies an indefinite amount of time.

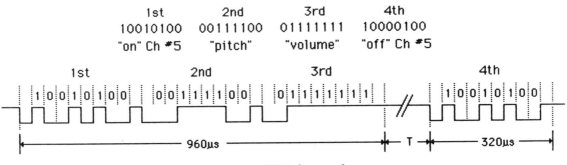

FIG. 11-9. *MIDI data packet.*

FIGURE 11-10 is a table of all of the 4-bit channel codes. There is a code that makes a synth read information regardless of the MIDI transmit channel called the OMNI mode. This three-byte code enables a synth to read all MIDI channels (FIG. 11-11). The four bit positions marked with an x imply that those four bits could be any of the 16 MIDI channel codes.

ch1....0000	ch5....0100	ch9....1000	ch13....1100
ch2....0001	ch6....0101	ch10....1001	ch14....1101
ch3....0010	ch7....0110	ch11....1010	ch15....1110
ch4....0011	ch8....0111	ch12....1011	ch16....1111

FIG. 11-10. *MIDI transmit/receive channel codes.*

BYTES		
1st	2nd	3rd

	1st	2nd	3rd
OMNI on	1011xxxx	01111101	00000000
OMNI off	1011xxxx	01111100	00000000

FIG. 11-11. *OMNI mode.*

There are many other codes in MIDI applications that control sound parameters. It's not practical to know all these numerical codes in order to use them; it's only necessary to know what features exist. Other control-related functions include:

poly mode—Enables the synth to function polyphonically. Most keyboards are eight-note polyphonic, meaning that as many as eight notes can be played simultaneously.

mono mode—Disables the polyphonic mode allowing only one note to be played at a time. It could be worth sacrificing polyphonicity for a "thicker" monophonic sound.

program change—A received code that selects or changes a sound program.

A synth has several types of manual controls that generate MIDI messages. Keyboards have *pitch bend* and *modulation* wheels, or in place of wheels, a *joy stick*.

pitch bend—This control slightly deviates the pitch of a sound plus or minus its normal pitch.

modulation—Deviates the pitch back and forth at a specific rate, giving a vibrato effect.

touch sensitivity—The key velocity that is used during play controls the dynamics of the volume level. The harder the keys are struck, the louder the sound.

after touch—The amount of pressure applied to the keys, after the initial velocity. It is used to alter a sound parameter as an effect.

sustain—Usually controlled by a foot pedal that has a switch action to sustain notes played after key release.

SEQUENCING

Computers are typically used in MIDI applications for sequencing. The term *sequencer* describes a device used as a digital recorder. A computer serves as a digital recorder because it can store binary MIDI messages and then reproduce them in the order or sequence they were received. FIGURE 11-12 shows a typical setup in which a computer becomes a sequencer.

229

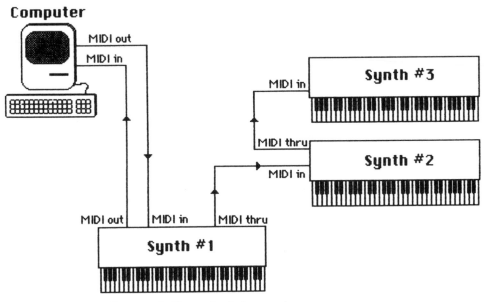

FIG. 11-12. *Computer being used as a sequencer.*

For example, say a musician wants to play synth #1 as the controller that sends MIDI information to the computer and then has the computer play it back through all three synths. First, a sequencer program must be down-loaded into the computer from a disk drive. As the computer is put into the record mode, a metronome click should be audible. As the musician plays, the computer receives and stores MIDI messages characterizing the performance of the keys played. After the recording is finished, the computer goes into the playback mode. The MIDI messages are reproduced, received by synth #1, and then relayed to synth #2 and #3. A number of interesting advantages are apparent here. During the playback, the musician can change sound programs and explore possibilities. A tempo change can be made to make the playback faster or slower. The playback can even be transposed to a different key.

Expand the setup by adding a drum synthesizer, which is also a sequencer, shown in FIG. 11-13. Assuming there is a drum program in the machine already, you could hear it with the playback it was intended for. Sequencers use special MIDI codes called *system real time* messages. When a playback is initiated, the computer sends a *start* MIDI message that has meaning only to the drum synth. The drum machine now needs some tempo information, so a continuous series of pulses called a MIDI clock is sent by the computer to synchronize the drum machine with the playback. A *stop* command terminates the playback, and a *continue* command resumes the playback.

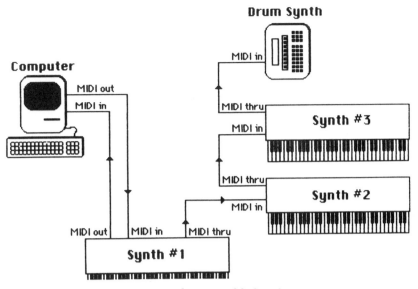

FIG. 11-13. *Drum synthesizer added to the MIDI chain.*

A drum synth can be played via a keyboard as shown in FIG. 11-14 because a drum synth can respond to certain keys, depending on the manufacturer. Usually there is a provision on the drum machine to alter the key assignments for the snare, toms, hi-hat, kick drum, etc. In fact, it is useful to know the industry standard of MIDI key numbers. FIGURE 11-15 shows a keyboard layout and its key number assignment. Below it is a list relating key number to note to octave. Middle C begins the 3rd octave.

BINARY AND HEXADECIMAL NUMBERS

Up to now, MIDI codes were expressed as binary number using 0s and 1s. For convenience, these numbers are translated to decimal form or hexadecimal form. The decimal system is the one we use in our everyday lives. To convert binary to decimal, recall that every bit cell has a value in powers of 2. FIGURE 11-16 shows a table of 2 to the 7th power. The second row is the value of these powers. The decimal value of the 8-bit code is determined by adding up all the numbers wherever there is a value of 1. In the example illustrated, the binary code 01101001 = 64 + 32 + 8 + 1 = 105.

A *hexadecimal* expression is another counting system based on a 4-bit value (FIG. 11-17). The 8-bit binary code can therefore be represented by two digits. In the example 01101001, the four left bits 0110 equal 6, and the four right bits 1001 equal 9. The hexadecimal value for 01101001 is therefore 69. The table in FIG. 11-18 is a handy conversion chart for all three numbering bases.

231

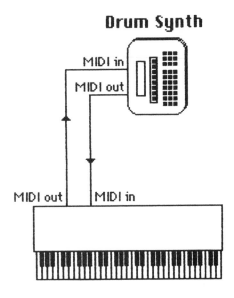

Drum Synth

MIDI in

MIDI out

MIDI out   MIDI in

FIG. **11-14.** *MIDI connection from keyboard to drum synth.*

MIDI INTERFACE DEVICES

MIDI applications can get much more complex than the examples set here. Addressability might involve many synthesizers and more than one sequencer or computer. Addressability has been demonstrated by "daisy chaining" the synths using the THRU terminals. The rule is that you should not daisy chain more than three or four synths. The MIDI signal degrades with each hop. Enough degradation causes bit errors. Another rule is that MIDI cables should not exceed 15 meters (≈ 50 feet). When daisy chaining, use short cables. If you want to address several synths, use a device called a *thru box* as shown in FIG. 11-19. You can then address a multiplicity of synths and still maintain a solid transmission. Thru boxes typically have a MIDI input and four outputs.

Another useful device is a MIDI patcher. This is like a patch bay where you can conveniently make MIDI routing connections from a central location as shown in FIG. 11-20. This device can substitute the need for a thru box. Most patchers are programmable so that you can electronically make a setup, store it, and recall the setup whenever you want it. Yamaha makes one that has eight inputs and eight outputs. This can accommodate routing among devices in many configurations. The electronic patching allows routing a MIDI signal to more than one device (but not merging MIDI signals). Basically, a patcher is a programmable thru box that splits the MIDI transmit signal. A device that *can* combine two MIDI signals from two transmit sources is called a *merger* box (FIG. 11-21).

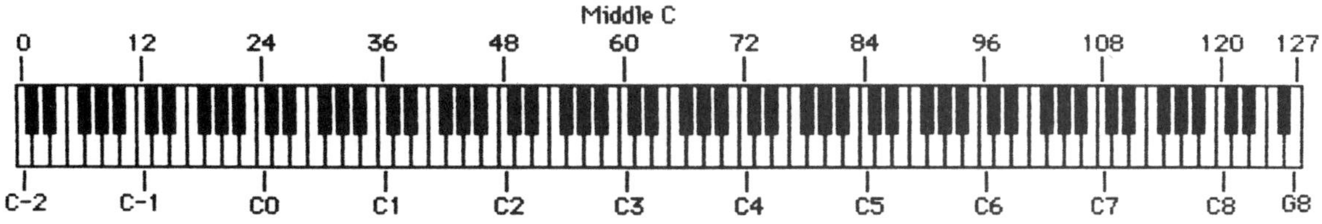

Middle C

```
0      12     24     36     48     60     72     84     96     108    120  127
```

Full Range of MIDI Key Numbers

C-2   C-1   C0   C1   C2   C3   C4   C5   C6   C7   C8   G8

0......C -2	12......C-1	24.....C0	36......C1	48.....C2
1......C#-2	13.....C#-1	25.....C#0	37.....C#1	49.....C#2
2.....D -2	14.....D-1	26.....D0	38.....D1	50.....D2
3.....D#-2	15......D#-1	27.....D#0	39.....D#1	51.....D#2
4.....E -2	16.....E-1	28.....E0	40.....E1	52.....E2
5.....F -2	17.....F-1	29.....F0	41.....F1	53.....F2
6.....F#-2	18.....F#-1	30.....F#0	42.....F#1	54.....F#2
7.....G-2	19......G-1	31.....G0	43.....G1	55.....G2
8......G#-2	20......G#-1	32.....G#0	44.....G#1	56.....G#2
9.....A -2	21.....A-1	33.....A0	45.....A1	57.....A2
10......A#-2	22.....A#-1	34.....A#0	46.....A#1	58.....A#2
11......B -2	23......B-1	35.....B0	47.....B1	59.....B2

60......C3	72......C4	84......C5	96......C6	108......C7	120......C8
61......C#3	73.....C#4	85......C#5	97......C#6	109......C#7	121......C#8
62......D3	74......D4	86......D5	98......D6	110......D7	122......D8
63......D#3	75......D#4	87......D#5	99......D#6	111......D#7	123......D#8
64......E3	76......E4	88......E5	100......E6	112......E7	124......E8
65......F3	77......F4	89......F5	101......F6	113......F7	125......F8
66......F#3	78......F#4	90......F#5	102......F#6	114......F#7	126......F#8
67......G3	79......G4	91......G5	103......G6	115......G7	127......G8
68......G#3	80......G#4	92......G#5	104......G#6	116......G#7	
69......A3	81......A4	93......A5	105......A6	117......A7	
70......A#3	82......A#4	94......A#5	106......A#6	118......A#7	
71......B3	83......B4	95......B5	107......B6	119......B7	

FIG. 11-15. *MIDI key/note assignment.*

233

	2^7	2^6	2^5	2^4	2^3	2^2	2^1	2^0
	128	64	32	16	8	4	2	1
example	0	1	1	0	1	0	0	1

decimal value = 4+32+8+1 = 105

FIG. 11-16. *Binary-to-decimal conversion.*

0000 = 0	1000 = 8
0001 = 1	1001 = 9
0010 = 2	1010 = A
0011 = 3	1011 = B
0100 = 4	1100 = C
0101 = 5	1101 = D
0110 = 6	1110 = E
0111 = 7	1111 = F

FIG. 11-17. *Binary-to-hexadecimal conversion.*

Another interesting device is a *MIDI/trigger converter.* A trigger is an electronic term for a one-shot pulse. Electronic percussion instruments like Simmons and Boss pads have a trigger input (a one-shot pulse is needed to activate the device). The converter has several programmable trigger outputs to drive many devices. The triggers are assigned a MIDI note and channel. Thus, when the converter receives a MIDI signal that matches up with a trigger assignment, the one-shot fires for that output. This mode of operation is called a *MIDI-to-trigger conversion* (FIG. 11-22). The converter can also be operated in the reverse mode (trigger-to-MIDI conversion). In this mode, triggering sources deliver a pulse that commands the converter to send a MIDI note, channel, and dynamic information corresponding to the trigger input assignment. This comes in handy, for example, when a live drummer wants to access a drum synth sound using triggering pads (FIG. 11-23).

Another type of converter directly related to analog recording is a MIDI *clock/tape sync* converter. There are two modes of operation: *write* (encode) and *read* (decode). In the write mode (FIG. 11-24), this converter receives MIDI clock signals and converts them to *tape sync* signals to be recorded on a track. In the read mode (FIG. 11-25), the tape sync track is fed into the converter for conversion back to a MIDI clock signal. This application is used on a regular basis. A MIDI clock signal is necessary to synchronize a sequencer with the prerecorded tracks.

Binary	Dec.	Hex.	Binary	Dec.	Hex.	Binary	Dec.	Hex.	Binary	Dec.	Hex.
00000000	0	0	01000000	64	40	10000000	128	80	11000000	192	C0
00000001	1	1	01000001	65	41	10000001	129	81	11000001	193	C1
00000010	2	2	01000010	66	42	10000010	130	82	11000010	194	C2
00000011	3	3	01000011	67	43	10000011	131	83	11000011	195	C3
00000100	4	4	01000100	68	44	10000100	132	84	11000100	196	C4
00000101	5	5	01000101	69	45	10000101	133	85	11000101	197	C5
00000110	6	6	01000110	70	46	10000110	134	86	11000110	198	C6
00000111	7	7	01000111	71	47	10000111	135	87	11000111	199	C7
00001000	8	8	01001000	72	48	10001000	136	88	11001000	200	C8
00001001	9	9	01001001	73	49	10001001	137	89	11001001	201	C9
00001010	10	A	01001010	74	4A	10001010	138	8A	11001010	202	CA
00001011	11	B	01001011	75	4B	10001011	139	8B	11001011	203	CB
00001100	12	C	01001100	76	4C	10001100	140	8C	11001100	204	CC
00001101	13	D	01001101	77	4D	10001101	141	8D	11001101	205	CD
00001110	14	E	01001110	78	4E	10001110	142	8E	11001110	206	CE
00001111	15	F	01001111	79	4F	10001111	143	8F	11001111	207	CF
00010000	16	10	01010000	80	50	10010000	144	90	11010000	208	D0
00010001	17	11	01010001	81	51	10010001	145	91	11010001	209	D1
00010010	18	12	01010010	82	52	10010010	146	92	11010010	210	D2
00010011	19	13	01010011	83	53	10010011	147	93	11010011	211	D3
00010100	20	14	01010100	84	54	10010100	148	94	11010100	212	D4
00010101	21	15	01010101	85	55	10010101	149	95	11010101	213	D5
00010110	22	16	01010110	86	56	10010110	150	96	11010110	214	D6
00010111	23	17	01010111	87	57	10010111	151	97	11010111	215	D7
00011000	24	18	01011000	88	58	10011000	152	98	11011000	216	D8
00011001	25	19	01011001	89	59	10011001	153	99	11011001	217	D9
00011010	26	1A	01011010	90	5A	10011010	154	9A	11011010	218	DA
00011011	27	1B	01011011	91	5B	10011011	155	9B	11011011	219	DB
00011100	28	1C	01011100	92	5C	10011100	156	9C	11011100	220	DC
00011101	29	1D	01011101	93	5D	10011101	157	9D	11011101	221	DD
00011110	30	1E	01011110	94	5E	10011110	158	9E	11011110	222	DE
00011111	31	1F	01011111	95	5F	10011111	159	9F	11011111	223	DF
00100000	32	20	01100000	96	60	10100000	160	A0	11100000	224	E0
00100001	33	21	01100001	97	61	10100001	161	A1	11100001	225	E1
00100010	34	22	01100010	98	62	10100010	162	A2	11100010	226	E2
00100011	35	23	01100011	99	63	10100011	163	A3	11100011	227	E3
00100100	36	24	01100100	100	64	10100100	164	A4	11100100	228	E4
00100101	37	25	01100101	101	65	10100101	165	A5	11100101	229	E5
00100110	38	26	01100110	102	66	10100110	166	A6	11100110	230	E6
00100111	39	27	01100111	103	67	10100111	167	A7	11100111	231	E7
00101000	40	28	01101000	104	68	10101000	168	A8	11101000	232	E8
00101001	41	29	01101001	105	69	10101001	169	A9	11101001	233	E9
00101010	42	2A	01101010	106	6A	10101010	170	AA	11101010	234	EA
00101011	43	2B	01101011	107	6B	10101011	171	AB	11101011	235	EB
00101100	44	2C	01101100	108	6C	10101100	172	AC	11101100	236	EC
00101101	45	2D	01101101	109	6D	10101101	173	AD	11101101	237	ED
00101110	46	2E	01101110	110	6E	10101110	174	AE	11101110	238	EE
00101111	47	2F	01101111	111	6F	10101111	175	AF	11101111	239	EF
00110000	48	30	01110000	112	70	10110000	176	B0	11110000	240	F0
00110001	49	31	01110001	113	71	10110001	177	B1	11110001	241	F1
00110010	50	32	01110010	114	72	10110010	178	B2	11110010	242	F2
00110011	51	33	01110011	115	73	10110011	179	B3	11110011	243	F3
00110100	52	34	01110100	116	74	10110100	180	B4	11110100	244	F4
00110101	53	35	01110101	117	75	10110101	181	B5	11110101	245	F5
00110110	54	36	01110110	118	76	10110110	182	B6	11110110	246	F6
00110111	55	37	01110111	119	77	10110111	183	B7	11110111	247	F7
00111000	56	38	01111000	120	78	10111000	184	B8	11111000	248	F8
00111001	57	39	01111001	121	79	10111001	185	B9	11111001	249	F9
00111010	58	3A	01111010	122	7A	10111010	186	BA	11111010	250	FA
00111011	59	3B	01111011	123	7B	10111011	187	BB	11111011	251	FB
00111100	60	3C	01111100	124	7C	10111100	188	BC	11111100	252	FC
00111101	61	3D	01111101	125	7D	10111101	189	BD	11111101	253	FD
00111110	62	3E	01111110	126	7E	10111110	190	BE	11111110	254	FE
00111111	63	3F	01111111	127	7F	10111111	191	BF	11111111	255	FF

FIG. 11-18. *Binary/decimal/hexadecimal conversion chart.*

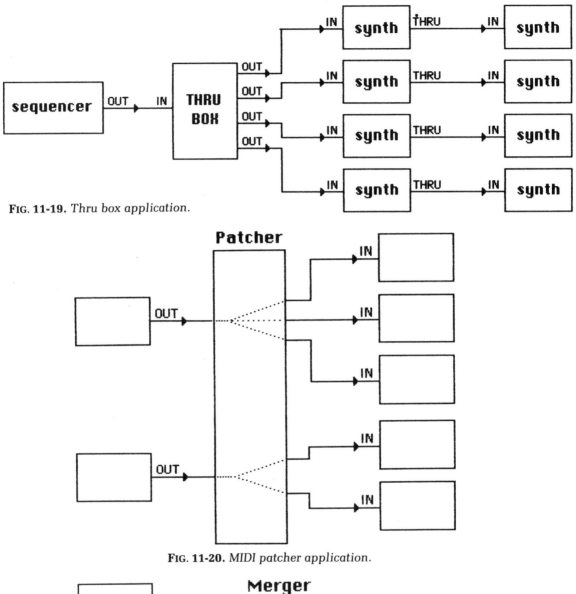

FIG. **11-19.** *Thru box application.*

FIG. **11-20.** *MIDI patcher application.*

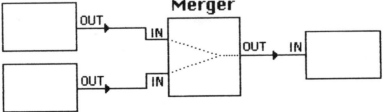

FIG. **11-21.** *MIDI merger application.*

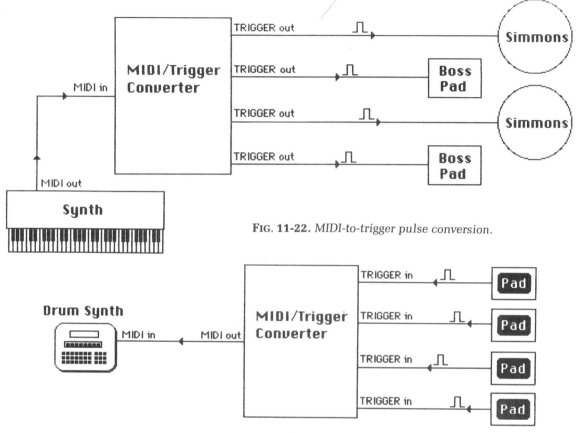

FIG. 11-22. *MIDI-to-trigger pulse conversion.*

FIG. 11-23. *Trigger pulse-to-MIDI conversion.*

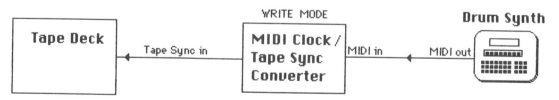

FIG. 11-24. *MIDI-to-tape sync pulse conversion.*

FIG. 11-25. *Tape sync-to-MIDI conversion.*

237

12

Recording Techniques and Production Decisions

BEFORE BEGINNING TO RECORD ONTO TAPE, THERE IS A PLANNING STAGE. Determine ahead of time how to allocate tracks. Because there is a limited number of tracks, there might be a need to submix or "bounce" tracks to accommodate all segments.

PREPRODUCTION PLANNING

Consider the following scenario. A band would like to record a bass, a rhythm guitar, a lead guitar, three sequenced keyboard parts using the same synthesizer, a sax, a lead vocal with two backup vocals, and a drum synth with a kick, snare, hi-hat, three toms, ride and crash cymbals, hand claps, and a tambourine. The itemized list is shown in FIG. 12-1. Item #7 is a clock signal referred to as *tape sync* that synchronizes the keyboard tracks with the drum machine. After this is done, you can record over this track and use it for something else. But right now there are 21 items and only 16 tracks. Some of the items must be combined.

The question is "What sounds in the song don't overlap?" The band decides that crash and hand claps are not played at the same time nor are the ride and tambourine. Therefore, submix the crash and hand claps onto one track and the ride and tambourine onto another track. Now four items are covered using two tracks. The band would like to have the three toms panned with #1 on the left, #2 down the middle, and #3 to the right. That means spreading the three toms over two tracks, but they need a good balance on the submix because it won't be practical to treat the toms individually, especially during a drum fill. Finally they want to combine keyboard #2 and #3. Because these keyboard parts have to be recorded one at a time using the same synthesizer, they can first record onto two individual tracks and then bounce these two tracks onto one track. The original two tracks can then be reused for other items.

1. BASS
2. RHYTHM GUITAR
3. LEAD GUITAR
4. KEYBOARD #1
5. KEYBOARD #2
6. KEYBOARD #3
7. MIDI SYNC (for keyboard sequencing)
8. SAX
9. LEAD VOCAL
10. BACK-UP #1
11. BACK-UP #2
12. KICK
13. SNARE
14. HI-HAT
15. TOM #1
16. TOM #2
17. TOM #3
18. RIDE
19. CRASH
20. HAND-CLAPS
21. TAMBOURINE

FIG. **12-1.** *Instrument and vocal schedule for a recording.*

RECORDING PROCEDURES

Now comes the task of assigning the tracks. There is an important rule: the least significant, least played parts, or those with the least high-frequency content should be placed on an "outer" track (i.e., 1 or 16). The reason is because the outer tracks are closest to the tape edges and any incidental tape damage will more than likely happen on the edge. If a part that is not played very often is placed on an outer track, the odds are more favorable that a tape damage will not be where the main part of the signal is. For example, put the toms and the bass guitar on an outer track.

Phase 1: The first thing to do is to lay down the drum tracks and the clock sync. Then use the sync track to sequence the keyboard tracks #2 and #3. Keyboard #1 can be sequenced at the same time the drum tracks are being recorded. From the previous analysis, use seven tracks for drums, a track for sync, and a track for key #1, as shown in FIG. 12-2.

The outputs from the drum synthesizer drive the LINE IN console inputs. The console DIRECT OUT outputs are used for the kick, snare, and hi-hat. Four submasters are needed for everything else: sub #1 and sub #2 for the three toms, sub #3 for ride and tambourine, and sub #4 for the crash and hand claps. A DIRECT OUT is needed for keyboard #1. The diagram in FIG. 12-3 shows the setup.

239

```
Track #4 - KEYBOARD #1
     #9 - SYNC
    #10 - RIDE CYMBAL / TAMBOURINE
    #11 - CRASH CYMBAL / HAND-CLAPS
    #12 - HI-HAT
    #13 - SNARE
    #14 - KICK
    #15 - TOM #1 / TOM #2
    #16 - TOM #3 / TOM #2
```

FIG. **12-2.** *Initial track sheet schedule (Phase 1).*

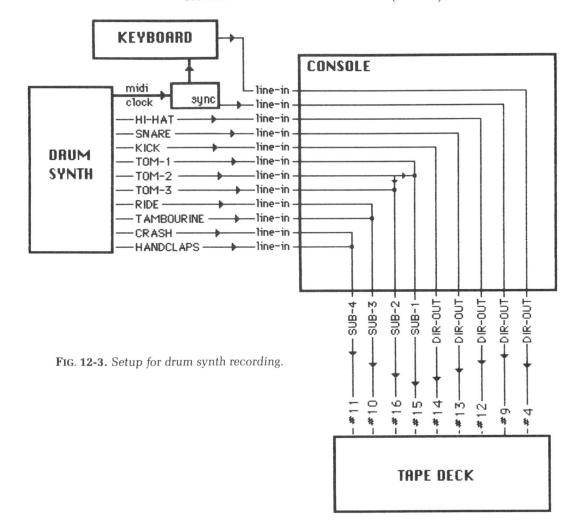

FIG. **12-3.** *Setup for drum synth recording.*

Note that there is a little box that converts the MIDI clock from the drum synth into a tape sync. The MIDI clock is also passed on to the keyboard to run its programmed sequencer.

The channel submaster assignment buttons 1 and 2 should be pushed in for the three tom channels. Tom #1 channel must be panned fully left so all of the signal goes out sub #1 onto track #15. Tom #2 channel must be panned down the middle so that the signal is mutually distributed out subs #1 and #2 going onto both tracks #15 and #16. Tom #3 channel must be panned fully right so that all of this signal exits sub #2 onto track #16 only.

Phase 2: The next step is to clock in the remaining two keyboard parts onto tracks #2 and #3 using sync track #9. Then bounce these tracks as one onto track #5. Later you can record over tracks #2 and #3. The track #9 output signal drives the FSK converter box to generate a MIDI clock for the keyboard again (this occurs twice—once for track #2 and then for track #3). Refer to diagram in FIG. 12-4.

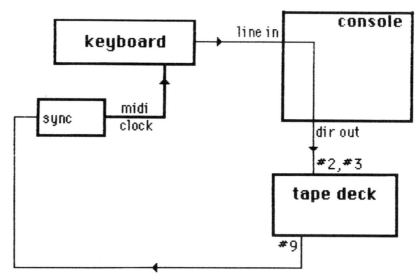

FIG. 12-4. *Recording sequenced keyboard parts.*

After both the keyboard tracks have been recorded, bounce them on track #5. Tape returns #2 and #3 then appear at console inputs #2 and #3. Select the TAPE position for the console input. Now choose a submaster to combine these two tape returns. It is important at this time to get the right blend of these two keyboard sounds because once they are committed to one track, the balance cannot be changed. Therefore, it is important to shut off tape monitors #2 and #3 and listen to #5 only. Refer to the diagram in FIG. 12-5.

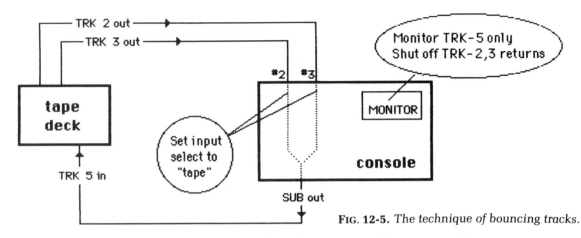

FIG. **12-5.** *The technique of bouncing tracks.*

An important rule to follow when bouncing tracks is to never bounce to an adjacent track! In our example, tracks #1 and #4 are considered to be adjacent tracks. Track #1 is adjacent to track #2 and track #4 is next to track #3. In the recording process, information being recorded on a track next to a track with the same information can couple and superimpose, creating a feedback squeal the same way a mike feeds back in a PA system. FIGURE 12-6 shows an update of the track sheet with tracks #2 and #3 bounced onto track #5.

TRACK	PART
1	
2	KEYBOARD #2
3	KEYBOARD #3
4	KEYBOARD #1
5	KEYS #2/#3
6	
7	
8	

TRACK	PART
9	MIDI SYNC
10	RIDE/TAMB
11	CRASH/CLAPS
12	HI-HAT
13	SNARE
14	KICK
15	TOMS 1/2
16	TOMS 2/3

FIG. **12-6.** *Session track sheet.*

Phase 3: The rhythm section consists of instruments like bass, rhythm guitar, and sax. Drums and percussion are part of the rhythm section, but since drums in this example have already been recorded using a drum synth, it will not be part of this phase. When using "live" drums, it is important that the whole rhythm section records together, plus the musicians need good eye contact to keep a "tight" sound. Attempts to dub in a "live" drummer usually don't work well and should be avoided. Drums or percussion instruments always get recorded first. If this is not possible, use a "click" track to keep the tempo consistent. This way, a live drummer has a sporting chance to lock in on the tracks.

In order to interface the bass with the balanced mike input, use a device known as a *direct box*. Most bass or guitar instruments are unbalanced, requiring a $1/4$-inch phone plug to make the connection. This is incompatible with the three-pin XLR microphone jacks, but the direct box makes this conversion. There are both passive and active direct boxes available. FIGURE 12-7 features two devices made by DOD, the models 260 and 265. Both models have two high-impedance instrument level inputs and one XLR output. The purpose of two inputs is that one of them can be used as a "foldback" or feed-through to relay the signal to another device such as an amplifier (see FIG. 12-8). The DOD 265 has a selectable pad to cut down hot signal sources. A ground lift switch is provided to defeat hum. FIGURE 12-9 features the Countryman Type 85 FET (field-effect transistor) active direct box. The AMP input accepts preamp or line level signals, and the INST input is selectable to accept an instrument or eight-ohm signal sources.

Bear in mind that consoles like the Tascam M-520 console have instrument inputs on channels #1 and # 2, which means an instrument could plug directly into the board. But when using a direct box to address a mike input, try the ground switch if there is an ac hum. When using a direct box, treat it as though you are using a microphone. Select the MIC position on the board. For instance, choose channel input #1 for the bass and connect DIRECT OUT #1 to TRACK IN #1. This completes the patch bay connection linking the console to the deck. On the track sheet, indicate that the bass is being recorded on track #1. The channel fader is used to adjust the signal drive for a nominal 0 dB on the deck's track #1 VU meter. Use the track #1 tape monitor on the console to adjust the volume.

A couple of production decisions must be made here. Listen to track #1 when the bass is not playing. If there is an audible hiss, consider patching in a noise gate. Some instrument transducers are sensitive to light dimmers. Override any dimmers if this is the cause. Static sometimes comes through when for example a guitarist does not make physical contact with the guitar strings.

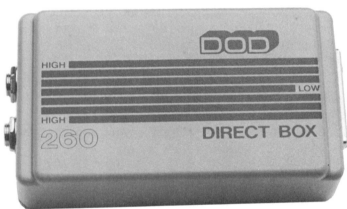

FIG. **12-7.** *DOD 260 and 265 direct boxes.*

FIG. **12-8.** *A typical direct box application.*

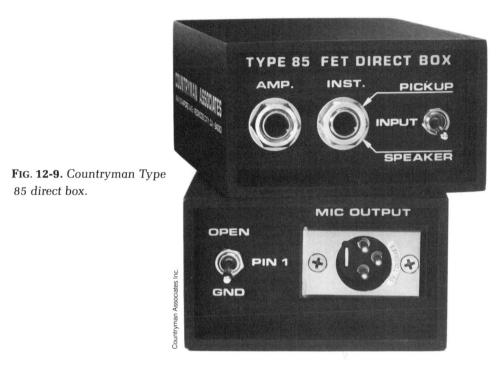

FIG. **12-9.** *Countryman Type 85 direct box.*

Therefore, request that musicians deliberately make manual contact during passages when not playing. Listen carefully and watch the deck's VU meter. Radical change in the dynamics might be a call to patch in a compressor, but be sure that the attack setting does not interfere with important transients in the player's techniques (such as ''string pops'') and don't forget about the trim setting to avoid front-end overload. Refer to FIG. 12-10 for this setup.

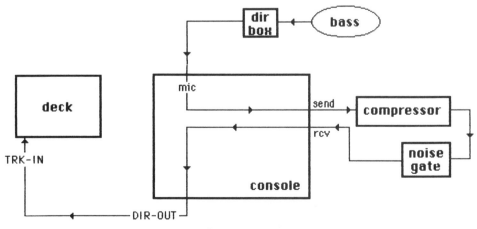

FIG. **12-10.** *System diagram for instrument recording.*

Next, set up the rhythm guitar and sax player. The sax and guitar are acoustical instruments and therefore require microphones. Since a sax has more acoustical power than a hollow-body acoustic guitar, there's a need to isolate the guitar so the sax doesn't bleed (cross talk) into the guitar mike. Therefore, put the guitar player in an isolation booth. Use a condenser mike on the guitar to fully capture any soft passages and use a moving-coil dynamic mike on the sax. Both microphones should be the unidirectional cardioid type. In a similar manner, make patch bay connections routing the signal from the mike, to the console, to the deck. Consider patching in compressors for these miked instruments. Put the rhythm guitar on track #2 (recording over old keyboard #2 track), and put the sax on track #9 (recording over the MIDI sync track). Mark this down on the track sheet.

The condenser mike used on the acoustic guitar should be placed about a foot and a half away from the guitar hole, or far enough away to reject the player's breathing or motion noises. In the control room, listen for a spectral balance of the highs and lows. If the lows are too dominant, consider patching in a high-pass filter or using a shelving-type equalizer. Experiment, positioning the mike to favor the high-pitched strings. If the sound is still a little muddy, try reducing the mids with the parametric equalizer on the board. Place the sax mike about a foot above the bell. Check for input overload on the player's "punchy riffs." Adjust the compressor to avoid VU overload on the tape deck.

Get a monitor mix going on all the recorded tracks. The sax, bass, and guitar player will want to hear themselves considerably louder than the recorded drum and keyboard tracks, so keep the latter levels lower. Now set up a mike to do a "scratch" vocal. This is not a serious vocal take but is for the benefit of the sax and guitar player to get a feel for the song and to get oriented as the song progresses. This scratch vocal must not bleed into the sax and guitar mikes.

As an added and helpful effect, patch in some reverb to stimulate the performers. Use the AUX 1 output to drive a unit and route the returns to the LINE-IN channel inputs. For convenience, send the wet signals on AUX 3 / 4 (prefade position) and monitor these sends. This is a way only to hear the reverb without recording it. The engineer might choose to record the scratch vocal and record over it later or send the vocal signal out on AUX 3 / 4 just for monitoring purposes. This is usually done when a scratch vocal is used for cues or instructions as the musicians are recording. If the sax or guitar player wants to hear reverb on their track, there are two approaches: either turn up the AUX 1 mike channel or use AUX 1 of the tape return channel. The latter is preferred because the reverb can be heard on the playback as well. On the playback, someone might want to do another take. A player or players can try as many times as they want until they are satisfied with their performance.

There are a couple of interesting features about multitrack tape decks that come in handy when dubbing tracks. Consider a situation in which the sax's register sounds flat with respect to the other instruments, and any mouthpiece adjustments do not help the tuning. In the control room, compensate by using the pitch control on the deck, slowing down the tape speed to match the sax register. This way it will sound in tune at the normal playback speed.

Another valuable feature are punch-ins. For example, the bass player did everything just right except for a one-note error. Instead of doing the whole part over, you can "punch-in" that segment or a phrase of notes around that error. Start the tape in the playback mode a few measures in front of the "glitch," and place it in a record/stand-by status. The bass player then plays along with his track and at some point prior to the error, engage the record mode and record over the last take. Then "punch-out" the track to discontinue. Care must be taken when doing this operation. If possible, punch-in and punch-out where there is a rest or absence of playing.

With completion of this phase, move on to dub in the lead guitar, lead vocal, and backup vocals. The track sheet update is shown in Fig. 12-11.

TRACK	PART	TRACK	PART
1	BASS	9	SAX
2	Rhythm GUIT	10	RIDE/TAMB
3	KEYBOARD #3	11	CRASH/CLAPS
4	KEYBOARD #1	12	HI-HAT
5	KEYS #2/#3	13	SNARE
6		14	KICK
7		15	TOMS 1/2
8		16	TOMS 2/3

FIG. 12-11. *Track sheet update.*

Phase 4: Save the most complicated parts for last. Lead instrument and vocal parts require more attention. Lay down the lead guitar track first, recording on track #3 over a previous keyboard line. If a guitar player wants to use an amplifier with some type of distortion, use a unidirectional cardioid mike. Place the mike about 6 to 8 inches from the cabinet grill. Instead of aiming it at the dead center of the speaker, explore off-center or off-axis positions. If the volume is high and the speaker cone is pushing a lot of air, try an off-axis miking position so the wind does not labor the microphone diaphragm. Remember this when miking a kick drum, too. Refer to the setups in FIG. 12-12.

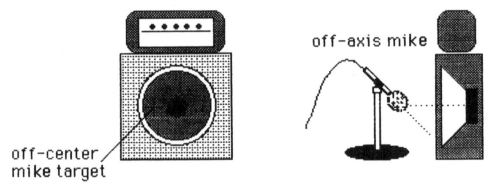

off-axis mike

off-center
mike target

FIG. 12-12. *Microphone placement for amplifier.*

It is just as important to make sure that there is sufficient volume to overcome amplifier hiss and static, especially if a ''fuzz'' or distortion box is being used. To have a good signal-to-noise ratio, the signal should be strong in comparison to the noise when the guitarist is not playing. In this case, a noise gate can be used effectively (see Chapter 6).

When finished recording the lead guitar, next record the lead vocal track and do the backup vocals last. Use a cardioid pattern-type mike for the lead vocal. When positioning the mike, consider an off-axis technique to minimize the vocalist's breath from striking the diaphragm. Most performers are in the habit of ''eating the mike'' from their stage experiences. The singer should stay about 6 to 8 inches from the mike, which should be placed about nose high to avoid the breath path (see FIG. 12-13). Pops that occur when singers say words beginning with p give recording engineers the most problems. Ask the singer to aim slightly away from the mike when singing such words.

Another habit that stage performers develop is body and head motion.

FIG. **12-13.** *Microphone placement for vocals.*

Changes in distance from the mike can result in audible discoloration. The vocalist must learn to adjust to recording conditions. When adjusting levels in the control room, watch the behavior of the vocalists. They sometimes attempt to back away or come closer to hear themselves louder over the music. Correct this by adjusting their monitors so they don't get too close. The point is to make a monitor adjustment to both keep the singer at the proper distance and suit the singer's ears. Patching in a compressor is usually a must in order to accommodate the wide dynamic range of a vocal track. First bypass the compressor, adjust the trim on the board, and use the fader to get a 0 dB reading for nominal vocal parts. Then turn on the compressor and make the proper threshold and compression ratio adjustments for a natural sound without tape saturation overload.

On the session track sheet, indicate that the lead vocal part was recorded on track #6. Tracks #7 and #8 are open for the backup vocals, so the band decides that two vocal parts go on one track and one other harmony part goes on the remaining track. Treat the single harmony part as you did the lead vocal and record it on track #7, and the dual vocal goes on track #8 (this track selection is totally arbitrary). The question is should the dual vocal be done on one mike, or should two mikes be used? Sometimes singers like to blend their own sound, in which case use a single mike with a bipolar pattern. On the other hand, if one singer dominates the other, use two mikes and control their relative levels in the control room. If a bipolar pattern is used, have the singers face each other with the mike in between (recall that a bipolar pickup pattern is optimal with sound coming from opposite directions) as shown in FIG. 12-14. If using two mikes in the same room, separate the singers, and have them face each other using cardioid mikes. Then submix in the control room using a compressor on each mike input (see FIG. 12-15).

249

FIG. **12-14.** *Recording two vocals using a figure eight polar mike pattern.*

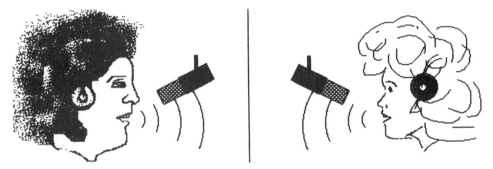

FIG. **12-15.** *Recording two vocalists facing each other.*

When the last of the backup vocals is done, the track sheet should now be completed and look like the one in FIG. 12-16. This completes the multitrack cycle. The next phase is the *mixdown*, in which all of these tracks are blended to achieve stereo and other effects (covered in the next chapter).

The previous sample session used a drum synthesizer. It is important to cover some aspects using a live drummer. In either case, "live" or "synth," always have a count-off to start a song. This is important especially when dubbing tracks so the musician knows when to come in on the song. A live drummer should clap the drum sticks or rap a closed hi-hat for a count-off.

Miking drums is very different from miking other sources. The engineer is dealing with a very fast attack and wide dynamic range. The initial attack is a pulse that is much higher in dB than what follows. When a drummer strikes a tom, you hear the stick making contact with the head followed by the sound of the vibrating head until it dampens out. This vibration is the majority of what you hear. The graph in FIG. 12-17 shows the decay profile of a tom. The peak transient is the stick striking the drum head. Since the peak is significantly higher in dB than the sound of the vibrating head and the channel trim was set to accommodate this maximum peak, the signal would seem weak. The trim should be set to accommodate the body of the sound (as shown in the figure).

TRACK	PART	TRACK	PART
1	BASS	9	SAX
2	Rhythm GUIT	10	RIDE/TAMB
3	Lead GUITAR	11	CRASH/CLAPS
4	KEYBOARD #1	12	HI-HAT
5	KEYS #2/#3	13	SNARE
6	Lead VOCAL	14	KICK
7	Back VOCAL	15	TOMS 1/2
8	Dual VOCAL	16	TOMS 2/3

FIG. 12-16. *Final track sheet.*

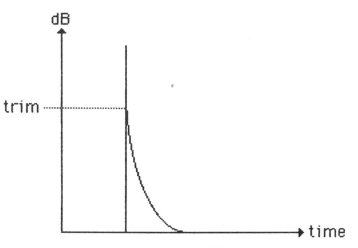

FIG. 12-17. *Dynamic profile of a tom.*

This setting means that the peak transient will break the trim threshold, flashing the LED overload indicator, however this is acceptable because it is so transient that no distortion is audible. A good way to achieve this trim setting is to first adjust the channel fader to the halfway position. Then adjust the trim for a normal VU reading of about 0 dB on the deck.

251

Certain considerations should be made when miking double-headed drums such as a snare (so are toms if the bottom head is not removed). A single mike can benefit from the tones that emanate from both heads. In the case of the snare, sound from both the top and bottom makes up the total sound. Therefore, rather than placing the mike over the top head only, place it outside the drum's perimeter where the snare rattle can be picked up. The top-to-bottom ratio depends on where you place the mike. Experimentation is helpful in getting the right balance (see FIG. 12-18). Miking double-sided toms is given the same consideration, although the top head should be favored to capture the percussiveness of the impact. If the bottom head is removed, the miking from the bottom will give a similar benefit.

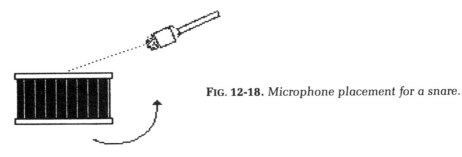

FIG. 12-18. *Microphone placement for a snare.*

Today's "kick" or bass drums only have a blanket thrown inside to mellow the sound yet have the percussive attack of the beater. The beater striking the head should sound somewhat like a basketball bouncing off a wooden gymnasium court. The mike should be placed inside as shown in FIG. 12-19. Aim the mike a little off-axis to protect the mike diaphragm from the kick air blast, or fold the blanket in front of the mike to act as a barrier.

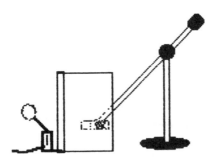

FIG. 12-19. *Microphone placement for a "kick" (bass) drum.*

Probably the most difficult thing about recording drums is the fact that it is a multi-mike situation. All the microphones are colocated, meaning that it is difficult to achieve isolation of each piece, so there is a crosstalk everywhere.

When the snare is played, all the tom mikes pick it up, too. Even though the snare mike picks up most of it, the bleed from other mikes will not be in phase with snare signal. Because the other mikes are farther away, these signals lag behind the main snare signal, causing phase cancelling. A couple of techniques are employed to offset this. One is by using noise gates on the snare, kick, and toms (but never on cymbals) because a noise gate can help isolate the signal by rejecting the more distant sounds. Do not use a noise gate on a tom if you are trying to capture an overhead cymbal too. Cymbals have a long decay and make the noise gate chatter when passing through its threshold.

Another approach to discourage phase cancellation is to use the phase-reversal switches on the console. Experiment with various combinations of NORMAL to REVERSE positions. This is strictly trial-and-error. It can improve the presence of a piece, but in general, the rule is to use the least number of mikes as possible. For example, use one mike to cover two toms instead of one for each tom. Also, don't forget to exercise the 3:1 principle.

13

Mixdown

THE MULTITRACK RECORDING PHASE IN THE PRODUCTION CYCLE HAS BEEN completed. The final phase is the stereo mixdown. This is the stage when the master tape is produced and can finally be used for record, cassette, CD reproductions, etc. Typically, the master tape is a $^1/_4$-inch tape, half-track stereo recording at 15 ips with noise reduction of some sort. Two machines are required to do this. The multitrack deck is in the playback mode with its outputs routed through the console. All of these signals are mixed on a pair of buses and recorded on the two-track mastering deck.

SETUP

The first operation is to configure the console for the mixdown. The sample session demonstrated a 16-track recording, therefore set console channels 1 to 16 to the TAPE position (FIG. 13-1). This setting routes all 16 tape returns to each channel. No patching is required because all of the tape returns are already wired as part of the system. However, patching is required for the effects and any channel patching. Don't forget the connection from the console to the mastering deck.

On the Tascam M-520 board, select a submaster pair as a stereo pair to feed the mastering deck's left and right inputs. For purposes of discussion, select submasters #1 and #2 by depressing these two buttons for each channel. The channel ON button must also be pushed in for each channel (FIG. 13-2). On the patch bay, connect SUB 1 OUT to the 2-TRACK LEFT input and SUB 2 OUT to the 2-TRACK RIGHT input. Monitor the two-track tape returns by depressing the 2 TRK A button in the monitoring section on the board (FIG. 13-3). The next thing to do is label all the tracks on the console's labeling strip using a grease pencil or china marker. The labeling from 1 to 16 should be consistent with the track sheet.

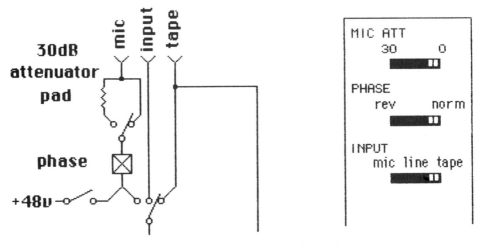

FIG. 13-1. TAPE *select position for channels 1 to 16.*

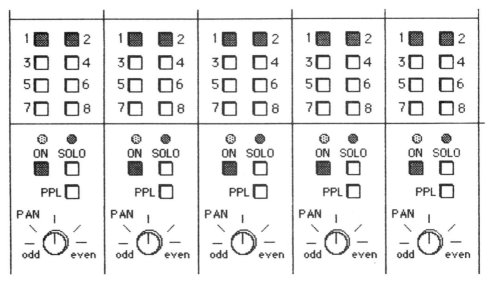

FIG. 13-2. *Stereo sub assignments for tape and effect returns.*

Now is the time to choose which effects or channel patch devices will be necessary. Bear in mind that there are four auxiliary sends and four channels (17 thru 20) for effect returns. Input channels #17, #18, #19, and #20 should be set in the LINE position rather than the TAPE position (at which the first sixteen channels should be set). Route these four effect return channels onto SUB 1 and SUB 2 also. The principle here is that the wet signals merge with the dry signals.

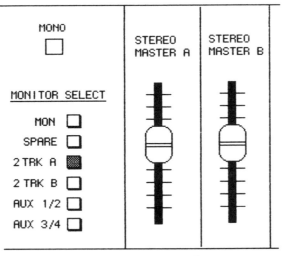

FIG. 13-3. *2TRK A monitor select.*

Most effect devices have stereo outputs. Using four signal processors would imply a total of eight wet signal returns, which is of course a problem with only four channels reserved for effect returns. This can be overcome by using a line mixer. The block diagram in FIG. 13-4 should be helpful in explaining this. All of the effect outputs are merged as a left and right total, routed into channel inputs #17 and #18, and placed on SUB 1 and SUB 2. This requires 14 patch bay connections.

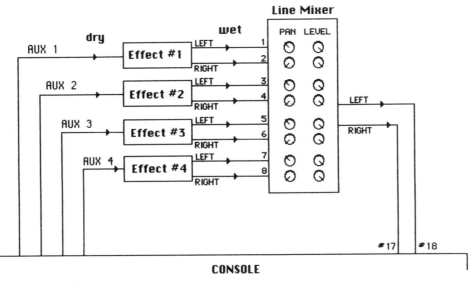

FIG. 13-4. *Line mixer used to submix stereo effects returns.*

Suppose you want to add a fifth effect. There are two ways to handle it. One method is to drive effect #5 with a vacant submaster and (arbitrarily) choose sub 8. Then depress #8 assignment buttons on those channels you want this effect to apply. The stereo outputs of effect #5 can now be routed to channels #19 and #20 for effect returns (FIG. 13-5). Once again, the wet signals coming through channels #19 and #20 will be placed on the mix buses sub 1 and sub 2. There is a limitation that must be pointed out here. If more than one channel is going to use effect #5, then the amount of drive per channel is dependent on the fader position of those channels as opposed to an AUX send control that drives an effect independently. If you only want to use effect #5 for one channel, then the sub 8 fader can act as an auxiliary send. Sub 8 was used as an example, but bear in mind that an even-numbered sub only works with a signal panned right or "down the middle." If the channel signal is panned left, you would need to use an odd-numbered sub.

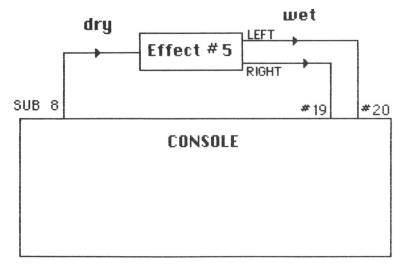

FIG. 13-5. *Submaster used as an effect send.*

Another way is to channel patch an effect. Up to now, effects were considered as being wet signal devices, implying that channel patching an effect in the direct signal path would sacrifice the dry signal. Most effects have a mix control that allows the dry signal to pass, too. Thus far in sample applications, only the wet signal was passed. The mix control on the effect changes the ratio of dry to wet. The output can be made all wet, all dry, or somewhere in between. Note in FIG. 13-6 that the forward signal is dry and the return is a mixture of dry and wet.

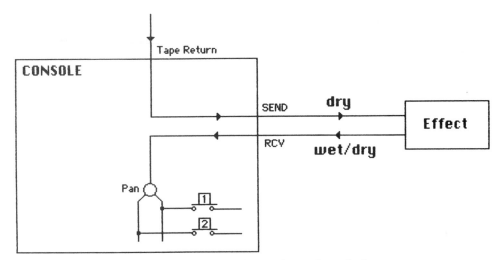

FIG. **13-6.** *An effect used as a channel patch device.*

Besides patching in effects, some dry signal devices like compressors, gates, or equalizers can legitimately be channel patched. If the material has some explosive dynamics, you might consider putting a stereo compressor in the sub buses, or just compress those tracks that cause the dynamic problem. FIGURE 13-7 shows a compressor application in the stereo subs #1 and #2. Be conservative when using compression in the stereo situation. Use just enough to capture some potential overload. If only a couple of tracks do most of the overloading, just channel patch compressors singly in those tracks.

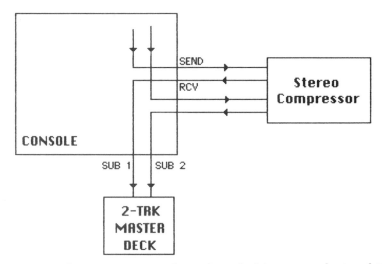

FIG. **13-7.** *Stereo compressor channel patched in stereo subs 1 and 2.*

When all of the patching is completed, start working on the mixdown. Start by positioning the sub 1 and sub 2 faders half way. Ignore the effects for now. Solo each track and experiment with equalizer changes if the sound needs enhancing. If dbx Type 1 noise reduction is being used, consider channel patching a high-pass filter or using a shelving-type equalizer to roll off the lows in the bass and kick drum tracks. When using dbx, there is a tendency for the lows to be boosted, making the bass sound "flabby."

PREMIX

Now get a balance going without applying the effects. Start mixing the drums first and then bring in the bass. Then bring in the rhythm guitar and keyboard parts and experiment with panning. Use the session track sheet from the previous lesson as an example (FIG. 13-8). Pan tom tracks #15 to the right and #16 to the left. Place the hi-hat on the right. Place the ride/tamb partially left and the crash/claps partially right. Keep the kick and snare down the middle. Put the rhythm guitar partially left and the key #2/#3 partially right. Put the sax on the right. Get a balance going with these instruments before working on the lead parts. At this point, the faders should be about halfway because you will need the headroom to bring out the lead parts. When you get a balance, check the VU meters for mix buses sub 1 and sub 2. Pull back on sub faders if meter deflections are in the red. Adjust control-room volume if you need more monitoring without disturbing the VU levels. Now bring in the lead instruments and all vocals and get an overall balance. Take notes on where fader or equalizer adjustments are going to be made in various places. Do all this without using effects, because getting a good dry sound will eliminate a lot of confusion when applying effects.

FIG. 13-8. *Session track sheet.*

TRACK	PART
1	BASS
2	Rhythm GUIT
3	Lead GUITAR
4	KEYBOARD #1
5	KEYS #2/#3
6	Lead VOCAL
7	Back VOCAL
8	Dual VOCAL

TRACK	PART
9	SAX
10	RIDE/TAMB
11	CRASH/CLAPS
12	HI-HAT
13	SNARE
14	KICK
15	TOMS 1/2
16	TOMS 2/3

Now decide what effects are to be used. Perhaps use gated reverb for the snare, toms, and possibly the kick drum for a contemporary sound. You could use two reverbs—one for a small room setting and the other for a larger room setting. What about echo, chorusing, and some exciter, particularly for the backup vocals or even the lead vocal, too? FIGURE 13-9 shows the effects list.

```
EFFECT #1 - gated reverb
EFFECT #2 - small room reverb
EFFECT #3 - large room reverb          FIG. 13-9. Effects schedule.
EFFECT #4 - echo (digital delay)
EFFECT #5 - chorousing
EFFECT #6 - exciters 1 and 2
```

Assign the first four effects to the four auxiliary sends. Using the line mixer, all of the effect returns should come in on channels #17 and #18 LINE inputs. If, for example, you wanted chorusing on the rhythm guitar only, channel patch it. Drive the exciter channels #1 and #2 with sub 5 and sub 6, and have the returns come in channels #19 and #20 LINE. If you intend to use the exciter on the lead vocal, backup vocal, and dual vocal tracks, then depress sub buttons #5 and #6 for each channel. Position sub 5 and sub 6 faders to control the amount of drive to the exciter. Position effect return faders on channels #17, #18, #19, and #20. Adjust the chorus effect MIX dial for a dry/wet ratio. Don't forget that when using a sub as a send for a track that is panned left, choose an odd-numbered sub to get a drive signal, and vice versa because odd-number subs respond to pan left and even ones respond to pan right.

MIXING METHODS

Now when this is all accomplished, it's just a matter of making parameter adjustments on the effect devices for the desired sound. There is one interface consideration that is important. Try to drive the effect units hard and keep return gain reduced to optimize the best signal-to-noise ratio. An effect might sound hissy if the return level is high with a small send signal. Be careful not to overload the effect input and getting a distorted wet return.

After getting this far, it's time to schedule in the effects by turning up the auxiliary sends on the channels. For example, if you want gated and small-room reverb on the snare and toms, turn up AUX 1 and AUX 2 respectively on channels #13, #15, and #16. If you only want gated reverb on the kick drum, then turn up AUX 1 just on channel #14. If you want large-room reverb and exciter on all the vocal tracks, then turn up AUX 3, SUB 5 and SUB 6. Effects can be selected as PRE or

POST fader, meaning that the signal is taken before or after the fader control. In most cases, POST is desired because any fader changes keep the dry-to-wet ratio proportional. In the PRE setting, fader changes do not influence the effect level, which means that as you reduce the fader level, the effect will stay the same and sound louder with respect to the dry signal.

When everything is reasonably under control, make a few takes on the master deck. Put the deck in the REPRO mode and monitor the actual playback of the deck so you know what you are really getting. Prior to this, only the stereo signals applied to the deck input have been monitored. Now, you can hear the playback while the recording is in progress. Both tape decks are in motion. While the master deck is recording, you can monitor the signals from the decoded output of the noise reduction circuits.

Now use an external pair of VU meters to monitor the decoded output and ignore the console or master deck VU meters (the master deck registers the encoded signals). FIGURE 13-10 shows the stereo signals from the console subs applied to the mastering deck. Note that the stereo signals are being monitored at the decode outputs. Sometimes in the encode-decode process, the frequency response is disturbed. With dbx, the low end tends to rise and the bass and kick drum sound louder. That is why patching in a high-pass filter or shelving equalizer to roll off the lows was recommended earlier.

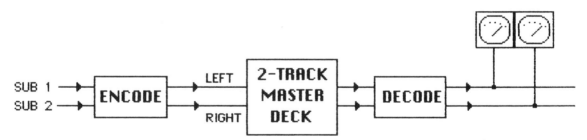

FIG. 13-10. *Post-decode VU monitoring of stereo signals.*

Subfaders will have to be readjusted to produce a nominal 0 dB level on the decode VU meters. The goal is to avoid an overload that penetrates deeply into the red. Overloads particularly threaten disc lathe cuts for record pressings. The higher the level, the wider the groove that is cut into the acetate or vinyl. A disc cutter gauges the cut based on the tape reference level. An unexpected overload can overdeviate the cutting lathe beyond its allowable limits. Cassette duplications and CDs are more forgiving. CDs (compact discs) can handle a wide dynamic range before overloading and still have excellent signal-to-noise ratio.

There are generally two ways a song ends—either abruptly or by a fade-out. The submix faders have to be uniformly reduced for a successful fade-out. Fade-outs should be rehearsed a few times to get a feel for when and how long the fade will begin and last. The real time indicator is useful for a cue. When a take is finally successful, you must "leader" the start and end of the song. Put the master deck in the EDIT mode to unlock the reels. Rotate the reels manually back and forth with your eye on the playback head and find the space on the tape between the end of the count-off and the beginning of the song. Using a white grease pencil, mark where that place on the tape is. Place the tape in the splicing block and cut it with a razor blade. Spool off about five feet of white paper leader and splice it in with adhesive editing tape. The block provides a choice of either a straight or angled cut (FIG. 13-11). The idea behind the angled cut is that the splice will not pass across the deck's head all at once; any noise introduced by the cut is distributed over a time period. Bear in mind that at 15 ips, one inch of tape displaces in $1/15$th of a second. If an angle splice is about a $1/4$ inch wide, this time period is only $1/60$th of a second. A straight cut obviously has no measurable time period because the whole cut crosses the head at the same time. So if a straight cut doesn't cause any audible problems, use it.

Editing Block

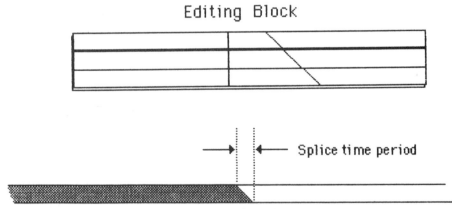

FIG. 13-11. *Editing block.*

A leader is required at the end of the song as well. Be careful not to chop out the reverb decay at the end of the song. Exactly where the reverb decay ends might be hard to detect by just rocking the reels, so play out the decay first to be sure.

POSTMIX

When all of the songs are mixed and leadered, the final thing to do is apply the reference tones. Three frequencies should be used to represent low, mid, and

Strata Recording Studios

1215 MacDade Blvd.
Folsom, PA 19033
(215) 237-8134

Multitrack Productions

Date _____

Client _____

Address _____

City _____ State ____ Zip _____

Phone # ( ) ____ - _____

Engineer _____ Producer _____

Project: _____

Leader	Title	Time
1	TEST TONES "0"dB – 100,1K,10K	
2	Song A	
3	Song B	

■ **Stereo Master**
☐ **Master Copy**

Stereo Format
■ 1/2-Track
☐ 1/4-track

Tape Storage
■ Tails Out
☐ Heads Out

Speed
☐ 30 ips
■ 15 ips
☐ 7-1/2 ips
☐ 3-3/4 ips

Noise Reduction
■ dBx Type 1
☐ Dolby A
☐ Other _____
☐ None

Test Tones
■ 100Hz
■ 1KHz
■ 10KHz

"0"dB Reference
■ NAB Standard – 250nw/m²
☐ EIA Standard – 320nw/m²
☐ Other _____

Output levels
☐ Pre-NR decode
■ Post-NR decode

FIG. 13-12. *Sample master tape box label.*

263

high references. These calibration tones represent the 0 dB reference. Even though standard calibrations are used, it will give another potential user a point of reference and a confidence check. The Tascam M-520 console provides 40 Hz, 1 kHz, and 10 kHz tones. About 15 seconds of each of these tones should be placed at the beginning of the tape at 0 dB playback levels. A leader should mark the beginning of the first tone, followed by the first song or program. This could be done before or after the mixdown. The oscillator output is fed into a channel LINE input and on the mix buses feeding the mastering deck.

The final steps are storing the tape tails out and labeling the reel and the box. Labeling should include the order of the leadered material by title, the tape speed and format, the reference tones used, the reference fluxivity (nano-webers/meter), and the noise reduction type. FIGURE 13-12 shows a sample box label. This information will eliminate a lot of confusion in the hands of the next user, be it a record pressing, CD, or cassette duplication house. The client (recording artists) should make a copy of the master if they intend to make duplications of some sort, because most mass-duplication outfits ask for a master copy, and will not be responsible for damage to a tape.

APPENDIX
Mathematics Review

THROUGHOUT THE CHAPTERS, THE READER IS BOMBARDED WITH MANY mathematical expressions. This appendix, therefore, covers some of the algebra, vector math, and logarithms necessary to make sense of the principles and theories addressed.

Algebra is the craft of manipulating unknown *variables* (letters used as a substitute for numbers) for the purpose of deriving expressions and definitions for the variables. The major foundation behind this is the *justice scale* principle. In order to keep the scale in equilibrium, whatever is done on one side must be executed on the opposite side to maintain the balance. For example:

$$iR = V$$

Adjacent letters mean multiplication (iR is i times R). If the left side is divided by R, then to be consistent, the right side must be divided by R.

$$\frac{iR}{R} = \frac{V}{R}$$

The Rs cancel on the left side, leaving just i.

$$i = \frac{V}{R}$$

As another example, solve for b in:

$$ax + bx = y$$

First subtract ax from both sides:

$$ax + bx - ax = y - ax$$

On the left side, since $-ax$ plus ax is zero, then only bx remains on the left side.

$$bx = y - ax$$

Now divide both sides by x to isolate b.

$$\frac{bx}{x} = \frac{y - ax}{x}$$

$$b = \frac{y}{x} - a$$

The variable b has been solved in terms of y, x, a. Given real numbers for y, x, and a would determine a real number value b.

Scientific notation is a way of conveniently expressing either very large or very small numbers in powers of 10. For example, 5,000,000,000 is 5×10^9 in scientific notation. A number like 0.0000025 is expressed as 2.5×10^{-6} in scientific notation. In the first case, 10^9 means multiply the whole number 5 by 1,000,000,000—or simply add nine zeros. In the second case, 10^{-6} means to divide the number 2.5 by 1,000,000—or simply move the decimal point over to the left six places. The rule for *multiplying* two numbers in scientific notation is to multiply the numbers and add the powers. For example:

$$(5 \times 10^9)\,(2.5 \times 10^{-6})$$
$$= 12.5 \times 10^{(9-6)}$$
$$= 12.5 \times 10^3$$

The rule for *dividing* two numbers in scientific notation is to divide the numbers and subtract the exponents. For example,

$$\frac{(15 \times 10^8)}{(5 \times 10^6)} = 3 \times 10^2 = 300$$

The rule for adding or subtracting two numbers in scientific notation is to reference them both to a common power of 10 and then add or subtract the numbers. For example,

$$(15 \times 10^8) + (5 \times 10^6)$$
$$= (1500 \times 10^6) + (5 \times 10^6)$$
$$= 1505 \times 10^6$$

Vector math employs trigonometry. FIGURE A-1 is a review of the cosine, sine, and tangent angle functions. In a coordinate system, a vector is described

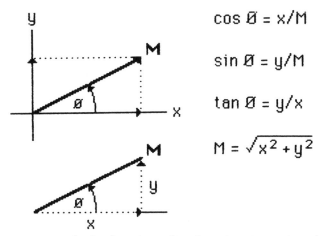

FIG. A-1. *Vector math: the functions of cosine, sine, tangent, and magnitude.*

as a magnitude M and an angle θ. The magnitude is an absolute value that can be expressed in terms of vertical and horizontal components y and x respectively. The sum M of these components is:

$$M = \sqrt{x^2 + y^2}$$

If components x and y were in the same direction, the sum would simply be $M = x + y$ as shown in FIG. A-2. If $x = 3$ and $y = 4$, then $M = 7$. But as vertical and horizontal components:

$$M = \sqrt{(3)\,(3) + (4)\,(4)}$$
$$= \sqrt{9 + 16}$$
$$= \sqrt{25}$$
$$= 5$$

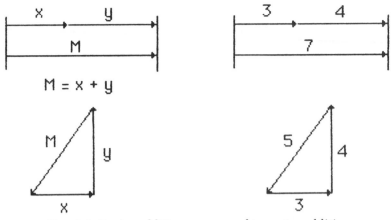

FIG. A-2. *Scalar addition as opposed to vector addition.*

Since tan(θ) = y/x, then θ = arctan (y/x). For the example, θ = arctan(4/3), so θ = arctan(1.33). Either using trig tables or a scientific calculator, calculate θ as 52.43 degrees. The arctan is also called the inverse tangent (tan^{-1}). The vector is now defined in the form **M**$\{\theta\}$ as **5**$\{52.43\}$. The rule for *multiplying* two vectors is to multiply the magnitudes and add the angles:

$$\mathbf{M_1}\{\theta_1\}\ \mathbf{M_2}\{\theta_2\}\ =\ \mathbf{M_1 M_2}\{\theta_1 + \theta_2\}$$

For example:

$$\mathbf{6}\{24\}\mathbf{7}\{12\}\ =\ \mathbf{42}\{36\}$$

The rule for *dividing* vectors is to divide the magnitudes and subtract the denominator angle from the numerator angle.

$$\frac{\mathbf{M_1}\{\theta_1\}}{\mathbf{M_2}\{\theta_2\}}\ =\ \frac{\mathbf{M_1}}{\mathbf{M_2}}\{\theta_1 - \theta_2\}$$

for example:

$$\frac{\mathbf{18}\{52\}}{\mathbf{6}\{12\}}\ =\ \mathbf{3}\{40\}$$

Given the magnitude and angle, the x and y components can be calculated where x = Mcos(θ) and y = Msin(θ). For example, the components for **20**$\{60\}$ are see (FIG. A-3):

$$x\ =\ 20\cos(60)\ =\ 20(0.5)\ =\ 10$$
$$y\ =\ 20\sin(60)\ =\ 20(0.866)\ =\ 17.32$$

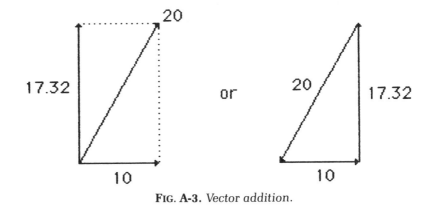

FIG. **A-3.** *Vector addition.*

The rule for adding or subtracting two vectors is to first convert them into their respective x and y components and then add both x components and both y components. The magnitude of the new vector is the square root formula, and the angle is the $\tan^{-1}$ of the y/x ratio. For example:

$$\mathbf{V} = 7\{30\} + 4\{60\}$$

$$X_1 = 7\cos(30) = 7(0.866) = 6$$
$$X_2 = 4\cos(60) = 4(0.5) = 2$$
$$\mathbf{X} = X_1 + X_2 = 8$$
$$Y_1 = 7\sin(30) = 7(0.5) = 3.5$$
$$Y_2 = 4\sin(60) = 4(0.866) = 3.46$$
$$\mathbf{Y} = Y_1 + Y_2 = 6.96$$

$$\mathbf{V} = \sqrt{\mathbf{X}^2 + \mathbf{Y}^2}$$
$$= \sqrt{8^2 + 6.96^2}$$
$$= 10.6$$

The angle is $\theta = \tan^{-1}(6.96/8) = 41$ degrees

Therefore (see FIG. A-4):

$$\mathbf{V} = 7\{30\} + 4\{60\} = \mathbf{10.6\{41\}}$$

In electronics, complex impedances are vectors where the x component is the *real* part and the y component is the *imaginary* part. Resistors are treated as real values (are expressed on the positive x-axis), and capacitive (X_C) and inductive (X_L) impedances lie on the imaginary y-axis. The capacitive values are

FIG. A-4. *Example of vector addition.*

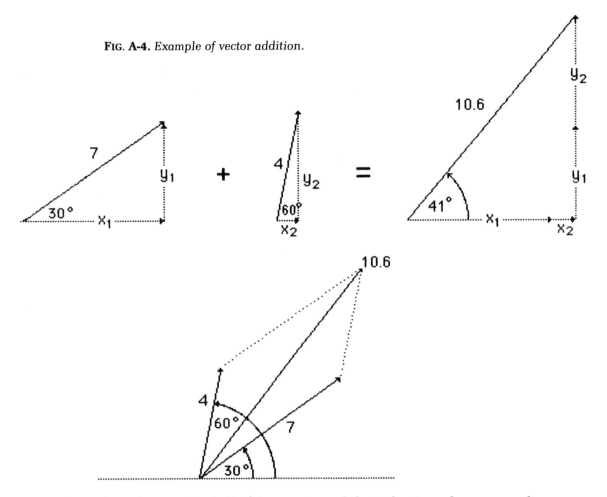

located on the negative half of the y-axis, and the inductive values are on the positive half. Refer to FIG. A-5. Recalling that the capacitor impedance X_C is a function of frequency, calculate X_C for purposes of demonstration at 8000 Hz for the illustration in FIG. A-6.

$$X_C = 1/2\pi fC$$
$$= 1/(2)(3.14159)(8000)(0.01 \times 10^{-6})$$
$$= 1990 \; \Omega$$

Because X_C lies on the negative imaginary axis, it is written as $-j1900$. Then $X_{R/C} = R - jX_C = 3000 - j1990$. The magnitude of $X_{R/C}$ is:

$$|X_{R/C}| = \sqrt{3000^2 + 1990^2} = 3600 \; \Omega$$

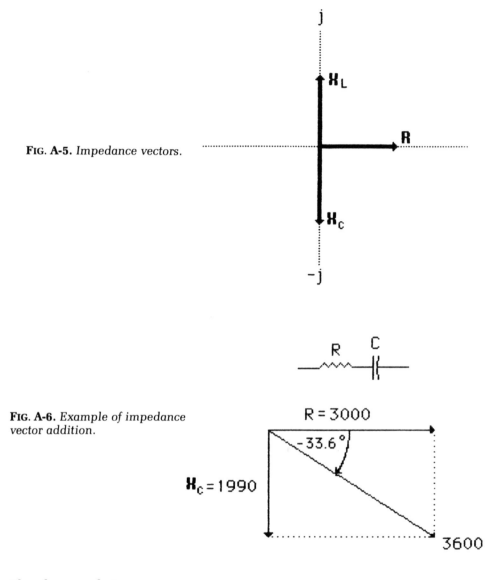

FIG. A-5. *Impedance vectors.*

FIG. A-6. *Example of impedance vector addition.*

The phase angle is:

$$\theta = \tan^{-1}(-1990/3000)$$
$$= \tan^{-1}(-0.663)$$
$$= -33.6 \text{ degrees}$$

Then in vector or phasor form:

$$X_{R/C} = 3600\{-33.6\}$$

271

Voltages and currents in analysis are considered to be sinusoidal waveforms expressed as either sine or cosine functions such as:

$$v(t) = V\sin(\omega t + \theta) \text{ or } i(t) = I\sin(\omega t + \theta)$$

They can be treated as vectors in which V is the voltage magnitude and θ is the phase angle, expressed as $\mathbf{V}\{\theta\}$, and current (I) is the current magnitude with some phase angle θ, expressed as $\mathbf{I}\{\theta\}$.

Logarithms are exponents using number 10 as a base. The expression:

$$\log (a) = x$$

is the same as saying:

$$10^x = a$$

As an example:

$$\log (100) = 2$$

because:

$$10^2 = 100$$

As another example:

$$\log (1000) = 3$$

then:

$$10^3 = 1000$$

If $10^2 = 100$ and $10^3 = 1000$, then what is the log of 500? The answer to this is not as obvious. Using logarithm lookup tables or a scientific calculator:

$$\log (500) = 2.69$$

where:

$$10^{2.69} = 500$$

Note that because 500 falls between 100 and a 1000, the exponent 2.69 falls between 2 and 3.

Glossary

absorption coefficient—Describes the damping property of materials as the ratio of absorbed sound energy over the incident sound (S_a/S_i).

acoustics—The science of sound.

acoustic suspension—A sealed, airtight speaker enclosure.

A/D converter—Analog-to-digital converter. Typically used in sampling where the converter takes a signal's amplitude and converts it to a binary number.

addressable—Describes any device that can receive serial or parallel data transmissions.

alias frequency—A parasitic frequency generated as a consequence of sampling a frequency greater than one-half the sampling-rate frequency. The alias frequency is the difference over one-half the sampling rate.

alternating current—Current that reverses polarity and alternates its direction in a circuit path.

ambience—Natural room acoustics.

amperes—Abbreviation A. Units for current.

amplifier—A device that boosts signal voltage or current levels.

amplifier sensitivity—The maximum input level before clipping.

amplitude—The signal voltage level.

analog—Refers to signals with an infinite series of discrete amplitudes.

AND gate—Digital logic device in which all inputs must be high to yield a high.

anechoic chamber—A special test chamber with a surface of very dense sound-absorption material to prevent reflections.

anode—The positive pole on a diode.

attack—A control on signal processors to regulate the rise time of a signal.

attenuation—The amount of gain reduction of a signal expressed in dB.

audio—Pertaining to sound or the frequencies of the human hearing range.

audio analyzer—Test gear that registers the acoustic energy level for discrete frequency bands.

autolocate—A feature on tape transports that automatically searches for a counter position.

auxiliary—A send output on a mixing console used for connection to effects devices.

azimuth—A tape head alignment position that makes the track segments on the head parallel to the tape motion.

baffle—A partition or surface for speaker mounting that prevents forward sound pressure from dispersing to the rear.

balanced—An electronic system using two conductors for signal flow and a separate shield for grounding.

bandpass filter—A filter that rejects low and high frequencies but passes middle frequencies.

bandstop filter—A filter that passes low and high frequencies but rejects middle frequencies.

bandwidth—A frequency range.

base—The transistor terminal that receives the signal to be amplified.

bass reflex—A loudspeaker enclosure that is not sealed, allowing air movement through a port on the cabinet face (*baffle*).

bass trap—A hollow structure with a flexible surface used to absorb acoustical low-frequency content.

BETA—A Sony VCR tape format.

biamping—Using two independent amplifiers to drive a two-way speaker system in which each amplifier is dedicated to cover only the frequency range of the speaker component it is driving.

bias—The recording signal (greater than 150 kHz) used in analog tape machines to be modulated by the incoming audio signal.

bidirectional—A microphone polar pattern that has a figure eight profile in which sound reception is directional along the "0" and "180" degree axis.

binary—A numbering system using just 1s and 0s (a base 2 system).

biphase—Describes a binary serial data transmission format in which 1s and 0s are determined by positive or negative transitions.

biphase mark—A serial data transmission used for SMPTE time code in which a 1 is recognized if a transition occurs in a bit cell whether it is positive- or negative-going.

bit—A binary 1 or 0.

bit cell—A time frame defined by the maximum pulse width for a data rate.

bit resolution—The number of bits used in sampling for quantitative assignment. Sixteen-bit resolution means a numbering range up to 2^{16} or 65,536 counts.

bleed—Crosstalk or spillover of sound from one mike to another.

Bode plot—Amplitude (dB) versus frequency response curves on semilog graphs in which the frequency axis is logarithmic.

bounce—A recording technique in which several tracks are submixed onto another track.

bus—Any signal path that is common to a multiple of inputs or outputs.

byte—A binary word, which is made up of a number of bits.

capacitor—A passive electrical circuit element composed of spaced metallic surfaces that hold and release a charge.

capstan—A rotating shaft that acts as the main tape drive on a transport by pinching the tape between itself and the pinch roller.

cardioid—A unidirectional microphone polar pattern that is heart-shaped. Pickup sensitivity is highest for sound approaching the front and is lowest for sound approaching from the rear.

carrier—A radio frequency (RF) transmission that can be modulated to carry information.

cathode—The end of the diode that is the exit for current.

CD—Compact disc.

channel patch—The process of inserting a signal processor in the direct signal path.

charge—The state of a device that contains current particles (electrons).

chase-lock—The initial activity that takes place when interlocking two tape decks using a synchronizer in which the slave deck chases the master until their time codes match.

choke—Another term given to an inductor when its function is to initially block or "choke" current when a voltage change-up is applied.

chorusing—An effect that creates the illusion of listening to multiple identical sources.

clip—Distortion where a sinusoidal signal's positive and negative peaks flatten as the result of overdriving a device's input.

clock—The time base signal that sequences digital devices.

coaxial—A term typically used to describe an unbalanced cable with a shield and one center conductor.

collector—The transistor terminal in the amplifying path that receives current (if an npn) or from which current exits (if a pnp).

colocation—In the same vicinity.

coloration—A distortion in the acoustical frequency response of a listening environment that impairs the spectral purity.

comb-filter effect—The frequency response profile with dips and peaks across the band.

compander—The dual function of compression and expansion associated with noise reduction devices.

comparator—An active circuit component that compares the incoming signal against a reference voltage, yielding a high or low voltage on the output based on whether or not the input signal is above or below the reference.

compression ratio—The change of input over change in output of a compressor.

compressor—A signal processor that controls the dynamics (limits the amplitude) of a signal by reducing it when the incoming signal exceeds the threshold assignment.

condenser—Another word for capacitor that also describes a microphone with a capacitor-type transducer.

console—A recording mixing board with input channels, subgroups, and a monitoring section.

control room—The portion of a studio that contains the console, tape decks, and signal-processing equipment.

convoluted—A term to describe air foam that has peaks and valleys for sound diffusion.

CRCC—Cyclic redundancy check code.

crossfade—Fader operation in which one fader increases level (fade-in) while another fader reduces it (fade-out).

crossover network—A frequency-dividing network that separates the incoming signal into several audio bands and distributes the signals to each amplifier or speaker cone.

crosstalk—Spillover or bleed from one channel into another.

cue—A tape counter position, or on consoles, a monitor send.

current—Electron flow in a circuit expressed in amperes.

cutoff—On filters, the frequency at which the output has fallen 3 dB.

cycle—The time period of a repetitive waveform.

D/A converter—Digital-to-analog converter. Receives binary data and converts it to an analog signal.

DASH—Digital *audio* stationary *head.* A digital recording tape format with selectable sampling rates (48 kHz, 44.056 kHz, and 44.1 kHz), 16-bit resolution, and four tracks per channel.

DAT—Digital *audio* tape. A format for rotary head systems.

dB—An abbreviation for *decibel,* used to represent logarithmic power ratios where dB = 10 log (P_2/P_1).

dBm—An absolute power level (for +4 dBm systems) based on a 1-milliwatt (0.001 W) reference where dBm = 10 log (P/0.001).

dBV—An absolute power level (for −10 dBV systems) based on a 1-volt reference where dBV = 20 log(V/1).

dead room—A room that has no perceptible reverberation characteristics or hard reflective surfaces.

decay—The time duration for a signal to diminish to an undetectable level.

decibel—A logarithmic power ratio that represents acoustical power (sound pressure) levels (SPL) or electrical levels (watts) in the form 10 log (P_2/P_1).

decode—The electronic process of converting a signal or data transmission back to its original form or format.

de-esser—A high-frequency limiter that softens harsh vocal "ess" sounds.

degaussing—The process of demagnetizing a tape head.

diaphragm—The transducer element in a microphone that converts mechanical vibrations into an electrical signal.

diffuser—An irregular surface area for the purpose of diffusing sound to break up standing waves and echoes.

DIN connector—Stands for *Deutsche Industrie Normen* which is a five-pin connector used mostly in MIDI applications.

diode—An electronic component that allows current to flow only in one direction.

direct box—An interface that connects an unbalanced source with a balanced microphone input.

direct current—Current that goes only in one direction in a circuit path.

direct out—The per-channel output on a console.

distortion—Excessive disturbance in the frequency spectrum or an abnormal response from such cases as overdriving a device or clipping a power amp.

Dolby—Trademark for a noise reduction system.

Doppler effect—The acoustic phenomenon that alters or bends the apparent pitch of a sound source as it moves away or toward the listener.

drop out—The temporary loss of a signal or drop in decibels due to tape damage.

dry—Describes a signal without any effects.

dub—To record additional tracks after the initial recording. Sometimes called *overdub.*

ducking—A processor function that attenuates a source by external control. The presence of the external control signal reduces the gain of the source.

dynamics—Change of volume or power level of signals.

dynamic range—The minimum to maximum level change of the source or performance specification of a device, usually expressed in dB.

echo—Discrete repeats of a signal.

edit—To change or correct a program be it a razor-blade tape splice or software modification.

effect—A processor that enhances a program such as reverb or echo.

efficiency—A measure of performance given by the ratio of output over input (expressed as a percentage).

electrolytic—A type of capacitor usually used for values beyond 0.47 μF. Typically used in power supplies.

electrons—The particle flow of current.

emitter—The terminal of a transistor in the gain path from which current exits (if an npn type) or that receives current (if a pnp type).

encode—The conversion of a signal to another format.

envelope—The transient dynamic profile of a signal.

equalization—The boosting or reduction of a signal level for some portion of its bandwidth.

exciter—An effect that enhances the clarity or ''presence'' of a sound.

expander—Resembles a noise gate function in which softer sounds are made quieter and stronger ones louder.

fader—A slide-control type potentiometer to regulate signal level output from a console.

fall time—The time duration for a signal to drop from some nominal level to almost no level.

farad—Abbreviation F. The unit for capacitor values.

feedback—The condition when the output is fed back into the input that causes a gain if it superimposes on the input or reduces a gain if it phase cancels the input.

figure eight—Describes a bidirectional polar response.

filter—An equalization circuit used to operate on a selected portion of the audio spectrum to either boost or cut levels for those frequencies.

flanging—A comb-filter effect resembling a sonic wind sweeping through the spectrum that emphasizes and de-emphasizes frequencies by introducing phase-shifted delayed signals.

flat response—A term used to describe the frequency response profile of unity gain across the audio spectrum by being uniformly level from end to end.

Fletcher-Munson curves—Frequency response curves that describe human hearing in terms of the required level for frequencies to be perceived as equal volume. Midrange frequencies require less level than lows and highs to have the same apparent volume.

flip-flop—A digital device used commonly as a frequency divide-by-two circuit.

floating room—A special construction technique in which all of the intersecting room surfaces are jointed with resilient flexible hardware to improve soundproofing.

flutter—A tape drive anomaly in which tape skewing causes transient high-frequency drop outs.

flutter echo—An acoustical effect that occurs when a sound source between two parallel, hard surfaces bounces back and forth.

flux—Magnetic lines of force.

FM—Frequency modulation. Where a carrier frequency is deviated plus and minus the frequency imposed upon it (the modulating frequency). In digital recording, FM is used as a data-encoding technique.

foldback—An input signal that is relayed to another device.

frequency—Abbreviation f. The number of cycles, or waveform periods, completed per second. Frequency is inversely proportional to the time frame (*period*, t) for one cycle ($f = 1/t$).

fundamental frequency—The first harmonic of a signal, which has the lowest frequency but the highest amplitude. All succeeding harmonics are higher in frequency with significantly lower amplitudes.

gain—The power ratio of output over input, typically expressed in decibels as dB = 10 log (P_{out}/P_{in}).

gate—In recording, it means noise gate, a processor used to squelch unwanted signals or noise. *Gate* also describes electronic logic devices.

gated reverb—Combination effect of a noise gate and reverb.

glitch—An error in an analog or digital signal.

gobos—Portable partitions used to improve acoustical isolation between sound sources.

graphic equalizer—An equalizer that can boost or cut frequencies at fixed frequency intervals.

ground—Reference voltage potential of zero.

ground loop—A condition when the ground path becomes resistive and exhibits a voltage, so it is then no longer a zero reference point.

half-normalled—A pair of patch bay points in which one is electrically connected to the signal path of an adjacent one where when a plug is inserted, one point interrupts the path and the other doesn't.

half-track stereo—A tape head format in which only half of the tape width is used by one of the tracks.

harmonics—A series of related frequencies that are an integral of the fundamental or first harmonic.

headroom—The available peak signal margin prior to distortion.

heads in—A spooled tape condition on a take-up reel where the end of the tape is the outermost layer (same as *tails out*).

heads out—A spooled tape condition on a supply reel where the beginning of the tape is the outermost layer (same as *tails in*).

helical scan—A tape-to-head relationship that describes the method in which the tape is read. Used in video and DAT recorders.

henry—Abbreviation *H*. Units for inductor values.

hertz—Abbreviation *Hz*. Units for frequency. Also called *cycles per second* (cps).

hexadecimal—Numbering system that uses base 16.

high-pass filter—A passive network to reject lows but pass highs.

horn—A speaker component with a flared neck used in two-way speaker systems to cover the upper range.

hypercardioid—A microphone polar pattern that has more intense unidirectional characteristics than a cardioid but worse rear rejection.

idlers—Feedback mechanisms on tape decks that control supply and takeup reel torque.

imaginary—The vertical *y*-axis for phasor math applications in electronics.

impedance—The quantitative expression to correlate current flow through a circuit element with an applied voltage for a certain frequency.

incident—The sound wave that first strikes a surface.

inductor—A coil of wire or choke used in circuit applications.

infinity—An indefinitely large number. Also defined as any number divided by zero.

input—The terminal on a device or circuit that accepts a signal.

intermod—Stands for *intermodulation*, which is the unwanted byproduct of mixing signals called *spurs*.

inverter—A device that changes the signal phase one-half cycle or 180 degrees.

inverting amp—An amplifier that inverts the signal's phase 180 degrees.

isolation booth—A booth to optimize isolation from other activities on the same floor space (as in a studio).

jumper—A short patch card.

keyed gate—A special function in which an external signal keys the gate on or off and not the signal that is being gated itself.

kilo—A prefix that means multiply by 1000.

Kirchhoff's voltage law—A circuit law that says that the sum of the voltage drops across each component in the loop must equal the voltage source.

lag—The amount of signal delay in terms of phase shift.

lead—Amount of signal lead in terms of phase shift.

LED—Light-emitting diode. Used as light indicators.

limiter—A circuit with a compression ratio better than 10:1.

line in—An input to a device such as a console channel.

line out—An output that sometimes means *direct out* in other consoles.

live room—A room with some ambient reverb characteristics.

load—An impedance source driven by a device's output.

lobe—A microphone polar pattern (also called ''shotgun'') that is the most intense unidirectional pattern.

logarithm—an exponential math function in which a number is in terms of 10 to some power.

lossy—A device or circuit that is resistive and responsible for signal loss or attenuation.

low-pass filter—A passive network that passes lows while rejecting highs.

LSI—Large-scale integration. A whole microcircuit packaged as one device.

magnitude—A vector resultant in terms of its x and y components.

master—In a synchronous application, it is the device that is not being controlled by the time code.

mega—A prefix for one million.

MFM—Modified *frequency* modulation. A biphase data transmission technique used by some manufacturers for digital recording applications.

micro—A prefix that means one millionth.

microphone—A device or transducer that converts acoustical energy (sound) into an electrical pulse.

microprocessor—A digital device used in computers as the central processor.

MIDI—Musical instrument digital interface. A binary protocol used for synthesizer digital control applications.

midrange—the middle portion of the audio spectrum.

milli—Prefix for one thousandth.

mix—The blend of several signal sources.

mixdown—The final phase in a recording production where all the tracks are mixed into a stereo format.

mixer—Any device that will merge several inputs as one output.

monitor—Another term for *listen*. Or, another term for *loudspeaker*.

mosfit—A special enclosure that isolates tape decks from the control room listening environment.

moving coil—The diaphragm of a dynamic microphone.

MTR—Multitrack recorder.

multiplexer—A device that takes parallel data inputs and converts them to a serial data transmission.

NAND gate—A digital logic device equivalent to an AND gate with an inverter following the output.

negative-going transition—The data transition going from a high level to a low level.

noise—Any unwanted signals.

noise gate—A signal processor used to squelch unwanted signals.

noise reduction—Signal processing dedicated to treat noise problems associated with the analog recording process.

noninverting amp—An operational amplifier configuration with no phase reversal.

NOR gate—A digital logic device that is equivalent to an OR gate followed by an inverter.

normalled—A patch bay configuration in which a pair of points are mutually connected with make-or-break insertion contacts.

notch filter—A bandstop filter with a very narrow rejection bandwidth.

NRZ—Nonreturn to zero. A serial data transmission in which a 1 is represented by a high level and a 0 by a low level.

Nyquist criterion—States that the digital sampling frequency should be at least twice the highest intended audio frequency.

octave—A frequency span in which the high frequency is twice the low frequency.

off-axis—Any radial position other than the zero reference axis.

ohms—Units for resistor values.

Ohm's law—Theory that the voltage drop across a component or circuit is equal to its resistance times the current through the device.

omnidirectional—A polar pattern for a microphone that is mutually sensitive in all radial directions.

on-axis—The zero-degree reference axis.

operational amplifier—Abbreviated *op-amp*, which is an integrated circuit that uses a feedback and an input resistor to determine gain.

OR gate—A digital logic device in which any high level on any input yields a high on the output.

oscillator—A circuit that generates a continuous periodic waveform.

output—The signal "send" terminal of a device.

overload—A condition in which a device is operating in excess of its power rating.

overtones—Another term for *harmonics*.

pad—An attenuator.

pan—To crossfade a signal from one output to another in a stereo fashion.

parallel impedance—Circuit components sharing a common voltage and common nodes.

parallel transmission—Simultaneous signal transmission on multiple signal paths.

parametric equalizer—An equalizer that features sweepable frequency, gain, and Q-factor controls.

PCM—Pulse code modulation. A method used in digital sampling to convert analog amplitudes into digital (binary) values.

PD format—Professional digital. A digital stationary tape head format.

period—Abbreviated t. The time frame for one cycle where $t = 1/f$.

phantom power—A $+48$ Vdc supply used to power condenser microphones.

phase angle—The vector angle of a complex impedance or relative lead or lag relationship of voltage or current.

phase cancellation—The cancelling of a signal when mixed with itself 180 degrees out of phase.

phase-locked loop—A stable crystal voltage-controlled oscillator (VCO).

phase shift—A signal lead or lag.

phasing—An effect similar to flanging in which two identical signals are phase modulated to create the effect.

pica—A prefix that means to multiply by 10^{-12}.

pinch roller—The relay-controlled roller on a tape deck that advances tape in conjunction with the capstan.

ping-ponging—Bouncing submixed tracks from one tape deck to another.

pink noise—A test noise source that rolls off at 3 dB per octave across the audio spectrum.

pitch—The frequency or musical note.

pitch shift—A frequency change or transposition.

plate reverb—A somewhat outdated mechanical reverb that uses a large metal sheet held taut with tension at each corner. At one end, a driver vibrates the plate with the dry signal, and at the other end, transducers convert these vibrations into electrical signals for a wet return.

polar pattern—A graphical representation of a microphone's radial pickup sensitivity or pattern with respect to off-axis position.

polarity—The plus and minus applied voltage orientation.

positive-going transition—The data transition going from a low level to a high level.

post—A console selector position that accesses a signal path after the equalization section or the fader.

post-emphasis—Part of the decode operation in a noise reduction system.

potential—The voltage from a node to the ground reference.

potentiometer—An adjustable resistive electronic component used as a voltage divider. Can be either in rotary form like effect sends or slider form like faders.

pre—A console selector position implying access to a signal path before the equalizer section.

preamble—A sync code prior to a data transmission.

preemphasis—Part of the encode operation in a noise reduction system.

presence—The sound quality of closeness.

pressure gradient—A term for ribbon microphones.

pressure zone microphone—A microphone mounted on a flat surface that can therefore be used in miking situations where reflections from hard surfaces would threaten phase cancelling.

primary—The input side or applied voltage windings of a transformer.

print through—On tape stored on a reel, the transfer of recorded information from one layer of tape to an adjacent layer.

proximity effect—The effect of boosted bass when you are close-miking a vocal.

pulse—A transient voltage signal.

pulse width—The time duration of a pulse.

punch-in—The method in the recording process of switching from the play to the record mode while the tape is in motion.

punch-out—The method in the recording process of switching from the record to the play mode while the tape is in motion.

Q-factor—The quality or narrowness of a bandpass filter, defined as the center frequency of the band divided by the 3 dB down bandwidth.

quarter-track stereo—A tape head format in which only one quarter of the tape width is used by one of the tracks.

quasi-parametric—An equalizer featuring sweepable frequency and gain controls only.

radiation pattern—The directional characteristic of a monitor with respect to frequency.

rarefaction—The low air pressure or suction developed on the trailing side of a speaker cone as it moves back and forth.

real—The zero phase-reference x-axis for phasor math applications in electronics.

rectifier—A diode or a combination of diodes, configured to convert ac voltage into dc voltage.

reflection—The return path of an incident sound wave bouncing off a hard surface.

rejection—The amount of attenuation expressed in dB.

release—A gate function that works on the fall time of a signal that keeps the gate open a little while after crossing the threshold level.

reproducer—Another term for a tape deck's playback mode.

resistor—A passive component that impedes current flow. Units are ohms (Ω).

resolver—A rotary shaft in the tape path that is responsible for counter readout.

resonance—The optimum performance of a system or electronic network tuned for some frequency or frequencies such as bass traps or filter networks.

returns—The output from the tape deck that is routed back to the console.

reverberation—An acoustical phenomenon of multiple random reflections as the result of sound repeatedly striking hard surfaces in an enclosed area.

RFI—Radio frequency interference.

rise time—The time period for a signal to reach its maximum level.

rms—Root mean square. Represents an average for sinusoidal waveforms, which is the peak value divided by the square root of two.

roll-off—The slope of a frequency response curve.

sample hold—A function used in digital applications to temporarily store binary information from the A/D conversion process.

sampling—The analog-to-digital conversion process of a signal.

saturate—To operate at maximum capacity.

scientific notation—A method of expressing either very large or very small numbers in powers of ten.

secondary—The output voltage windings of a transformer.

sends—Usually rotary-type controls on consoles that drive effect devices.

sensitivity—The output performance of a device with respect to an applied input.

sequencer—A device that can receive and store digital control information as well as transmit it in the same order and time base it was received. Typically used in MIDI applications.

serial transmission—A single data path transmission.

series impedance—Consecutive components in a single path.

shelving filter—A filter that can cut or boost frequencies, giving a plateau response at either the low or high end of the spectrum.

shock mount—A suspension system that decouples microphones from any vibrations transmitted through the stand.

short—A conductive path or something that exhibits zero impedance.

shotgun—A microphone with a very directional pickup pattern used mostly in broadcast applications or in high-noise environments.

sibilance—The quality of presence in a vocal with emphasis on "s"-sounding pronunciations.

signal—Any electronic pulse or continuous waveform.

single-ended—A term for unbalanced input or output.

sinusoid—A periodic waveform defined by the sine or cosine trigonometric functions.

slate—A message or announcement recorded at the beginning of a take.

slave—In a synchronous application, the device being controlled by the time code.

slew rate—The transient performance of an amplifier in terms of voltage rise time expressed in volts per μs.

SMPTE—Society of Motion Picture and Television Engineers. Represents a time code displayed in hours, minutes, seconds, and frames that is used for video and audio synchronization applications.

S/N—Signal-to-noise ratio.

software—The assembly language or operating system for a computer.

sound—any vibration transmitted by air.

soundproofing—Methods to greatly attenuate sound transmission and achieve acoustic isolation.

speaker efficiency—The percent of electrical energy that converts into acoustical power.

speaker sensitivity—The amount of acoustical power measured at 1 meter that converts from a 1-watt input.

spectrum—A frequency bandwidth.

spillover—Bleed or crosstalk from one track or channel to another as the result of close miking.

SPL—Sound pressure level, expressed in decibels.

spooling—winding tape on an open reel.

standing waves—An acoustical phenomenon that occurs when a source is placed between parallel surfaces. The frequency whose wavelength is twice the distance between the parallel surfaces is reinforced or "standing."

steady-state response—The response of a network beyond the initial applied voltage.

stepdown transformer—A transformer that reduces applied primary voltage on its secondary.

stereo image—The perceived placement of signals originating from left and right directions.

stripe—to record a time code on a track.

subgroup—The submaster output section on a console.

submaster—A fader-controlled output of the subgroup.

submix—The grouping of several input signals into a single output.

summing amp—An operational amplifier that merges several signals and amplifies them as one output.

supercardioid—A unidirectional microphone polar pattern that has more off-axis rejection than the ordinary cardioid pattern.

superimpose—The electrical addition of two or more signals.

supply reel—The left-hand reel on a tape deck that discharges the tape in the play or record mode.

sync—An abbreviation for synchronize.

synchronizer—A device that can read and write time code and can control transport tape speed for a chase-lock application.

synthesizer—An electronic musical instrument.

tails in—A spooled tape condition on a supply reel where the beginning of the tape is the outermost layer (same as heads out).

tails out—A spooled tape condition on a take-up reel where the end of the tape is the outermost layer (same as heads in).

take—A recording.

takeup reel—The right-hand reel on a transport that accumulates tape in the play or record mode.

tape lifters—The vertical posts that push the tape away from the heads when in the fast-forward or rewind modes.

tape skew—Abnormal tape motion in which vertical forces acting on the tape cause mistracking or poor contact with the head.

tape sync—A time code placed on a track for synchronization applications.

THD—An amplifier specification that stands for total harmonic distortion.

three-to-one rule—A colocation mike placement principle in which the distance between two mikes should be at least three times the distance from the source.

three-way system—A monitor using three components to reproduce the audio range.

threshold—A specific level setting on a device such as a compressor or noise gate to serve as a reference point for operation when compared with an applied input signal level.

timing diagram—A graph that shows the input and output waveform timing relationships, particularly for digital circuits.

transducer—A device that converts mechanical energy into an electrical signal.

transformer—A device that converts the ac voltage applied to its primary windings to a higher or lower voltage on its secondary.

transient response—The initial behavior of a network with applied voltage.

transistor—An active device usually used for signal amplification.

transmission coefficient—The ratio of the transmitted sound energy that passes through a medium over the incident sound wave.

transmission loss—Expressed in dB as the amount of sound energy absorbed by a medium defined mathematically as TL = $10 \log(S_i/S_t)$ where S_i is the incident wave and S_t is the transmitted wave.

transport—Another term for *tape deck*.

triamping—Technique of using a frequency-dividing network and three amplifiers to drive each component individually.

triggering pulse—The type of pulse used in MIDI applications that drives a device and converts it to a note assignment.

tweeter—A high-frequency speaker system component.

two-way system—A monitor using two components to reproduce the audio range.

unbalanced—A two-conductor system in which the shield is a current return path.

unidirectional—A microphone directional response that is mostly sensitive to on-axis sounds.

unity gain—An output-to-input power ratio of 1, or in terms of decibels, 0 dB.

VCA—Voltage-controlled amplifier. Used in console automation to substitute manual fader and rotary pot movements in mixdowns. A digital address from the computer controls the amount of attenuation in the signal path.

VCR—Video cassette recorder.

vector—A magnitude with an angle referenced to the 0-degree axis.

VHS—A VCR tape format that stands for video home system.

voice coil—The windings at the base of a speaker cone.

voltage—Abbreviated V. The electromotive field force that causes current flow through a conductive medium.

voltage regulator—A device used to control consistency of dc voltage levels in power supply applications.

volume—Loudness.

VU—A metering term that stands for volume units.

watts—Abbreviated W. Units used for electrical power.

wavelength—The physical distance of a waveform displaced by one cycle.

webers—Abbreviated w. Units used for magnetic force fields.

wet—Used to describe a signal that has been processed by an effect device.

white noise—A test noise source that generates equal energy across the audio spectrum.

windscreen—A protective airfoam cover for microphones that resists vocal breath forces at close range.

woofer—A loudspeaker dedicated to handling the lower register of the audio range.

wow—A tape motion anomaly caused by tape speed fluctuations in the drive mechanism.

zenith—A tape head adjustment that pertains to the vertical alignment such that the head surface is parallel to the tape surface.

Index

mixing (*see also* mixdown), 156
   ducking, 129
   five items, two tracks, 85
   methods for, 260-262
   panning, 85
   premix, 259-260
   pulled down track, 129
   punched through track, 129
mixing-console architecture, 70-98
modes, standing wave, 54
modified frequency modulation
   (MFM), 181
modulation, 229
monitoring (*see also* speakers), 25-
   47, 92-95, 104-105
multi-effect processors, 100
multitrack tape heads, tape transports, analog, 154-156

N
NAND gate, 22, 23
noise
   generator for, 68
   noise gate to suppress, 123
   noise-reduction devices, 168-172
   pink, 65, 66, 68, 69
   signal-to-noise ratio, 123, 124
   weighting, 51, 52
   white, 65, 66, 68, 69, 130
noise gates, 100-101, 117, 123-128,
   258
noise measurement, 51, 52
noise-reduction devices, 128, 168-
   172
noninverting input, operational
   amplifiers, 16, 17
NOR gate, 22, 23
normalled configuration, patch bay,
   80, 81
notch filter, 135
NRZ encoding, digital audio recording, 179
Nyquist criterion, 178

O
off-axis coloration, 215
Ohm's law, 2
ohms, 2
omnidirectional microphones, 196,
   218
on- and off-axis positions, speakers,
   33
one-shot, noise gate, 127

opening microphones, 221
operational amplifiers, 16-18
OR gate, 22, 23
oscillation, 115, 116
outputs, system integration, 103
overload, 37, 38, 40
overtones, 116

P
panning, 85
parametric equalizers, 132, 135
parity bytes, digital audio recording,
   183
passive filters, 131, 133
passive vs. active devices, 14
patch bay (*see also* channel patching), 76-82
   balanced vs. unbalanced sockets,
   78
   mixdown, 256
   normalled vs. half-normalled configurations, 80, 81, 82
   plugs for, 78
   signal flow paths, 80-81, 85, 88
   system integration, 103
   tape deck, 104
   use of, 79-80
peak-to-peak signal, amplifier, 38-39
peak-to-peak voltage, 5
permanent magnets, 25, 26
phantom power supplies, 193
phase angle, 13, 271
phase cancellation, 35, 56, 253
phase lock synchronization, 167
phase relationships, 6-8, 12
phase shift, 12, 143
phasing, 100, 143-146
   lag and, 144, 145
   vocal eliminators and, 144
phasor math, 12
pink noise, 65, 66, 68, 69
pitch bend, 229
pitch shift, 100, 148
pitch, sound, 114
plate reverb, 140
polar patterns, microphones, 204-
   214, 219
polarization, microphones, 193
positron flow, 2
postmix, 262-264
potential reference, zero, 4
potentiometer, 10, 11
power, amplifier rating for, 38
power amplifiers, 46

power density, 42-44
power output, amplifier, 44
power supplies, 1, 19-22
preamble code, digital audio recording, 180
preamps, 40
premix, 259-260
preproduction planning, 238
pressure gradient microphones, 192
pressure zone microphones, 221
print through, tape transports, analog, 168
production (*see* recording and)
proximity effect, microphones, 215
pulse code modulation, 173-178
punch-in, 158, 247

Q

Q response, 135
quasi-parametric equalizers, 135

R

radiation patterns, 33, 34
rarefaction, 35
reactance, 5, 6, 8
real component, 269
recorder/reproducer (*see* tape transports)
recording and production, 238-253
recording console, layout of, 72
rectifier circuits, full- and half-wave, 20-21
reflections, 33
   echoes and, 140-141
   flush-mounted monitors, 35
   microphones, 222
   reverb and, 138-140
   sound absorption materials, 35
   wall-mounted monitor, 34
regulators, voltage, 19, 21, 22
release, 119
resistance, 2, 12, 41-42
resistors, 2, 3, 6, 7, 20-21
resolver, tape transports, analog, 153
resonators, 53, 56
reverb, 56-58, 86, 99-101, 138-140, 148
   system loop monitoring, 110, 112
   system loop recording via submaster, 112
reverb time, 139
reverse torque, tape transports, analog, 151

rise time, 114, 115
roll-off frequency, 14, 131, 133
rotary head digital recorders, 186-190

S

sample hold, 178
sampling rate, 173-178
saturation, 119
scalar math, 268
schedule, recording and production, 239
scientific notation, 266
scratch vocals, 246
sensitivity
   amplifiers, 45
   microphones, 215-219
   monitors, 42
sequencing, MIDI applications, 229-231
session track sheet, 242
shelving equalization, 131, 132
shields, 195
shock mounts, microphones, 220
short circuits, 8-9
shotgun microphones, 216
signal generation, 1, 3-5
signal-to-noise ratio, 45, 123, 124, 169
signal transient, 119
signals
   in-phase, 143
   phase shift in, 143
   routing, 106-113
sine, 267, 272
sine wave, 115, 116
sinusoidal signals, 3-6, 35, 272
skew, tape transports, analog, 154
slave tape transports, analog, 167
slew rate, 45, 46
SMPTE time code, 166-167, 183
snap action, 125
Society of Motion Picture and Television Engineers (SMPTE), 97
sound, 114-119
sound absorption materials, 35
sound pressure level (SPL), 42-44, 114, 218
soundproofing, 48-52
   absorption coefficient of materials, 56-57
   bass trap for, 54-56
   diffusers, 59
   Fletcher-Munson curves in noise measurement, 51, 52